Green Afternoons

Oregon Gardens to Visit

Green Afternoons
Oregon Gardens to Visit

by Amy Houchen

illustrations by Lee Hascall

Oregon State University Press
Corvallis

The paper in this book meets the guidelines for permanence and durability of the Committee on Production Guidelines for Book Longevity of the Council on Library Resources and the minimum requirements of the American National Standard for Permanence of Paper for Printed Library Materials Z39.48-1984.

Library of Congress Cataloging-in-Publication Data
Houchen, Amy.
  Green afternoons : Oregon gardens to visit / by Amy Houchen
      p. cm
  Includes index.
  ISBN 0-87071-429-5 (alk paper)
      1. Gardens—Oregon—Guidebooks. 2. Parks—Oregon—Guidebooks. 3. Oregon—Guidebooks. I. Title.
  SB466.U65074 1998
  712'.09795—dc21   97-50119
                                                                CIP

Oregon State University Press
101 Waldo Hall
Corvallis OR 97331-6407
541-737-3166 ✿ fax 541-737-3170
orst.edu / dept / press / osupress.htm

Table of Contents

Introduction i

Portland North of Burnside and Communities to the North 1

The Grotto 3
The Oregon Garden 5
Peninsula Park 7
University of Portland 10
Bybee-Howell Territorial Park, Sauvie Island 14
Columbia County Demonstration Garden, St. Helens 17
Hulda Klager Lilac Gardens, Woodland, Washington 19
Salmon Creek Poison Prevention Garden, Vancouver, Washington 21
Fort Vancouver, Vancouver, Washington 23

Southeast Portland and Southern and Eastern Suburbs 27

Ladd Circle and Squares 29
Crystal Springs Rhododendron Garden 33
Leach Botanical Garden 38
Gresham Regional Library Japanese Garden 42
Mt. Hood Community College, Gresham 44
The Gardens of Enchantment, Sandy 45
Risley Landing Gardens, Oak Grove 46
Heritage Garden, Oregon City 48

Oregon City - Tateshima Sister City Japanese
   Garden, Oregon City 50
Clackamas Community College, Oregon City 51

Southwest Portland and Washington County 56
Duniway Park 58
Elk Rock 61
The Berry Botanic Garden 65
Edna Holmes Garden 70
Fulton Display Garden 73
The Jenkins Estate, Aloha 74
Harold Eastman Memorial Rose Garden, Hillsboro
   79

Washington Park 80
International Rose Test Garden 82
The Japanese Garden 89
Hoyt Arboretum 98
Metro Washington Park Zoo 105
OMSI Herb Garden 112

Northern Willamette Valley 113
Emma Wakefield Herb Garden, Aurora 115
North Willamette Experiment Station, Aurora 117
The Grove of the States, Wilsonville 119
The Cecil and Molly Smith Garden, St. Paul 121
Minthorn House, Newberg 124
Linfield College, McMinnville 126

Salem-Dallas Area   128

Capitol Arboretum, Salem   130
Willamette University, Salem   133
Deepwood, Salem   138
Bush's Pasture Park, Salem   142
Brunk House, Salem   145
Delbert Hunter Arboretum and Botanic Garden and
    Japanese Garden, Dallas   147
Western Oregon State University and Gentle House,
    Monmouth   150

Corvallis-Albany Area   154

Albany Olde-Fashioned Garden   156
Peavy Arboretum, Corvallis   157
Chintimini Park, Corvallis   159
Oregon State University, Corvallis   160
Central Park, Corvallis   167
Avery Park, Corvallis   169
Lewis-Brown Farm, Corvallis   172

Eugene   174

Owen Rose Garden   176
University of Oregon   178
Hendricks Park   183
Mt. Pisgah Arboretum   186

Southern Oregon   188

Lotus Knight Porter Garden, Roseburg   190
Roseburg Veterans' Administration Hospital   191
Douglas County Demonstration Farm, Roseburg
    192

Victor Boehl Memorial Rose Garden, Grants Pass
  193
Palmerton Arboretum, Rogue River   194
Jacksonville Herb Garden   196
Old Rose Garden, Jacksonville   197
Southern Oregon Experiment Station and Claire
  Hanley Arboretum, Medford   198
Lithia Park, Ashland   201

The Coast   205

Tillamook Master Gardeners' Demonstration Garden
  207
The Connie Hansen Garden, Lincoln City   208
Gallagher's Park, Florence   211
Mingus Park, Coos Bay   212
Shore Acres, Coos Bay   214

Central Oregon   218

Seufert Rose Garden, The Dalles   220
Rorick House, The Dalles   222
Sorosis Park, The Dalles   224
Kalama Park, Redmond   226
Pioneer Park, Bend   227
Hollinshead Garden, Bend   228
Sunriver Botanical Garden   229

Gardens in the Works 231

Classical Chinese Garden, Portland   231
Sara Hite Memorial Rose Garden, Milwaukie   233
The Oregon Garden, Silverton   234
Jackson & Perkins Garden at Miles Field, Medford
    235
Pioneer Garden, The Dalles   236
Japanese Garden, Four Rivers Cultural Center,
    Ontario   237

General index   238
Plant index   242

Acknowledgements

Fortunately for me, people usually love to talk about their gardens and show them off. Librarians, archivists and others were also helpful in finding background material. Among those who provided some sort of assistance are (and to those whose names I spelled wrong or left out altogether, my apologies): Vi Adamson, Lee Allen, Mike Anders, Dale Archibald, Mike Bauer, Rocky Bauer, Larry Beutler, Bobbe Blacher, Jim Black, Shirley Bridgham, Bonnie Brunkow, Chip Buell, Jill Burns, Mike Cady, Erica Calkins, Pearl Campbell, Catharine Cobb, Frank Cochran, Linda Cook, Tom Cook, Dwayne Coyer, Joyce Cresswell, Jeannette Crosby-Kruljac, Pat Cummins, Jim Davis, Jane Dirks-Edmonds, Doug Dollarhide, Jim Dowd, Bob Downing, Jill Durow, Jess Eastman, Rick Edwards, Fran Egan, Sue Egger, Helen Elsmore, Skip Enge, Wanda Esson, Dorothy McKee Fender, Madeleine Fisher, John Galbraith, Isabelle Garlock, Jim Gersbach, Jim Gillespie, Charles Goodrich, Roger Gould, George Guthrie, Jim Haines, Dorothy Hall, Rick Hanes, Nora Hanke, Clayton Hannan, Jane Hart, Jane Hartline, Andrew Haruyama, Jerry Herrmann, Elizabeth Howley, Claire Iley, Julie Jackson, Darrell Johnson, Elaine Joines, Greg Jones, Tim King, Waldo Kleiber, Irene Knapp, Hoichi Kurisu, Eileen Landregan, John Lauer, Daisa Lawson, Celeste Lindsay, Susannah Lints, Jim MacDonald, Joe Majeski, Jerry Maul, Jan McClain, Henry McKenney, Linda McMahan, Miles McCoy, Michael McQuade, Gary Miller, Shirley Miller, Peter Mott, Elizabeth Neilsen, Don Neilson, Julie Reynolds Otrugman, Fred Paggi, Rod Park, Frank Patterson, Cindy Lou Pease, Otis and Shirley Pierce, Leslie Pohl-Kosbau, Thomas Pomeroy, Bob Renner, Fred Reentsjerna, Keith Richard, Michael Robert, Marcus Robyns, Bill Robinson, Ken Roll, Fran Rosenthal, Eric Ross, Randy Samuelson, Maureen Sanchez, Robert Scotton, Michael Sestric, Maxine Sickels, Jim Sjulin, Bessie Smith, Jim Smith, Vi Sobolek, Marjorie Speirs, Claudia Spiewak, Peg Stenlund, Bryce Stetler, George Strozut, Barbara Sullivan, Scott Sundberg, Catherine Taylor, Helmy Tewfik, Maureen Thomas, Sue Thomas, Robert Y. Thornton, Robert Ticknor, Donn Todt, Lena Tucker, Steve Webber, John Williams, and staff at the Government desk at Multnomah County's Central Library; Oregon Historical Society library, photo desk and manuscript room; the Canby *Herald*; the Southern Oregon Historical Society; the Oregon State Library; the City of Portland's Stanley Parr Archives and Records Center; and the University of Oregon's Knight Library, Special Collections.

Introduction

Gardeners visit gardens other than their own for various reasons: instruction, inspiration, reflection, respite from the demands of their own gardens, communion with kindred spirits. This book is for those who want to know where to find gardens to visit without a special invitation from the owner. All the gardens listed here (except, of course, those in the works) are, at the time of writing, reasonably accessible to the public. They may be open every day, at all hours, or only a few days during the season when their specialty is at its best, or for some other limited period, or by appointment. Admission may be free, a set charge, or by donation. Hours and admission policies change occasionally, so it's a good idea to call ahead and make sure the garden will be open when you want to see it.

This book uses the term "garden" broadly, to include not only traditional, stand-alone gardens but also plantings of interest in such places as parks, college campuses, farms, and community gardens. It includes an arboretum at a freeway rest area, old-fashioned flowers planted in the island of a visitor center parking lot, climbing roses dressing up the cyclone fence around a ballfield, and a display of ornamentals at an agricultural experiment station.

All but three of the gardens are in Oregon. Those three—Fort Vancouver and Salmon Creek in Vancouver and the Hulda Klager Lilac Garden in Woodland, Washington—seemed too close to Portland, and too interesting, to leave out.

Some garden descriptions are long, some are short.
They may be short for various reasons. Some gardens are
very small; some change annually; some are very simple
in design or planting; for some, no one would claim
knowledge of the plantings. All should be of interest to at
least some readers. The descriptions are intended to give
a flavor of the gardens, not to list every plant. If you want
to know whether a particular species or cultivar is grown
in a garden, call ahead. Where telephone numbers are
listed with a parenthetical reference, the number is not
that of the garden but of a person or entity that can
respond to inquiries about the garden.

You may be glad to travel a few miles to see a garden
that you would not drive hours to visit. Many of the
gardens are quite modest in size and scope—herb
gardens, in particular, are tiny—so read the descriptions
carefully before you go. Some very small gardens were
included because they show how to use a small space
well.

The garden listings include seasons of interest,
directions, public transit information (in the Portland
area), information on holding weddings, whether plants
are labeled, a listing of special events, a description of
what to see, and a section of background. Any gardener
knows that gardens don't just happen. They get started
for a reason; someone determines their site, shape and
scope; and someone keeps them going. Some of the
gardens started as estates or personal hobbies; others
were begun by plant societies, or restored and made
accessible to the public by historical-interest groups.
Some were founded as educational tools, and some are
part of the public face of institutions. Most, but not all, of
the Oriental gardens were begun by or in conjunction
with sister-city organizations.

Specialty collections, including roses and herbs, may be worth a trip to those especially interested in them even if they are not the main focus of a garden. Some gardens are of interest in only one or two seasons; others are rewarding all year long. Unless the garden has a conservatory, witch hazels, camellias, or species rhododendrons, it won't have much color in winter, even though it may well be worth seeing then for evergreens and the branch structure of deciduous plants.

Change occurs in all gardens. Plants grow, change, and die; tastes change; physical and financial circumstances alter. Varieties come and go; few gardens are as fortunate as the International Rose Test Garden in Washington Park, which can count on a body of volunteers to keep treasured old varieties in propagation although they're no longer available commercially. Gardens disappear: Lambert Gardens got built upon, and Monteith Riverpark lost its rose garden because it became too shady. Nature wreaks havoc: many gardens suffered losses in the Columbus Day Storm (an offshoot of Typhoon Frieda that swept through western Oregon and Washington, bringing high winds, on October 12, 1962); the unusual snow and cold during the winter of 1988-89; the storms during the winter of 1995-96 that brought wind, then cold, then ice, then floods and landslides; and the ice and snow late in 1996. New gardens are planted. Change means that this book is slightly out of date even as it is printed.

Gardens all require time, money, and effort. Funds for gardens run by public entities have been cut severely as other public concerns shouldered them aside in the budget process. If you have a particular interest in or fondness for a garden, it probably has a group of friends that would welcome your time, money, effort, or all three, to ensure its continuation and good health. Gardens don't thrive on neglect.

Finally, when you visit these gardens, take care to be a good guest. It would be a great loss to all if a few rude or destructive visitors provoked the owners to bar the public or quit maintaining the garden. Leave at home children who can't be restrained by either you or their maturity and all pets. Limit your consumption of food and drink to areas designated for them, if any. Take only pictures and memories; leave nothing behind except a donation.

Portland North of Burnside and Communities to the North

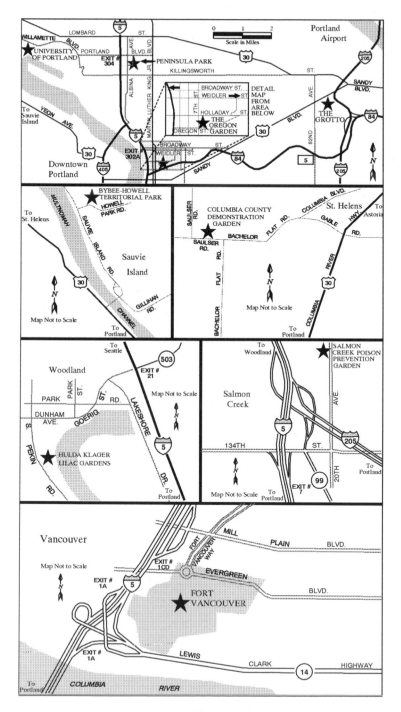

The Grotto

(The National Sanctuary of Our Sorrowful Mother)

8840 N.E. Skidmore (P.O. Box 2008)
Portland OR 97294-0008
(503) 254-7371

❧

Seasons of interest: All

Directions: From Interstate 84 in Portland, take the 82nd Avenue exit (no. 5) and proceed north to Sandy Boulevard. Turn right on Sandy. At the corner of 85th and Sandy, turn right into the Grotto; the entrance is well marked. There's no admission fee, but you must buy a token in the gift shop to ride the elevator from the lower level to the upper level.

Public transit: Tri-Met bus 12-Sandy Boulevard stops at 85th and Sandy.

Labels: None

Weddings: Weddings are not allowed in the gardens.

Background: The Sanctuary of Our Sorrowful Mother, familiarly known as the Grotto, was founded in 1923 by Father Ambrose Mayer, a Servite (Order of the Servants of Mary) priest then serving Assumption parish in St. Johns, and dedicated in 1924.

The grotto for which the sanctuary is known was carved from a stone cliff in 1925. Planting started early on, so many of the camellias and rhododendrons on the lower level are decades old. The redwoods lining Skidmore Street and the "redwood highway" from the monastery to 82nd Avenue were planted in 1936. The most recent garden development is the Marguerite M. Casey Peace Garden, dedicated in 1989, which is the setting for three Mystery Collages by Rainier artist Mary Lewis.

What to see: The gardens start at the entrance on Sandy Boulevard. Roses edge the entrance lawn. Planting areas within the parking lot contain fountains surrounded by plain and variegated hostas, bulbs, ferns, and evergreen azaleas.

Much of the garden is planted with natives, interspersed with hybrid rhododendrons and exotic evergreens. The greatest variety is at the top of the elevator. Along the path winding south toward the monastery are dogwoods, camellias, bleeding hearts and trilliums.

In front of the monastery is the Grotto's rose garden. Most of the roses are hybrid teas, but there are a few miniatures and climbers. From the rose garden, the path leads north past winged euonymus (*Euonymus alatus*) and Japanese maples (*Acer palmatum*) to the peace garden.

The peace garden winds along a stream past three mystery collages. Each of the collage areas is landscaped in a different color scheme. The Joyful Mysteries garden emphasizes blue and white, the Sorrowful Mysteries garden runs to deep reds, blues, and purples, and the Glorious Mysteries garden is planted in yellow and gold.

The Oregon Garden

N.E. Oregon Street between 7th and 9th Avenues
(503) 233-4048 (Ashforth Pacific)

৵৻৶

Seasons of interest: All

Directions: From Interstate 5 northbound, take the Weidler/Coliseum exit (no. 302A). Turn right on Martin Luther King, Jr. Boulevard, left on Holladay, right on 7th, and left around the statue of the pioneer family onto Oregon Street. There is metered parking on both sides of the street.

Public transit: On MAX, get off at the 7th Avenue stop and walk two blocks south. The garden is just east of 729 Oregon Square. Or take Tri-Met bus route 6-M. L. King Jr. Blvd. to Grand Avenue (which is the equivalent of 5th) and Pacific; walk three blocks east and one block south.

Labels: None, but permanent maps identify the plants, usually by their common names.

Weddings: The garden is not available for weddings.

Background: In the late 1980s, Pacific Development, Inc., redeveloped several blocks into Oregon Square. In the process the streets in the area became private and one of them, 8th Avenue, disappeared entirely. Where it formerly ran the developer built a garden, to provide a pleasant oasis amid the buildings and paving. All the plants were grown in the Willamette Valley. The garden was dedicated in August 1990.

What to see: This urban garden—tucked into a long, narrow strip between an office building and a parking lot—has plants of all types, from ground covers to trees. It offers something of interest every season; even in February, after the pansies have given up under assaults by rain and snow, color and scent are provided by heathers, winter daphne (*Daphne odora*), Chinese witch hazel (*Hamamelis mollis*), winter jasmine (*Jasminum nudiflorum*), and rosemary. Later in the spring, dogwoods, flowering cherries, azaleas, and rhododendrons provide color before the annuals come into their own.

The garden is in two parts: you can stroll through the west half on meandering or straight paths, or you can sit under the vine-draped pergolas on the east half.

Peninsula Park

Portland Boulevard and Albina Avenue
(503) 823-3636 (City of Portland Rose Gardens)

ᛞ

Seasons of interest: Summer, fall

Directions: From Interstate 5 take the Portland Boulevard exit (no. 304). Proceed east on Portland Boulevard to Albina Avenue; turn right on Albina, left on Ainsworth, and left on Kerby; park on Kerby. The rose garden is sunk into the south end of Peninsula Park, which this route partially circumnavigates.

Public transit: Take Tri-Met bus 40-Mock's Crest to Portland Boulevard and Albina.

Labels: None

Weddings: The garden can accommodate up to a hundred people. Call the City of Portland Reservation Center ((503) 823-2525).

Background: Peninsula Park's rose garden was designed in 1910 by Emanuel T. Mische, Portland's park superintendent from 1908 through 1914. Mische studied for a time at Kew Gardens in London, and spent nine years with Frederick Law Olmsted's sons—proprietors of Olmsted Brothers, the nation's leading landscape architecture firm—who considered him the best plantsman in the country. He was very methodical, and spent considerable time on details if he felt the effort justified. He described his design for Peninsula's rose garden as "severely formal of the French parterre type. . . . Scale, proportion and luxuriance of growth and choiceness of material will be its main charm."

The original plant list required 10,339 roses: 3,010 of the white hybrid perpetual 'Frau Karl Druschki;' 4,718 *Rosa wichuraiana* hybrids; 798 'Mme. Caroline Testout,' Portland's signature rose (see International Rose Test Garden, page 83); several hundred each of five other

7

hybrid teas; and three each of several hundred hybrid teas. A planting scheme from 1910 indicates that the roses were to be planted in color blocks: reds and pinks in the outer beds; yellow and, presumably, all those white 'Frau Karl Druschki' in the inner beds. Mische intended frequent replanting to keep the collection modern. In 1912, the year construction began, he suggested placing flowering potted plants around the fountain and dwarf box around the rose beds.

The garden soon lost its original planting scheme and luster. In 1936, the curator reported that many replacements of modern roses had been made and that the garden was in poor shape. By some time in the 1950s the fountain was inoperable and the pool dry; the potted plants had disappeared, and climbers had been planted at the edges of the beds around the fountain. In 1957, the garden was redesigned into large, uniform blocks of roses. Much of the uniformity was lost by the mid 1970s, but regained in the early 1990s. Portland's 1994 park bond issue provided funds to repair the fountain and plant roses at street level along the south end of the garden, for who cannot manage the steps. Construction is slated for spring and summer 1998.

What to see: This grand old garden is very formal. Majestic stairways; wide, patterned brick walkways; aged pollarded catalpas marking intersections of broad grass paths; box-edged beds filled with straight rows of roses; and the bandstand hovering above the north balustrade— all evoke a time and place far from a modest neighborhood in North Portland in the 1990s.

The roses, on the other hand, are not period pieces. Most date from the last few decades; there are no species roses, old garden roses, miniatures, or labeled award winners. This is a garden in which to stroll and admire its design, the blocks of color on the slopes, and the rings or bands of color in the flat beds.

University of Portland

5000 N. Willamette Boulevard
(503) 283-7306

Seasons of interest: All

Directions: From Interstate 5, take the Portland Boulevard exit (no. 304). Proceed west on Portland Boulevard; get in the right-hand lane and bear right on Willamette Boulevard. Follow signs to the University of Portland. You will need a parking permit—available at Pilot House, the first building on your right along the main entrance road—to park on campus.

Public transit: Tri-Met bus 1-Greeley goes to the University of Portland.

Labels: Some. A brochure with a history of the campus gardens and a map identifying some of the plantings is available from the Public Safety office on the west side of N. Warren Street (which runs north across N. Portsmouth from the Chiles Center), or the Public Relations office, Room 303, Waldschmidt Hall, south of Pilot House on the bluff.

Background: The University sits on a historic spot on a bluff above the Willamette River visited by William Clark in 1806. There has been a university here since 1891. Little of lasting horticultural interest occurred until the 1930s and 1940s, when Brother Ferdinand Moser, a math instructor, and another priest planted more than 570 trees on the campus and on land the University owned down the bluff to the high-water mark. Over three hundred of those trees remain. They are the only mature trees on campus except the Douglas firs (*Pseudotsuga menziesii*), the bigleaf maples (*Acer macrophyllum*) along Willamette Boulevard, and the native Oregon white oaks (*Quercus garryana*), some of which are more than three hundred years old.

Brother Moser also started the campus camellia collection with more than five dozen *Camellia japonica* varieties and hybrids, and the rhododendron and azalea collections.

Ted Deiss, a professional horticulturist who became superintendent of grounds on Brother Moser's death in 1964, donated a greenhouse and developed a master plan for the university's landscape. He planted many azaleas, rhododendrons, and flowering trees. In the early 1980s, a variety of conifers were planted beyond the baseball diamond's outfield fences. Several years later, southeast Asian species rhododendrons were planted around the Chiles Center, and species azaleas at the tennis center. Newer plantings continue the tradition of providing year-around horticultural interest.

Because the campus is in a protected spot above the river and in the lee of the West Hills, it enjoys winter lows an average five to ten degrees higher than the rest of the city, and lost only two trees in the major windstorm of December 1995. It does, however, experience drying east winds.

What to see: This campus is worth seeing any time of year. Fall is particularly spectacular, with bright fall leaves on deciduous trees set off by nearby evergreens. In winter and early spring, much of the interest is provided by camellias.

Over two hundred camellias, including over one hundred named varieties, snuggle in groves around many of the campus buildings. Along with dozens of *Camellia japonica* cultivars are several hybrids, Sasanqua camellias and a few other species, including a tea plant (*C. sinensis*). If you've only seen camellias in residential foundation plantings, sheared up the back to keep branches away from the house wall or flat-topped to avoid interference with a window or gutter, you may have a different view of their character after seeing them here. The camellias are planted far enough away from the buildings that they can reach their full potential sizes.

Species rhododendrons, all natives of China or Tibet, have been planted around the Chiles Center, the dome northeast of the main parking lot. Between the buttresses are light pink *Rhododendron racemosum*, *R. bernicosum*, and several forms of *R. davidsonianum*; light yellow *R. flavidium* and *R. lutescens*; white *R. morii*; and purples including *R. impeditum*, *R. fastigiatum*, and *R. augustinii* ssp. *elegans*. The trees at the back of the beds on the south side are Japanese snowbells (*Styrax japonicus*). The trees along the walk stretching southeast of the Chiles Center are columnar European hornbeams (*Carpinus betulus* 'Columnaris'); others around the dome are Carriere hawthorns (*Crataegus* x *lavallei*).

To the west of the dome, along the south edge of the baseball field, is a collection of conifers, including several pines and spruces. Southwest of the field, Orrico Hall faces south. Along the walk in front are ornamental grasses, several witch hazels, in bloom in January or February, and three Jacquemont birches (*Betula jaquemontii*). Further to the southwest, facing the south wall of the engineering school, a small rose garden includes such old favorites as 'Dainty Bess' and 'Betty Prior.' To the west, camellias line the north side of the tennis center, and azaleas anchor its northeast and southeast corners.

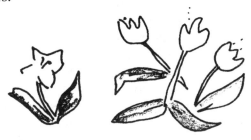

Continuing southwest, around the patio outside the
Commons are sedums, pines, azaleas, ornamental grasses,
and some annuals. Across the lawn from the Commons
and the engineering school is Buckley Center. At its
southwest corner are the viburnums *Viburnum* x
bodnantense, V. plicatum tomentosum, and *V. tinus.* The little
tree shading them is a Camperdown elm (*Ulmus glabra*
'Camperdownii'), grafted onto an American elm (*U.
americana*) rootstock.

Along the walk north of Buckley Center and south of
the library are striped-bark maples: *Acer davidii,* with
green and white stripes, and *A. capillipes,* with brown and
white stripes. The forsythia on the north side of the walk
is *Forsythia viridissima* 'Bronxensis,' a dwarf that spares
the gardener pruning. Tucked into a corner northeast of
the auditorium is a peace garden of azaleas, heather, a
witch hazel, and tulips. In the middle of the plaza to the
east is one of the campus's ancient Oregon white oaks.

In the southeast corner of the campus along the bluff
are groves of camellias. Near the edge of the bluff is a
1988 sculpture of William Clark, his slave York, and an
American Indian by Michael Florin Dente. The sculpture
is intended to be touched, and the immediate landscaping
is comprised of natives—salal (*Gaultheria shallon*),
mahonia, and vine maple (*Acer circinatum*)—tough
enough to withstand the attentions of art lovers.

Bybee–Howell Territorial Park

Howell Park Road
Sauvie Island
(503) 221-1741 (Oregon Historical Society)
(503) 797-1850 (Metro)

Season of interest: Summer

Directions: From Highway 30, approximately ten miles north of Portland, turn east to Sauvie Island; the intersection is well marked and has a traffic light. Cross the bridge and proceed north approximately one mile. Turn right on Howell Park Road, following signs to the park. Parking is a few hundred feet east, on the left, in a field. After parking, walk east past the house toward the barn; the orchard is just north of the barn. The park is open every day, but it is attended, and the house is open for tours, only during the summer; call for hours attended.

Public transit: Tri-Met bus 17-NW 21st Avenue-NW St. Helens Road crosses the bridge onto Sauvie Island, and stops at the base of the island side of the bridge.

Labels: None

Weddings: The grounds may be rented for weddings through the events manager at the Oregon Historical Society, (503) 306-5227.

Background: James F. Bybee homesteaded the land in 1845 and built the house in 1856. He sold the property to Benjamin and Elizabeth Howell in 1873. Multnomah County bought it from the Howell family in 1961. The park is now jointly administered by Metro Greenspaces and the Oregon Historical Society.

Although four ancient apple trees survive from the Howell era, it's not clear when the original orchard was planted, and what varieties grew there. Most of the younger trees date to 1969-70, when the Home Orchard

Society planted 120 varieties representing those grown in Oregon during the pioneer era. The society also planted thirty-eight pears, fifteen prunes and plums, four cherries, and four grapevines. In 1988 some Russian varieties were planted, as part of the historical society's North Pacific program, though there is no evidence that either Russian settlers or Russian apple trees were here in pioneer days.

The Portland Garden Club planted the herb garden behind the house in a paisley shape in the late 1960s. Another area at the northwest corner of the house was planted with two dozen herbs in the mid 1980s. The cottage gardens along the north and south sides of the house were started by Skip Enge, exhibit designer for the historical society, in the mid 1980s. They have developed in true cottage-garden style. He started by scattering a seed mixture, and later added plants as he divided perennials in his home garden. Each year he inspects the border to see whether it's in balance, and winnows out extra specimens of over-represented varieties. Some plants also disappear at the hands of over-zealous weeders.

What to see: The orchard contains approximately 140 varieties of apples, generally divided into early bearers in the front rows and later bearers in the back. The trees lack labels because scoundrels would strip the scion wood of rare varieties. The names, even if you don't know to which trees they belong, are delightful; they include Black Jersey, Cox's Orange, Horse, Irish Peach, Greasy Pippin, Mother, Peck's Pleasant, Sanctuary Delicious, Sops of Wine, and Westfield Seek No Further. The three dozen varieties of pears were also known to the pioneers.

The gardens are small and only sporadically
maintained at this writing. The herb garden behind the
house contains iris, chives, sweet woodruff (*Galium
odoratum*), several mints, sage, and thyme. The front herb
garden has melded into the border.

The borders to the south and north change annually,
depending on what has reseeded itself most vigorously or
given up the battle for survival, and what plants have
been added. Probably you'll find ornamental grasses,
rudbeckia, hollyhocks, purple coneflowers (*Echinacea
purpurea*), *Campanula carpatica* 'Blue Chips,' Shasta daisies
(*Chrysanthemum* x *superbum*), and *Heuchera* 'Palace
Purple.'

Columbia County Demonstration Garden

Columbia County Fairgrounds
St. Helens
(503) 397-3462 (Chip Buell)

❧

Seasons of interest: Summer, fall. Vegetables and annuals are planted in spring, and the garden is at its best from fair season (the last full week in July) into the fall.

Directions: From Highway 30 on the southern edge of St. Helens, turn west at the traffic light onto Gable Road, just south of the Safeway store. After seven-tenths of a mile, turn left onto Bachelor Flat Road. After another 1.1 mile, Bachelor Flat Road veers off to the left; proceed straight ahead on Saulser Road. The fairgrounds gate nearest the garden is a few hundred feet farther on the right; the main gate is four-tenths of a mile farther, around the corner.

Schedule tours through Mr. Buell, the county agent.

Labels: There are a few labels. Interpretive signs for some of the gardens discuss garden planning and techniques.

Background: The Columbia County Master Gardeners have maintained a demonstration garden here since 1987 to show new techniques and crops suitable for the area.

What to see: This garden provides a variety of inspirations for the home gardener.

To the right inside the entrance is a small pond, surrounded by sedums and bee balm (*Monarda didyma*). The flower bed just to the east includes gayfeather, speedwell, yarrows, daisies, and cosmos. To the left inside the entrance a shade garden includes feverfew (*Chrysanthemum parthenium*), hardy fuchsia (*Fuchsia magellanica*), and baneberry (*Actaea rubra*).

Herbs and edible flowers both have their own beds, as do perennial grasses, including arrow bamboo (*Pseudosasa japonica*), blue oat grass (*Helictotrichon sempervirens*), and giant silver banner grass (*Miscanthus sacchariflorus*). One bed is a nursery for daffodil seedlings, cover-cropped with calendulas. Others hold a variety of fruits and vegetables, including an edible landscaping bed with a tepee of beans above calendulas and nasturtiums. The east fence is lined with grapes, and apple trees form the southern boundary.

Hulda Klager Lilac Gardens

115 South Pekin Road
Woodland, Washington 98674
(360) 225-8996 (Hulda Klager Lilac Society)

❧

Seasons of interest: All

Directions: from Interstate 5, take the Woodland exit (no. 21). Follow the signs to the garden (only the first sign off the freeway is an official brown and white highway sign; the rest are multi-colored). The garden is open from 10 a.m. to dusk. A donation of $1 for those over twelve is requested.

Labels: Many of the trees and shrubs are labeled; smaller plants are not.

Weddings: The grounds may be rented for weddings and other events; call the Hulda Klager Lilac Society.

Special events: An open house (during which the house and gift shop are open) is held each year during lilac season (late April and early May; call for specific dates), and includes a sale of lilac plants.

Background: Hulda Klager was a German immigrant who moved to Woodland in 1877, at the age of thirteen. Her house and garden are on five acres of her family's farm. When she was forty and recovering from an illness, she read a book about Luther Burbank, the world-renowned plant breeder (1849-1926), who developed over eight hundred strains and varieties. She decided to start hybridizing plants. She worked with apples, roses, dahlias, and hardy fuchsias, and, two years after starting this work, began hybridizing lilacs. She developed dozens of varieties over the years and, by 1920, she began holding an open house each spring during lilac season to show off her garden. When she was eighty-three, the flood of 1948 washed away her plants, but customers brought cuttings and she replanted. She started holding

open houses again in 1950, and had two hundred
varieties of lilacs by 1958. She died in 1960, six weeks
before her ninety-seventh birthday.

What to see: This old-fashioned garden celebrates lilacs. It
is home to more than five dozen varieties, three dozen of
which were bred by Klager, including 'My Favorite
Sensation,' with white-edged purple blossoms.

But there is more to see than just lilacs. The driveway
curves around a lawn set with a flagpole flanked with
roses, and the garden sign is set in a bed of irises,
rhododendrons, gladioli, and asters. Huge old specimen
trees in the front yard include a variegated box elder (*Acer
negundo* 'Variegatum') shading impatiens and ferns, the
rarely seen true chestnut (*Castanea dentata*), and a monkey
puzzle (*Araucaria araucana*).

In front of the house is the flatiron garden, named for
its shape. The bed is full of tulips in the spring; summer
color comes from coreopsis, pelargoniums, and
marigolds. Dahlias and lilacs line the driveway to the
north; hardy fuchsias and tree peonies are south of the
house.

Behind the house, poor-man's-orchid and honeysuckle
hug the front of the shed, while trumpet vine (*Campsis
radicans*) and plume poppy (*Macleaya cordata*) try to cover
the south side. Hollyhocks grow between the supports of
the water tower, and an umbrella pine (*Sciadopitys
verticillata*) hovers nearby. Behind the house are nursery
beds and full-grown lilacs of all colors.

Salmon Creek
Poison Prevention Garden

Kaiser Permanente Salmon Creek Medical Office
14406 N.E. 20th Avenue
Vancouver, Washington
(360) 254-8436 (Washington State University Master
Gardeners)

Seasons of interest: May through October. Call the Master Gardeners for tours, offered every Saturday at 11 a.m. or by appointment.

Directions: From Interstate 5, take the 134th Avenue exit (no. 7). Proceed east on 134th; turn left on N.E. 20th, at a traffic light. Continue north half a mile. The Salmon Creek Medical Office is on the left. Park on the left side of the parking lot; the garden is in the southwest corner of the parking lot, near the Albertsons store.

Public transit: C-Tran buses 6, 21, 25, and 71 travel to 134th and N.E. 20th.

Labels: All plants are labeled with common and scientific names. A brochure available at the desk just inside the building's main door details the poisonous parts of the plants and the symptoms of poisoning they cause.

Background: This garden has its roots in Southern California. Thirty years ago, poisonings from oleander (*Nerium oleander*), an attractive flowering evergreen shrub widely grown there, were well publicized. Southern California has both human and horticultural immigrants from all over the world, and the humans may not know which plants new to them are toxic. So Kaiser built a Sinister Garden to help them learn, and now has three in that area. The Pacific Northwest also has many immigrants who are unlikely to know, for instance, that all parts of the ubiquitous rhododendrons are poisonous, so Kaiser decided to start a poisonous plant garden here. It worked with the Oregon and Washington poison centers and one of its own pharmacists to select appropriate plants for the garden, installed in July 1997.

The plants all have toxic properties, but, for the safety of the gardeners, plants that cause contact dermatitis, like poison oak, were left out.

The docents are all master gardeners who have received additional training.

What to see: None of these plants is very rare; the purpose of the garden is to educate the public as to which plants commonly found in northwest gardens have toxic properties. As the docents may mention, good garden etiquette—staying outside the fence, not picking flowers or berries, keeping children under control—is extremely important here.

Among the many attractive plants in the garden are blue and red cardinal flowers (*Lobelia siphilitica* and *L. cardinalis*); winter and garland daphnes (*Daphne odora* and *D. cneorum*), and smooth hydrangea (*Hydrangea arborescens* 'Annabelle'). The berries of the winterberry (*Ilex verticillata* 'Winter Red') provide winter color.

The plants represent a variety of sources for poisoning. Rhubarb leaves and holly berries and leaves are toxic if eaten; comfrey leaves are traditionally boiled into a tea that is harmful in strong or frequent doses; and the euphorbia's seeds and sap are skin irritants. The leaves and acorns of the Oregon white oak (*Quercus garryana*) include toxic tannins. Leaves and extracts from the ginkgos (*Ginkgo biloba* 'Autumn Gold') are irritants, and all parts of the red horsechestnut (*Aesculus* x *carnea* 'Briotii') are poisonous. Some of the plants, like the foxglove, have beneficial uses if purified and used in correct doses, but are harmful in casual, uninformed use.

Fort Vancouver

612 E. Reserve
Vancouver, Washington
(800) 832-3599

Seasons of interest: All

Directions: From Interstate 5, take exit 1C (Mill Plain).
Turn right on Mill Plain, then right on Fort Vancouver
Way. At the traffic circle, go three-quarters of the way
around the circle and proceed east on Evergreen
Boulevard. Turn right at the sign for the visitors' center,
and then right again. At the stop sign, continue straight
ahead. The garden is southwest of the parking lot, just
outside the stockade. There is no admission charge to the
garden (open 9-4 in winter, 9-5 in summer), but there's a
receptacle for donations; there is an admission charge to
the fort.

Public transit: C-Tran bus 32 stops on Evergreen
Boulevard at the entrance to the visitors' center.

Labels: Most varieties are labeled.

Background: The Hudson's Bay Company, a British fur-
trading business, started a fort in what is now the
Vancouver area in 1825; the fort on the current site was
built in 1829. The fort served as the company's Columbia
District headquarters and a commercial trading post, and
was expanded several times. It was an important factor in
establishing European settlement in the Oregon Country.

In 1860, the fort became the property of the US Army,
which burned the remaining buildings to the ground in
1866. Archaeological excavations began in the 1940s, and
in 1948 the fort site became a National Monument. It
became a National Historic Site in 1961, and work on
rebuilding the fort, starting with the stockade, began in
1966. An orchard was planted in 1963, but in a location
and with varieties that are not historically accurate. A

garden in the style of American pioneer kitchen gardens was started in the late 1960s. The current garden is planned to evoke an English kitchen garden—grown for both usefulness and pleasure—of 1845. It is not an exact replica of any garden from the fort's active days.

Since the Hudson's Bay Company was an English company, its original garden no doubt reflected current English gardening practices (transitional, from the late Georgian to the early Victorian era) rather than American ones. Rick Edwards, the park ranger and former rock musician who's been running the garden since the late 1980s, learned that English kitchen gardens, which served wealthy households, didn't just grow herbs, vegetables, and flowers in the ground, as American ones did. Their flowers were grown both in pots and for cutting, and they grew fruits including exotics such as lemons and figs. They also served as pleasure grounds for the family and guests of the house.

According to Edwards's research, the fort had no greenhouse, but did have coldframes and hotbeds. Thus the garden couldn't have grown pineapples, but did grow lemons, oranges, pomegranates, and figs. The lemons and oranges would have been started from seed, in order to be hardy enough to survive the winter without a greenhouse.

English kitchen gardens of a century and a half ago didn't have chemical fertilizers or pesticides, so the fort's garden doesn't use any today. Cover crops—crimson clover, buckwheat, winter rye, and Austrian field peas—provide nutrients and soil amendments. Nicotine is an authentic organic control of the period, but Edwards chooses not to use it. Garden practices he does follow include planting organically grown seedlings, crop rotation (on a seven-year cycle), companion planting, hand-picking of cabbage worms, and putting terra-cotta tiles under melons to speed ripening.

About ninety percent of the garden is planted in varieties appropriate to 1845 English gardening, as the search continues for authentic varieties. The remaining ten percent includes wheat (grown because it was a major trade crop for the fort, not because it would have been grown in the original garden), potatoes, and watermelon. Some of the melons grown at the fort were so tasty that John McLoughlin, the chief factor (business manager), posted a guard over them so that they didn't all disappear. Flower varieties that prove inauthentic are cut less slack. When a visitor pointed out that Shasta daisies were a twentieth-century cultivar, the fact was confirmed and the plant was gone by the next day.

Edwards tries to introduce a new design element into the garden each year, to give visitors an idea of what they can do in a small space. One such feature is the hop tunnel. The English of the period used hops ornamentally, and to create shade. They didn't eat corn, but the garden grows some Indian corn in tribute to the French Canadians at the fort, who did. Some of the produce is used in the fort's kitchen demonstrations; some is put in a cart at the front of the garden for visitors to sample.

What to see: The scarlet runner beans along the front
fence are planted each year on Queen Victoria's birthday
(May 24). Among the flowers in the front beds are love-
lies-bleeding (*Amaranthus caudatus*), widows'-tears
(*Tradescantia virginiana*) and four o-clocks (*Mirabilis jalapa*).
An herb garden nearby is to be divided into medicinal
and culinary areas.

The cutting garden includes tasselflower (*Emilia
javanica*) and red swallowwort (*Asclepias incarnata*), along
with such common flowers as dahlias and zinnias.

Among the many heirloom tomatoes are 'White
Beauty,' 'Yellow Perfection,' and 'Purple Calabash.' The
muskmelon is 'Nutmeg.' One bed grows wheat, and
there's another of colewort, a Scottish green.

At the south end of the garden, beyond a hop trellis
and just outside the stockade walls, are more flowers,
including such old favorites as beebalm (*Monarda didyma*),
cosmos, and calendulas. An uncommon one, which
provokes comment because it's showy in bloom, is
gooseneck loosestrife (*Lysimachia clethroides*). (If you think
you want it in your garden, be aware that it's very
invasive.)

Southeast Portland, and Southern and Eastern Suburbs

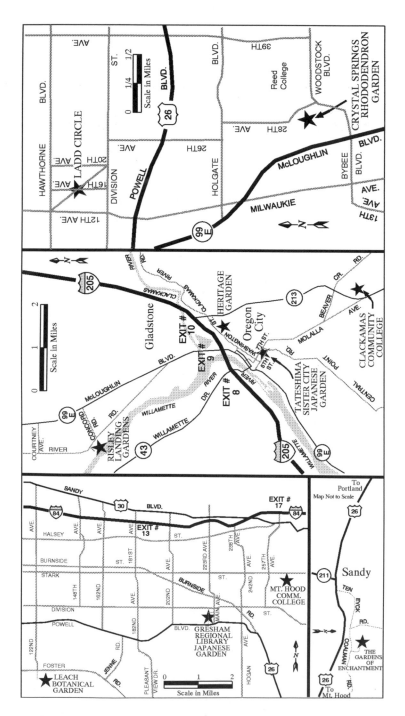

Ladd Circle and Squares

S.E. 16th and Ladd Circle
(503) 823-3636 (City of Portland Rose Gardens)

ॐ

Seasons of interest: Spring, summer, and fall

Directions: From Hawthorne Boulevard head south, or from Division Street head north, on S.E. 16th Avenue. Continue past the first square and park at the circle. The squares are easily visible from the circle, and each is just a block away. It's generally easier to walk to the squares from the circle than drive to them; Ladd's Addition has a diagonal street grid.

Public transit: Take Tri-Met Bus 10-Harold to Ladd Circle.

Labels: All the roses in the squares are labeled; the plants in the circle are not.

Background: The 1891 plat of Ladd's Addition named the circle Central Park and the squares East, South, West, and North parks. Building did not begin in earnest until 1905. The city planted floral displays of some sort in the squares by 1909.

The circle was graded and turfed in 1910 and was planted with annuals that summer and hardy shrubs in the fall. An early plant list for the circle includes hundreds of hybrid rhododendrons, winter daphne (*Daphne odora*), Spanish broom (*Spartium junceum*), and hydrangeas; lesser numbers of viburnums, barberries, winter currants, hawthorns, and *Stephanandra incisa*; and one oriental plane tree (*Platanus orientalis*). In 1911, the city planted "a floral display of tender exotics" in the circle. By then, the squares were planted with roses.

In 1912, the city decided to use the squares as part of a public rose education project in conjunction with the newly planted rose garden in Peninsula Park. New varieties first planted there were to be propagated and planted in the squares, and replaced in a few years with better or newer varieties. The public was to visit Ladd's squares and Peninsula Park not just to gaze upon the roses but to study them, and thereby become fit citizens of the City of Roses.

It is not clear when three of the squares (all except the north) arrived at their current design. The north square, which had matched the others, was radically redesigned in the mid 1970s. The narrow grass paths in the other squares must be hand-mowed; the north square got arc-shaped rose beds with wide swaths of grass to allow the use of a riding mower. Public protests prevented similar relandscaping of the other three squares. Traditionalists wanted the north square to be replanted in the prior design, although its new configuration offered a less densely packed prospect than the others, and was by no means ugly. In 1994, the Park Bureau compromised by replacing the yews in the center with square rosebeds and climbers.

The east square is shorter, north to south, than the others to accommodate Tri-Met buses. The rosebeds were shortened accordingly, and the difference is not very apparent.

The circle was relandscaped in the early 1980s to open up the view into the center and add lower-growing shrubs as a transition to the huge old originals. For some years many annuals and bulbs were planted; in recent years those have gradually given way to perennials.

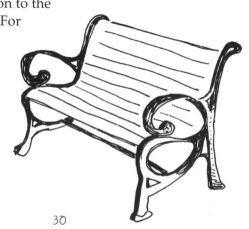

What to see: The squares display roses—hybrid teas, floribundas, grandifloras, and, around the center lawn of each, climbers. Except for Portland's signature rose, 'Madame Caroline Testout' (see International Rose Test Garden, page 83), which dates from 1890, none of the rose varieties was released into the trade after the establishment of these gardens.

Three of the squares (all except the north) are divided into four diamonds—north, east, south, and west—which are in turn divided into a center bed and wedge-shaped beds aligned to the compass points. 'Madame Caroline Testout' can be found in the east square, in the south bed of the east diamond. Other venerable roses in the east square include 'Étoile de Hollande,' a classic red hybrid tea of 1919, in the north bed of the south diamond; 'Sparkler,' a red polyantha from 1929 in the south circle; and 'Duquesa de Peñaranda,' an orange-pink from 1931 in the southwest bed of the south diamond. Among the newest roses in the east square are 'All That Jazz' from 1991, in the west circle, and 'Maid of Honor' from 1986, in the east bed of the north diamond. The climber in the center is 1960's 'Royal Sunset.'

In the south square several orangey roses line Orange Avenue. In the west diamond is 'Elizabeth of Glamis,' a deep salmon in the west bed and 'Tropicana,' an orange, in the center. The deep red-orange 'Voodoo' is in the southwest bed of the north diamond. If you like lavender roses, the only one in the south square is 'Heirloom,' in the southeast bed of the south diamond.

In the west square, 'Masquerade' in the south diamond of the south bed opens yellow and turns to red. In the north bed of that diamond is 'Graceland,' a butter yellow hybrid tea. Among the pinks are 'Fluffy Ruffles,' a pink polyantha in the north bed of the north diamond; 'Pink Favorite' in the center of the west diamond; and 'Dainty Bess,' a single, in the east bed of the west diamond.

In the north square, the beds are arcs of concentric circles, radiating from a central planting of climbers. Many of the roses run to oranges and warm reds, including 'Just Joey,' a ruffled apricot in the south bed of the outer circle, offspring of the deeper orange 'Fragrant Cloud' in the south bed of the middle circle; and 'Cathedral,' a deep orange in the southeast bed of the outer circle.

Back at Ladd Circle, the season begins in spring for the huge old rhododendrons and camellias. Later color and interest are provided by hydrangeas, iris, ornamental grasses, lupines, daylilies, and daisies.

Crystal Springs Rhododendron Garden

S.E. 28th and Woodstock
(503) 823-3640

Seasons of interest: Spring

Directions: From S.E. Powell Boulevard turn south on 26th Avenue; turn left on Holgate Boulevard and then right on 28th Avenue. Continue seven-tenths of a mile and turn right into the well-marked parking lot. The garden is open year round. Visitors twelve years and older must pay an admission fee when visiting Thursday through Monday, from March to Labor Day, between 10 a.m. and 6 p.m.

Public transit: Take Tri-Met bus 19-Woodstock to 28th and Martins.

Labels: Some plants are labeled.

Weddings: Various spaces in the garden accommodate up to one hundred and fifty people. Call (503) 256-2483 for information.

Background: Rhododendron collectors and nursery operators formed a rhododendron society in Portland in the summer of 1944 that soon incorporated as the American Rhododendron Society. One of the society's purposes, along with publishing a bulletin on various aspects of rhododendrons and promoting a rhododendron show, was to establish a test garden.

The society held its first rhododendron show on Mother's Day Weekend of 1945, began publishing a yearbook, and, at the very end of 1945, was given a site for the garden. Three members of the Jackson family, publishers of the *Oregon Journal* (a daily newspaper published in Portland from 1902 to 1982), bought twenty-five acres of land along Terwilliger Boulevard in southwest Portland and gave it to the state board of higher education—owner of the adjoining Sam Jackson Park—for use as a park. The American Rhododendron Society had already begun amassing rare rhododendrons. The garden was to consist mostly of hillside planting beds, reached by footpaths, with few roads and buildings. But the site proved too steep to be hospitable, and the society began looking for a new place for its test garden.

It found the island in Crystal Springs Lake, next to the city's Eastmoreland Golf Course. The site had proven too remote for the city's Shakespearean garden, which lasted only a couple of years there in the 1930s, but its four acres seemed appropriate for the society's need for a space for displaying rhododendrons, working out their nomenclature, and testing them under local conditions. When the Crystal Springs garden started, there were only two other rhododendron test gardens in the country: at the University of Washington Arboretum in Seattle, and at Morris Arboretum outside Philadelphia. The first two rhododendrons planted, in October 1950, were not test plants; they were forty-year-old 'Cynthia' hybrids, dug out of the front yard of Park Superintendent C. Paul Keyser.

Within ten years, the garden had three distinct parts: the entrance garden was under way, the test garden had been developed on the island, and the display garden had been begun on the peninsula. But, with the lack of a resident curator, testing was abandoned in 1964. In the early 1990s, a series of rocky terraces at the north end of the island were planted with perennials, bulbs, and small rhododendrons.

What to see: Crystal Springs is the liveliest rhododendron garden around. Not only is the color almost overwhelming when the gardens are at their peak in late April, but activity abounds: water flowing, squirrels

34

begging for grain or munching on rhododendron pistils and stamens, mallards muttering comfortingly and, in the borrowed landscape of Eastmoreland Golf Course to the north and west, golfers at play.

The garden includes hundreds of rhododendrons—mainly hybrids—and a range of trees and companion plants. Just inside the entrance, a high bridge beckons past a 'Milky Way' Kousa dogwood (*Cornus kousa* 'Milky Way'). Below the bridge, on the right, are the huge, rhubarb-like leaves of a large patch of Japanese Butterbur (*Petasites japonicus*). You can reach them by a path winding down to the left through the Jane E. Martin Entrance Garden, planted in memory of the wife of an early president of the American Rhododendron Society. On the left are evergreen azaleas atop a stone wall; on the right are an American linden (*Tilia americana*) and species rhododendrons.

Hostas, iris, and ferns hem the stream's clear rocky pools. A side path to the right leads along the stream past heather, primroses, and species rhododendrons to the lagoon, with a view across to the peninsula. Ahead, the path eases back up the hill past more hostas, fringecups (*Tellima grandiflora*), and lunaria beneath bigleaf maples (*Acer macrophyllum*) on the left and big pink rhododendrons including *Rhododendron calophytum* on the right. Just before you reach the bridge, the little tree on the right is *Parrotia persica*.

A few feet past the bridge, turn right and proceed out to the peninsula. The pale yellow rhododendron 'Goldfort' arches over the path. A bit further on, the path traverses a little grove of Loderi hybrids. The north end of the peninsula has a collection of evergreen azaleas and smaller rhododendrons including 'Blue River' and 'Crater Lake,' hybridized in or near Eugene. Among the trees are Japanese stewartia (*Stewartia pseudocamellia*) and small maples; other companions include Japanese snowbell (*Styrax japonicus*), scilla, and crape myrtle (*Lagerstroemia indica*). Along the west side of the peninsula are 'Lem's Cameo' and 'Hello Dolly,' hybridized in Seattle. On the southeast side of the peninsula, toward the bridge to the island, the slope down to the lake inlet is scented by waves of mollis hybrid azaleas.

On the island, the path along the lake proceeds past a wall topped with azaleas on the left; on the right, several red alders (*Alnus rubra*) and gnarled Amur maples (*Acer ginnala*) arch over the path and the water. Above the path along the water around the southern end of the island the many species rhododendrons include *R. ririei* and *R. discolor*.

Near the southern end of the island, the large lawn is a popular picnic spot. On the west side, just to the north of *Magnolia sieboldii*, eighty-year-old plants of 'Cynthia' provide a twenty-foot-high wall of rosy blossoms. Azaleas grow along the eastern and southeastern edges. In the southeast corner, *Magnolia campbellii* var. *mollicomata* shades candelabra primroses. In the northeast corner, the trees in front of the restrooms are uncommon: the Chinese fringe tree (*Chionanthus retusus*), bearing wispy white blossoms in May, and a big willow oak (*Quercus phellos*). At the north end of the lawn a dove tree (*Davidia involucrata*) towers over 'Lem's Walloper,' another Seattle-area hybrid.

Continue north to the exhibit hall. Across the path to the west, in April 'Beauty of Littleworth' has huge white trusses, and 'Dairy Maid' glows with pale yellow. To the northwest of the hall, a bed containing only large old plants of 'Loderi King George' is a good place to see the character of mature rhododendron trunks.

Continue north. The northern edge of the island has rocky tiers with a double waterfall. In the terraces are very small rhododendrons and a wide range of companions, including several erythroniums, daphnes, and lewisias; *Corydalis lutea*; and *Penstemon pinifolius*.

As you return to the parking lot, look to your left about halfway up the hill between the low island bridge and the high bridge. At the junction where a path takes off to the northwest is the garden's namesake rhododendron, hybridized by a breeder from Garden Home in southwest Portland.

Leach Botanical Garden

6704 S.E. 122nd Avenue
Portland, OR 97236
(503) 761-9503

Seasons of interest: All

Directions: From S.E. Foster Road, turn south onto 122nd Avenue. The entrance is two-tenths of a mile from Foster Road, on the left; the parking area is a few hundred feet south, across the white wooden bridge, on the right. The garden is open every day except Mondays and holidays. Guided tours can be arranged, and a written tour brochure is available.

The paths require careful footing; some are steep, and some have small obstructions such as roots and stones.

Public transit: Take Tri-Met bus 10-Harold or 71-60th - 122nd to 122nd and Foster. 122nd has no shoulders or sidewalks for the second tenth of a mile to the garden and visibility is poor, so walking to and from the garden requires considerable caution and agility.

Labels: Many plants are labeled.

Weddings: An indoor wedding chapel, with piano and room for eighty-five people, can be rented. If weather permits, French doors from the chapel can be opened onto the lawn.

Background: The garden began as the private garden of John and Lilla Leach. The Leaches purchased the original five acres of the garden in 1931 and built the house in 1936. They called their estate Sleepy Hollow. Mr. Leach was a pharmacist and civic leader in southeast Portland. Mrs. Leach had a degree in botany from the University of Oregon, and taught botany for several years before they married.

The Leaches made plant-collecting trips off the beaten path over much of the west. They found the Siskiyou Mountains of southern Oregon a particularly good source of plants. Because the Siskiyous were not entirely inundated by the ocean during the Cretaceous period, 65 to 75 million years ago, as was the rest of the state, they have a variety of soils, including serpentine, and considerable speciation that the rest of the state lacks. To Mrs. Leach, the most exciting day in all of their twenty years of exploring was in 1930 when, in Gold Basin in the Siskiyous, she discovered a new genus, *Kalmiopsis*. The species name, *leachiana*, honors her. She also discovered one other genus (*Bensoniella*), and a dozen species.

Mr. Leach worked on the gardens and once had an herb garden (in a spot now too shady for one), but Mrs. Leach generally decided what to acquire and plant. Her collections included Northwest natives and plants from the Southeastern United States. She also collected hollies, camellias, witch hazels, stewartias, euonymus, and viburnums.

Mr. Leach died in 1972, and the following year Mrs. Leach gave the property to the City of Portland on condition that it be maintained as a botanical garden. The city hemmed and hawed for a few years, allowing the garden to become overgrown, because it wasn't sure that the public would be sufficiently interested in a botanical garden. After it almost lost the garden because of neglect, the city decided in 1981 to restore and maintain the property. Two years later the Friends of Leach Garden formed to help the city maintain it, and the garden opened to the public. In 1984 the city purchased an additional four acres to the south, and began developing gardens there. The rock garden behind the house was planted around 1990; the beds in front of the house, in the driveway and patios, are more recent.

What to see: The garden is tucked into the Johnson Creek ravine, and spills over onto a plateau to the north. It includes many collections, emphasizing ferns and Northwest and Southeast natives.

The first collections you come to are above the driveway. At the gate is a fern collection. Farther east are small trees and shrubs including witch hazels, barberries, sarcococcas, and viburnums.

In the driveway, the first bed in from the street is home to plants of the Cascades, including *Penstemon cardwellii* and an alpine fir (*Abies lasiocarpa*). The next bed includes such natives of the Southeastern United States as sheep laurel (*Kalmia angustifolia*) and fragrant sumac (*Rhus aromatica*). In the patio in front of the gift shop, one bed features mahonia species and the other displays ferns native to Oregon. On the patio outside the front door of the main house, the bed nearest the door holds plants of the Siskiyous including *Iris innominata*, one of Mrs. Leach's discoveries, and the bed further south displays a dozen sedums.

Next to the gift shop are steps to the rock garden that stretches up the slope behind the house. Here are yet more sedums and penstemons, along with columbines, iris, alliums, lewisias, erigerons, and heucheras. West of the rock garden, the xeric (drought-tolerant) collection is colorful with irises in late spring, and it's also home to lace shrub (*Stephanandra incisa*) and several species of kinnikinnick (*Arctostaphylos*), ceanothus, and California fuchsia (*Zauschneria*). Farther northwest, in the dry conifer forest, is a collection of epimediums, and wildflowers under a tall stewartia (*Stewartia monadelpha*). Natives in the dry woods include vine maple (*Acer circinatum*), huckleberry (*Vaccinium* spp.), trilliums, and cascara (*Rhamnus purshiana*).

East of the dry woods is the Leach collection of collections. Just above the rock garden are the camellias,

40

including more than fifty cultivars of *Camellia japonica*. Up
the hill from the camellias are woodland flowers at the
eastern edge of the property and rhododendrons slightly
to the west. Farther up the hill along the eastern edge are
the hollies. Contrast the very prickly hedgehog holly (*Ilex
aquifolium* 'Ferox') with the smooth- and small-leaved
Japanese holly (*I. crenata*).

At the top of the hill, proceed through the gate. Metro's
composting center compares several methods and
includes a mulching demonstration. Gardens include a
test garden for the Oregon Fuchsia Society, an herb
garden, and a display of North American penstemons,
with separate beds for various regions of the country. The
garden's only *Kalmiopsis leachiana* lives in a trough in front
of the small plastic greenhouse.

Return to the house. Behind the house is a sidewalk
from which you can see the rest of the rock garden. Keep
heading east, past the garage, to the walkway down the
eastern edge of the property. You'll pass a few more
camellias along the fence line, and come to a bog display
of ferns and other plants that like wet feet including the
willow *Salix commutata*, squashberry (*Viburnum edule*),
and *Boykinia rotundifolia*. To the west are yet more ferns,
particularly *Polystichum*, *Osmunda* and *Dryopteris* species,
and an assortment of wild gingers (*Asarum*).

Across Johnson Creek, most of the vegetation is native
to the Northwestern states: a soft-barked coast redwood
(*Sequoia sempervirens*), licorice and sword ferns
(*Polypodium glycyrrhiza* and *Polystichum munitum*),
trilliums, knob-cone pine (*Pinus attenuata*) and, at the east
end of the top of the bank, the Curry County section,
which includes a few items the Leaches collected. An
interesting exotic is the cork oak (*Quercus suber*), native to
southern Europe and northern Africa.

Gresham Regional Library Japanese Garden

385 NW Miller

Seasons of interest: All

Directions: From Interstate 84, take exit 13. Continue south on 181st to Division. Turn left on Division and continue two and a quarter miles; turn right on North Main. Proceed two-tenths of a mile; turn right on 5th, left on Miller, and right into the library parking lot. The garden is west of the library building.

The gravel paths are somewhat difficult to walk on.

Public transit: Tri-Met buses 4-Division, 9-Powell, 26-Stark, 80-Kane, 81-Hogan and 84-Sandy / Boring stop at the Gresham Central Transit Center, 8th and Kelly, three blocks east of the library. MAX also stops at Gresham Central.

Labels: None

Background: The garden commemorates the sister-city relationship between Gresham and Ebetsu, Japan. It was begun after the library opened in January 1990. The bond issue for the library did not include the garden; most of the materials and labor were donated. Ebetsu chose the plants. The garden was designed by Cindy Lou Pease.

What to see: This small garden has a higher proportion of lawn than the other Japanese gardens in this book, and next to the library building are rudbeckias and yarrows, but its other plant material is, as one would expect, evergreens, flowering cherries, and small maples.

Among the garden's weepers and creepers are a Camperdown elm (*Ulmus glabra* 'Camperdownii'), a prostrate deodar cedar (*Cedrus deodara* 'Pendula'), and a European birch (*Betula pendula*). The conifer with almost white new needles, across the path from the bench near the north edge, is a dwarf Canadian hemlock (*Tsuga canadensis* 'Gentsch White'). The flowering cherries are Kwanzans (*Prunus serrulata* 'Kwanzan').

The garden is flat except for five mounds symbolizing the five communities served by the library: Gresham, Troutdale, Wood Village, Fairview, and Maywood Park.

Mt. Hood Community College

Stark Street east of 257th
Gresham

❧

Seasons of interest: All

Directions: From Interstate 84 east of Portland, take exit 17. Follow the signs to the college. At Stark Street, turn left onto Stark and proceed three-tenths of a mile. Turn right into the college, and then immediately left. The first building, on your right, is the horticulture building, flanked by parking lots.

Public transit: Tri-Met buses 80-Kane Road and 81-Hogan-257th serve the Mt. Hood campus.

Labels: A few plants are labeled.

Background: The garden was probably planned by Jean Waller, a college staff member, in the mid 1970s to serve horticulture classes studying plant identification.

What to see: This garden displays the immense variety within the conifers in an attractive and compact, if somewhat unkempt, garden. Those who love conifers will appreciate the diversity of the collection while those who think they're boring will be astonished.

Most of the conifers are arrayed on the hillside west of the building, and along the road to the north. Near the bench (like most of the other wooden structures, fallen into disrepair) is a low, wide mound of balsam fir (*Abies balsamea* 'Nana'). Droopers include a European larch (*Larix decidua*) and, hiding some of the fence to the south, an Atlas cedar (*Cedrus atlantica* 'Glauca Pendula'). Among the specimen deciduous trees are a London plane tree (*Platanus* x *acerifolia*) and a Spanish locust (*Robinia hispida*) grafted as a standard, the better to see its rosy blossoms, and nearby an *Enkianthus* shrub. East of the building are more conifers, with bulbs and peonies.

❧

The Gardens of Enchantment

43233 S.E. Oral Hull Road
Sandy
(503) 668-6195

Seasons of interest: The gardens are open by appointment only, from May 1 through October 15.

Directions: From Highway 26 at the east end of Sandy, turn north onto Ten Eyck Road. At the bottom of the first hill, proceed straight onto Coalman Road. Go nine-tenths of a mile, turn left, and continue to the end of the road.

Labels: Many, in both Braille and large Roman

Background: The Gardens of Enchantment were designed by Tom Halvorson and built in 1970-71 by the Multnomah and Clackamas chapters of the Oregon State Federation of Garden Clubs. They are the headquarters of the Touch and Grow Garden Club for the blind or nearly blind.

What to see: The garden is designed to appeal to all senses. Some of the terraced beds are much higher than the adjacent paths, yielding a new perspective on plants generally viewed from above.

Just inside the gate is the sound area, a fountain surrounded by benches. The path proceeds to the taste area where culinary herbs grow in a raised bed on the west side of the walk. On the east side, obviously not for consumption, are rhododendrons, azaleas, irises, and annuals. The next terrace down is for touch, with common plants like lamb's ears (*Stachys byzantina*), holly, and yucca and more exotic plants such as tree ivy, with its stiff, upright branches and folded leaves, and weeping pussy willow. The fragrance terrace, at the bottom of the garden, includes miniature roses, scented geraniums, dianthus, stock, and nicotiana. Across from the terrace, pear and apple trees mark the eastern border.

Risley Landing Gardens

16195 Oak Shore Lane
Oak Grove
(503) 654-8044 or
(503) 654-2337 (Oak Grove Garden Club members)

❧

Seasons of interest: All. The garden is open by appointment only.

Directions: The gardens are near McLoughlin Boulevard, Highway 99E. If proceeding south from Milwaukie, in Oak Grove turn right on Courtney, the first stoplight past the Bomber (a B-17 perched west of the highway and frequently used as a landmark); at River Road, a stoplight, turn left; proceed 1.1 mile and turn right on Oak Shore Lane. If proceeding north from Oregon City, turn left at Concord Road; after six-tenths of a mile, turn right on River Road; after two-tenths of a mile, turn left on Oak Shore Lane. The gardens are at the end of the lane, where it intersects River Forest Place, and are well marked.

Public transit: Take Tri-Met bus 34-River Road to River Road and River Glen Court; walk south one block to Oak Shore Lane.

Weddings: The garden may be rented for groups of up to one hundred.

Labels: Some

Background: Risley Landing, settled by Orville Risley in the early 1850s, is a part of the Jacob S. Risley Donation Land Claim of 1866. Risley Landing was used by river traffic from the 1850s, finally falling into disuse when an electric train line connected Portland and Oregon City in 1893. All that remains of the landing is its foundation. The sandy beach below the landing is flooded in winter.

Hugh Starkweather, a great-grandson of Orville Risley, left 1.12 acres at the landing to the Oak Grove Garden

Club. After much clearing—the property was overgrown with blackberries—the club planted perennials and annuals in 1988, and erected a gazebo, designed by Jacob Risley IV, another Risley descendant and landscape architect, in 1989.

What to see: The garden isn't historic; a dozen oaks are all that remain from landing days of more than a century ago. But it's an attractive small garden with paths meandering around a gently sloping site above the Willamette River, and something in bloom almost any time of the year.

The garden has a small collection of rhododendrons, and several irises. Natives are included in many of the other plantings, including the small rock garden south of the pavilion, which has lewisias, *Sisyrinchium californicum*, *Claytonia parvifolia* var. *flagellaris*, and three euonymus.

Heritage Garden
End of the Oregon Trail Interpretive Center

1726 Washington Street
Oregon City
(503) 657-9336

Seasons of interest: Spring, summer, early fall

Directions: From Interstate 205 southeast of Portland, take the Park Place exit (no. 10), and follow the brown and white signs to the center. The garden is in the southwest corner of the interpretive center, beyond the circle of flagpoles.

Public transit: Tri-Met buses 32-Oatfield, 33-McLoughlin, 34-River Road, 35-Macadam, 79-Canby-Clackamas Town Center and 99X–McLoughlin Express serve the Oregon City Transit Center. From there you can catch a trolley to the End of the Trail Center. Call the Center for trolley operating hours.

Labels: None. There are several interpretive signs about pioneer gardening, however, and *Hatchet, Hands & Hoe*, a book about pioneer gardening by Erica Calkins, discussing plants and their uses, can be purchased at the Center's gift shop.

Background: The garden surrounds the markers on Abernethy Green marking the end of the Oregon Trail. It was planned and planted by local heirloom gardener Erica Calkins and other volunteers in 1992 to be ready for the 1993 sesquicentennial of the Oregon Trail. (The interpretive center wasn't completed until 1995.) The garden is a living memorial to the pioneers; not only are the plants those they would have grown, but some of the plant material came from pioneer families, and some of the roses from old churchyards and homesteads. The plants are all tough enough to survive neglect when the gardeners can't find time to garden. By the summer of 1997, the garden had already survived two floods.

What to see: This pioneer-inspired garden includes six subgardens of plants the pioneers knew and used.

The kitchen garden has such food staples as corn, beans, and tomatoes as well as sage for flavoring. The dooryard garden, running more to medicinal plants and flowers, includes foxglove and mints. In the rose garden are 'Harison's Yellow' (*Rosa* x *harisonii*), a sweet briar rose (*R. eglanteria*), Rosa Mundi (*R. gallica* 'Rosa Mundi') and several cabbage roses (*R. centifolia*). The flower garden includes hollyhocks (*Alcea rosea*) and love-in-a-mist (*Nigella damascena*). The crop garden is for hops, corn, and wheat. The native and naturalized garden includes such medicinal plants and housekeeping helpers as flax (*Linum perenne*) and giant mullein (*Verbascum thapsus*).

Oregon City–Tateshima Sister City Japanese Garden

5th and Washington
Oregon City

Seasons of interest: All

Directions: From Interstate 205 southeast of Portland, take the Park Place exit (no. 10). At the first light, turn right onto Washington. The garden is at the southeast corner of the Oregon City Senior Center, which sits between 5th and 6th and Washington and John Adams streets.

Public transit: Tri-Met bus 33-McLoughlin stops at 5th and Washington.

Labels: None

Background: The garden was designed by the Environmental Learning Center at Clackamas Community College and built under its supervision by the Oregon City community and its sister city. Much of the plant material was donated.

What to see: This small garden is planted along a winding path and an aggregate stream bed. Among the features is a small level bridge over the stream and a Japanese lantern. The plant material includes azaleas, rhododendrons, Japanese maples (*Acer palmatum*) and red pines (*Pinus densiflora*), Kousa dogwoods (*Cornus kousa*), birches, and ornamental grasses.

Clackamas Community College
Horticulture Department Gardens
Environmental Learning Center Garden
Home Orchard Society Arboretum

19600 South Molalla Avenue
Oregon City
(503) 657-8400, extension 2351 (Environmental
Learning Center)
(503) 631-3574 (Jim Black) (Home Orchard Society)

❧

Seasons of interest: All

Directions: From Interstate 205, take the Park Place exit
(no. 10). Proceed south on Highway 213 and follow the
signs to Clackamas Community College to the light at
Molalla Avenue; turn left at the entrance to the college.
Bear right at the entrance and follow Douglas Loop and
the signs to Clairmont Hall. For the horticulture
department gardens, park in front of Clairmont. For the
Environmental Learning Center garden and Home
Orchard Society Arboretum, continue past Clairmont,
turn right at the Environmental Learning Center sign, and
continue past the recycling center to the parking lot on
the left.

The Environmental Learning Center's garden is open
from 8 a.m. until dusk. Children must be accompanied by
parents or teachers, and no pets or bicycles are allowed.
There is an admission fee.

The arboretum is open from April through October on
Saturdays, from 8 a.m. to 3 p.m. If you cannot visit on a
Saturday, make arrangements for another time with Mr.
Black.

Public transit: Tri-Met buses 32-Oatfield, 33-McLoughlin
and 99X-McLoughlin Express serve the college.

Labels: Many plants are labeled.

Background: The horticulture department's gardens were developed and planted for instruction, student practice, and community enjoyment.

The Environmental Learning Center gardens are, in virtually every sense, a recycled and recycling garden. Starting in 1974, three and a half acres that had been the site of a berry processing plant (holding ponds, roads, drainage ditches, and parking lot) were turned into a shade and water garden. The soil, a compacted heavy clay subsoil, was amended by composts made with plant materials from the college grounds. The parking lot, where the drainage was the worst, became a wetlands. One bridge is built of recycled plastic, and recycled concrete and tires form retaining walls. Some of the water features are designed to purify and recycle the water. Even some of the plants are recycled; they were collected, by permit, from Deschutes National Forest lands, to forestall their destruction by a road grader. The garden is also, in essence, a backyard wildlife habitat; the plants were chosen as food sources or homesites for wildlife.

The Home Orchard Society started its arboretum in 1986 to display fruits and fruit trees that can be grown by home gardeners in the Northwest. Several other garden clubs have donated money or materials to the cause.

What to see: Three entities have gardens at Clackamas Community College, and each garden is quite different from the other two.

The horticulture department display includes nine subgardens: dwarf conifers; grasses; herbs; an All-America Selections (AAS) display garden; annuals; perennials; rhododendrons; roses; and witch hazels.

The dwarf conifers planted on the rim of the eastern side of the parking lot demonstrate the range of habits and colors available. A dwarf balsam fir (*Abies balsamea*

'Nana') forms a small, dense green mound and a Hinoki cypress (*Chamaecyparis obtusa* 'Nana Lutea') is a small yellow cone. An Atlas cedar (*Cedrus atlantica* 'Pendula Glauca') rises five feet before dropping at an acute angle toward the ground.

To the south, in front of the greenhouses, is the display of ornamental grasses. A Eulalia grass (*Miscanthus sinensis* 'Gracillimus') unfurls its thirty-inch blades like whips in mid-crack. Quaking grass (*Briza media*) holds its puffed-rice-like inflorescence on two-foot stalks above an eight-inch clump of green.

In front of and along the side of the west greenhouse, a small herb garden includes several each of lavenders, rosemaries, mints, and thymes.

West of Clairmont Hall are a series of gardens edged with Japanese box (*Ilex crenata*). The northernmost features shrub and climbing roses with fragrance, disease resistance, and interesting thorn and foliar colors. The selection includes several *Rosa* x *alba*, several *R. gallica*, and *R. damascena* 'Ispahan.'

Just south of the rose garden, the All-America Selections garden displays AAS choices of flowers and vegetables from the past few years and for the current year. East of the AAS garden, toward the greenhouses, is another small herb bed.

The next garden to the south changes every year; students design the central bed and four corner beds to display annuals, and each bed has a different color and planting scheme. The southernmost garden contains semi-circles of perennials, including several coral bells (*Heuchera* spp.) and thalictrums; peonies; iris; and leopard's flower (*Belamcanda chinensis*).

To the south is a Metro home composting demonstration area. Beyond the sidewalk along the east side of the beds are ten witch hazels. Except for those, which bloom in January and February, the gardens are best seen from June through October.

The Environmental Learning Center's garden is designed like a Chinese hill garden. The larger hills, on the inside of the garden, interrupt the view and make the garden seem larger than it is. The garden also uses coarse-textured foliage on the inside, through which you can see other parts of the garden, and fine-textured foliage on the outer edge, to shield the view of the world outside the garden. The falling water masks the sounds on a nearby road and aerates the water. Several wetland bridges allow contemplation of still water from various perspectives. The garden surrounds a birds of prey exhibit and a fish rearing facility. There are plans to replace the exotics—among them camellias and English ivy—with native plants. The conifers here include a Koster blue spruce (*Picea pungens* 'Koster'), a balsam fir (*Abies balsamea*), a bigcone Douglas fir (*Pseudotsuga macrocarpa*), and a Scotch pine (*Pinus sylvestris*). The hardwoods include an Amur maple (*Acer ginnala*), Pacific (*Cornus nuttallii*) and Eastern (*C. florida*) dogwoods, and a mountain ash. The shrubs include ninebark (*Physocarpus capitatus*), native rhododendrons, glossy abelia (*Abelia* x *grandiflora*), a Pfitzer juniper (*Juniperis chinensis* 'Pfitzerana'), *Pernettya mucronata*, and a wintergreen barberry (*Berberis julianae*). To maintain its effectiveness as a wildlife habitat, the garden is left unmanicured.

Just inside the gate of the Home Orchard Society Arboretum an edible landscape display shows how to grow fruits and enhance wildlife habitat in an informal backyard setting. It includes espaliers, grapes on an arbor, rhubarb, and berry bushes. In the pome section beyond are more than a hundred varieties of apples, and approximately three dozen different pears, including Asian varieties. A section of historical fruit varieties displays those more than a hundred years old but still

worth growing. The exotic fruit area includes kiwi fruit, pineapples, guava, and several plum-apricot crosses. Among the stone fruits are plums, peaches, and nectarines, as well as cherries grown on different rootstocks for comparison of dwarfing characteristics. The small-fruit area includes strawberries, cane berries (rasp, black, boysen and logan), and table grapes for juice, eating fresh, or as raisins. Along the back fence are eleven different blueberries.

Southwest Portland and Washington County

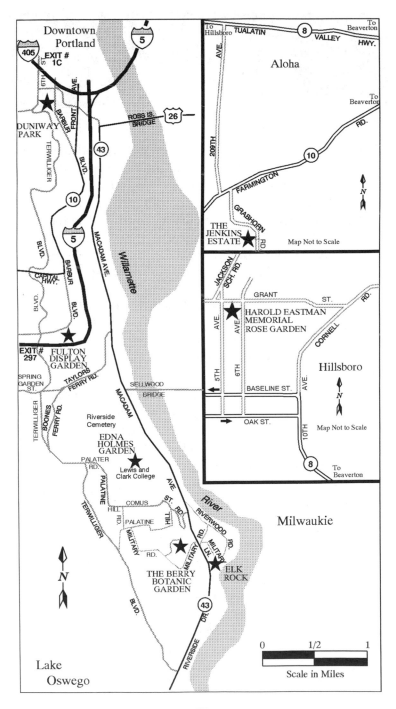

Downtown Portland

EXIT # 1C

405

5

6TH ST.

FRONT AVE.

BARBUR

DUNIWAY PARK

TERWILLIGER

ROSS IS. BRIDGE

26

43

BLVD.

10

5

MACADAM AVE.

Willamette

BARBUR

BLVD.

CAPITAL HWY.

BLVD.

EXIT # 297

FULTON DISPLAY GARDEN

SPRING GARDEN ST.

TAYLORS FERRY RD.

SELLWOOD BRIDGE

MACADAM

Riverside Cemetery

EDNA HOLMES GARDEN

BOONES FERRY RD.

TERWILLIGER

PALATER RD.

Lewis and Clark College

PALATINE

TERWILLIGER

COMUS

HILL RD.

PALATINE RD.

MILITARY

RD.

AVE.

11TH ST. RD.

River

RIVERWOOD RD.

MILITARY RD.

MILITARY LN.

THE BERRY BOTANIC GARDEN

ELK ROCK

43

Milwaukie

N

BLVD.

RIVERSIDE DR.

Lake Oswego

To Hillsboro

TUALATIN

8

VALLEY HWY.

To Beaverton

Aloha

209TH AVE.

FARMINGTON

10

GRABHORN RD.

RD.

To Beaverton

THE JENKINS ESTATE

Map Not to Scale

JACKSON SCH. RD.

GRANT ST.

HAROLD EASTMAN MEMORIAL ROSE GARDEN

CORNELL RD.

5TH AVE.

6TH AVE.

BASELINE ST.

OAK ST.

10TH AVE.

Hillsboro

N

Map Not to Scale

8

To Beaverton

0   1/2   1

Scale in Miles

N

57

Duniway Park

S.W. Terwilliger Boulevard and Sam Jackson Park Road

❧

Season of interest: Spring

Directions: From Interstate 405 from the north take the 6th Avenue exit (1C). At the top of the ramp continue to the next light and turn right on 6th. From the south, from Interstate 405 take the 6th Avenue exit (no. 1C). At the top of the ramp proceed north on 6th; get into the left-hand lane, turn left on Hall or College, and then left on Broadway; continue on Broadway (getting into the right lane) back across Interstate 405; it curves to the left. Turn right on 6th.

At the light at 6th and Sheridan, turn left. Park on Sheridan, or continue in the right lane; around the corner is a small public lot on the right, in front of the track. Walk west along Sheridan and then Terwilliger to reach the garden.

There is no public parking adjacent to the garden. The nearest public parking, two-tenths of a mile south, on the east side of Terwilliger, can't be recommended; cars parked there are frequently broken into.

Public transit: Take Tri-Met bus 8-Jackson Park to Terwilliger and Sam Jackson Park Road.

Labels: Few

Background: Portland is a city with a reputation for turning sows' ears into silk purses. It tore up a four-lane highway to build a park; it replaced a parking garage with a public square; and, on a more modest but just as ironic note, it remodeled its incinerator into an archive. But that's all fairly recent. Much earlier in the ear-to-purse business, it transformed a garbage dump into a fragrant garden.

The transformation was neither quick nor easy. Early in the twentieth century, what is now Duniway Park was

known as Marquam Gulch, and it was the upper part of a
steep ravine cluttered with shacks and crossed by a
railroad trestle. The Olmsted Brothers, brought to
Portland to consult on park development, suggested that
the city build a parkway hugging the hills southwest of
town. The resulting Terwilliger Parkway crossed the
ravine, offering a view of the shacks. The neighborhood
booster association wanted to fill the gulch with sanitary
fill (noncommercial refuse covered with dirt). At first the
garbage got dumped but not covered, and the children of
immigrants living in the ravine played in the garbage for
lack of a better playground. After the mayor promised to
clean up the area, the city in 1918 bought twelve and a
half acres and dedicated them as a park in memory of
Abigail Scott Duniway, Oregon pioneer and suffragette.
By 1923, the park was still a hole in the ground, although
there were plans for a memorial entrance in honor of Mrs.
Duniway, a playground, a community house, sunken
gardens, tennis courts, and an athletic field.

By 1934 much of the upper end of the gulch had
disappeared under fifty to ninety feet of fill and was a
smooth terraced park, although without the planned
features. A few years later an eminent Washington lilac
grower died, and his collection of eight hundred plants
was for sale. The Portland Garden Club bought them all
and hired John Duncan, the superintendent of Spokane
parks who had designed Hoyt Arboretum, to advise on
site selection. He suggested the west end of Duniway
Park, and the lilacs were planted there in 1938. Ten years
later, when a Portland businessman moved from the east
side of town to the west he gave his collection of almost
two hundred lilacs to the city for planting in Duniway
Park, and a couple of years after that the city received two
dozen more plants from the collection of retired nursery
owners who lived near Multnomah. Lilacs don't live

forever, so the garden now has substantially fewer than a thousand plants.

What to see: There are dozens and dozens of lilacs here, in pink, white, and the range from mauve to purple. Some of the flowers are big (as lilacs go) and flat; some are long tubes. The plants range from a couple of feet tall to tree-sized. Most are varieties of *Syringa vulgaris*, but on the north side in the middle the low plants with almost round leaves and small, very fragrant mauve blossoms are *S. microphylla* 'Daphne,' and on the south side are several Japanese tree lilacs (*Syringa reticulata*) that bloom in June.

Elk Rock
the Garden of the Bishop's Close

11800 S. W. Military Lane
Portland, OR 97219
(503) 636-5613 (Episcopal Diocese of Oregon)

Seasons of interest: All

Directions: Proceed south on Highway 43 in southwest Portland 1.7 miles beyond the Sellwood Bridge; turn east onto Military Road, and then immediately right on Military Lane. The garden is at the end of the lane.

It is open daily. Hours change with the seasons, and are always somewhat shorter than the hours of daylight. Pets, picnicking, and games are prohibited. Children under sixteen must be supervised. Groups must make reservations, and those of twenty or more must pay a fee. There are no public restrooms. The house is diocesan headquarters and is not open to the public.

Public transit: Tri-Met bus 35-Macadam stops at Highway 43 and Military Road.

Labels: Many plants are labeled.

Weddings: The garden is not available for weddings.

Background: In the early 1890s, Elk Rock became the home of Peter Kerr, a Scottish-born grain merchant, his partner, and his brother. They formed the Cliff Cottage Club, and lived in the cottage on the thirteen-acre parcel until they married. Kerr was the last to do so, in 1905. After two daughters were born to him and his wife, they built a larger house, at the beginning of World War I. John Olmsted, who had also consulted on the development of Portland's park system and planned the grounds of the Lewis and Clark Exposition early in the century, designed the gardens. Emanuel Mische, Portland's park superintendent from 1908 to 1914 and a former Olmsted employee, helped select the plant material.

After Kerr's death, in 1957, his daughters gave the estate to the Episcopal Diocese of Oregon as a living memorial to their parents. The estate is referred to as the Bishop's Close because at one time there were plans to have the bishop's residence built here.

While it hasn't been static—Kerr was an avid gardener and kept working on it, and changes have been made in the four decades since he died—the garden has matured quite gracefully, as an Olmsted garden should.

What to see: The design of the garden, the variety of evergreens, the selection of flowering plants, and the interesting forms of the deciduous plants give interest all year long.

Even at the peak of the flowering season, in late April and early May, when many rhododendrons, azaleas, and other plants are in bloom, the most engaging color is green. From the grass and tiny rock plants on the ground to the surrounding shrubs and perennials to the mature trees hiding much of the sky, this is an excellent garden in which to explore the shades, textures, and intensities of green that growing plants produce.

The magnolia collection includes about three dozen species and varieties, dispersed over the grounds. Other collections include witch hazels and rhododendrons.

The main parking area surrounds a large tulip tree (*Liriodendron tulipifera*), and is bordered by potentilla, Mexican orange (*Choisya ternata*), and two magnolias— southern (*Magnolia grandiflora*) and bigleaf (*M. macrophylla*). Take the path to the south, along the west side of the house (pausing to make a donation and pick up a map—helpful, but it lists mainly trees) past peonies and conifers. Just past a tiny pool almost hidden by a maidenhair fern (*Adiantum pedatum* var. *aleuticum*), rock

steps lead west up the hill through the rock garden past
more ferns, peonies, epimediums, Kenilworth ivy
(*Cymbalaria muralis*), yuccas, and small rhododendrons.

At the top of the path is the most formal part of the
garden. To the north, the gravel walk skirts the box-
bordered gravel beds of a small witch hazel collection:
Hamamelis mollis and *H.* x *intermedia* 'Ruby Glow' and
'Jelena.' If it's summer you have missed the blooming
season, but look at the yellowish-green, fuzzy, molar-
shaped fruits. Across the path from 'Jelena' is *Berberis
darwinii*; further south, across from 'Ruby Glow,' is a
flowering cherry. To the south are evergreens, including
more box, four large square columns of yew and, in the
southeast corner of the southernmost section, *Taiwania
cryptomerioides* with swooping branches and spiky short
silvery needles.

Down the hill, another walk parallels the west edge of
the lawn. Among the magnolias along the walk is a small
Magnolia stellata 'Jane Platt' (named for one of Kerr's
daughters; she made her own estimable garden a few
miles away). The path also passes numerous mature
rhododendrons, irises, hostas, a pink mountain laurel
(*Kalmia latifolia*), a Japanese stewartia (*Stewartia
pseudocamellia*) with intriguing exfoliating bark, a
Magnolia x *soulangiana* shading a white bleeding heart
(*Dicentra spectabilis*), and a *Cornus florida* 'Rubra' above a
peony.

Take the path veering southeast past a sweet gum
(*Liquidambar styraciflua*) towering over a white mountain
laurel (*Kalmia latifolia*) and across a small stretch of lawn.
To the south, the huge evergreen is an Atlas cedar (*Cedrus
atlantica*). A few steps northwest of the altar, look to the
northeast at the tapestry of evergreens—Hinoki cypress
(*Chamaecyparis obtusa*), Japanese cedar (*Cryptomeria
japonica*) with its pale yellow new growth, and *Magnolia*

liliiflora 'Nigra.' In the center of the lawn, a stream flows
through pools edged with green and variegated hostas,
several cultivars of *Acer palmatum*, ferns, minor bulbs, and
Mahonia pumila, much smaller and duller than Oregon
grape. Shade is provided by an Oregon white oak
(*Quercus garryana*), a Chinese red birch (*Betula albo-sinensis*
var. *septentrionalis*), and a Chinese fringe tree (*Chionanthus
retusus*). In a grove just to the north are a heavily pecked
dawn redwood (*Metasequoia glyptostroboides*) and the
rarely seen Chinese Katsura tree (*Cercidiphyllum japonicum*
var. *sinense*) with shaggy bark. The more common Katsura
(*C. japonicum*) is a few feet east of the grove, near the
fastigiate sugar maple (*Acer saccharum*) 'Newton Sentry.'

At the east edge of the lawn is a path along the cliff
above the river. To the south, the striped-barked *Acer
forrestii* stands just north of the bridge over the stream.
Further south, pass the green, red, and yellow bull's-eyes
of *Euphorbia wulfenii*, a couple of oakleaf hydrangeas
(*Hydrangea quercifolia*), and a southern magnolia (*Magnolia
grandiflora*) on your way to the fishpond, which is home
to yellow and pale pink water lilies. Beyond the pond, the
undergrowth has gone native. Return along the east edge
past the bridge and continue north past several
columbines and irises, lily of the valley, mullein, and
peonies.

At the north end of the house, a small garden within
balustrades is home to *Magnolia delavayi* against the north
wall of the chapel, and *Osmanthus delavayi* in the
northeast corner.

The Berry Botanic Garden

11505 S. W. Summerville Avenue
Portland, OR 97219
(503) 636-4112

❧

Seasons of interest: All. Call for an appointment.

Directions: From Interstate 5, take the Terwilliger exit (no. 297). Proceed south on Terwilliger. Where Terwilliger curves to the right past Lewis and Clark Law School, proceed straight ahead on Palater, following signs to Lewis and Clark College. After one-tenth of a mile, turn right on Palatine Hill Road. After nine-tenths of a mile, turn right on Military Road. After half a mile, turn left on Summerville.

From Highway 43 south of Portland, continue 1.7 miles south from the Sellwood Bridge. Turn right on Military Road. You will quickly come to a stop sign; turn left. Continue half a mile, and turn right on Summerville.

The garden is at the end of the street on the left, marked by a mailbox. There is an admission charge. Pets are not allowed; children must be supervised. At this writing, the garden's driveway and parking lot cannot accommodate busses.

Public transit: Take Tri-Met bus 35-Macadam to Highway 43 and Military Road.

Labels: Most plants are labeled.

Background: The Berry Botanic Garden began as a collector's garden. Rae Selling Berry corresponded with other plantspeople and subscribed to plant-hunting expeditions in China, Tibet, and Nepal in the 1930s. When her collection outgrew her house and yard in southeast Portland and the yard of a neighbor, she moved the garden to its current location, which she chose for its natural bowl shape. She and her husband built the house in 1938.

Mrs. Berry amassed hundreds of species in her garden, but not without focus. One of her interests was primulas, and she founded the Oregon Primrose Society. An avid collector and hybridizer of rhododendrons, she was a charter member of the American Rhododendron Society. She contributed plants to Crystal Springs Rhododendron Garden and helped James Barto of Junction City (see Hendricks Park, page 183) start collecting and hybridizing. She also collected trees, shrubs, and understory plants from eastern Asia; alpines and other rock garden plants; and lilies. She died at age ninety, in 1976. Friends and gardening enthusiasts anxious to preserve her collection bought the property. In 1979 they founded the nonprofit Berry Botanic Garden.

The garden is not, of course, exactly as Berry left it. Plants have died and been replaced; the log beds that originally held her alpine collection have been rebuilt with rocks; the house has been transformed into offices and extended to provide a visitors' center; a large greenhouse replaced an older, smaller one; and a conservation program and collection of natives have been added. Yet, the garden can instill in visitors an appreciation for Berry's adventurous spirit, and perhaps a tinge of regret that their own gardens are filled with commonplace plants when the plant world offers such variety, even within seemingly narrow categories.

What to see: Berry planned her garden to give pleasure year-round, so there's always something to see. And because of the way she designed the garden, and the way it has been developed since her death, there are three ways to tour it.

The first, for those who have only a short time to spend or who are unable to climb the slopes on the edges of the garden, is to circumnavigate the house, noting the carved front door as you go. Here are items representative of the

rest of the garden, such as the *Rhododendron augustinii*
against the front wall of the house, and winter-blooming
wintersweet (*Chimonanthus praecox*) and *Mahonia* 'Arthur
Menzies' in an ell at the back, across the patio from a
raised rock garden. At the south end of the house, a water
feature from alpine troughs, under construction at this
writing, is to attract birds, and it is to be surrounded by
nectar plants to attract both birds and butterflies.

A second way to see the garden is simply as an
attractive landscape. The shrub border beyond the front
and side lawns may look natural at first glance, but it's a
carefully orchestrated blend of natives (the firs, mahonia,
and salal that Berry allowed to stay) and exotics that
provide interest in every season, with a burst of fall color.
Among the imports are some—such as Meyer's lilac
(*Syringa meyeri*) and Kousa dogwood (*Cornus kousa*)—that
were uncommon when she planted them, so the garden
offers a rare chance to see them as mature plants. Behind
the house with the winter-blooming plants mentioned
above are cyclamen, which she planted for their
interesting leaf patterns as well as their flowers.

The third way to tour the garden is in appreciation of
the plants. The five main collections are rhododendrons;
alpine and rock garden plants; natives; primulas; and
lilies. Smaller collections include peonies, bog plants,
shortias, and ferns. A wide variety of other unusual plants
add depth and interest.

If you come to see the rhododendrons, you can easily
feel that the garden is a rhododendron garden with
accouterments. Two hundred of the eight hundred species
of rhododendrons are grown here. They range from
creepers to trees, with all sorts of leaf shapes, flower
types, and flower colors. Rhododendrons are planted in
or around almost every other collection. Across the front
lawn from the house, the border includes such tree-sized

rhododendrons as *R. yunnanense* with pale mauve
blossoms and *R. decorum* x *vernicosum* with white and
pale pink blossoms. Smaller specimens include 'Little
Bert' with red bell-shaped flowers, *R. fastigiatum* with
small purple flowers, and *R. hodgsonii* with huge leaves.

Successful rhododendron gardens depend on other
species to complete the garden picture. The overstory
here is not just the usual Douglas firs, but also contains
deciduous trees including silver bell (*Halesia carolina*).
Closer to the ground are natives including trilliums,
Disporum smithii and mahonia. Other smaller plants
include violets, cyclamen, hostas, sweet woodruff (*Galium
odoratum*), and vetches in blue, purple, several shades of
pink, and white.

Along the south edge of the lawn, primulas hold forth
at the front of the garden. Among them are such Asian
species as *Primula denticulata*, *P. alpicola*, and *P. sikkimensis*.
Back in the shade and wrapping around the southwest
corner are more rhododendrons, including such smaller
species as *Rhododendron emateium*, *R. leucaspis*, and *R.
kaempferi*.

Larger rhododendrons are planted along the western
border, behind the rock garden that occupies the slope

behind the house. Subcollections include gaultherias, daphnes, violas, lewisias, cactuses, prostrate clematis, and penstemons. Pots set in sand in a raised brick frame hold tiny conifers, saxifrages, cactuses, primulas, lewisias, talinums, and ferns. A wooden platform to the north holds troughs with yet more tiny plants.

North of the house, past the peonies, pass between the greenhouse (which you can't enter without a staff or volunteer escort) and the wooden building. Between the two buildings is a small pool, with pitcher plants (*Darlingtonia californica* and several species of *Sarracenia*) as well as other bog plants. East of the greenhouse is yet another group of penstemons. Go toward the gazebo. You're now "in the pink"; surrounding you on three sides are pink rhododendrons demonstrating great variety in plant size, leaf form, flower form, and growth habit. One grove, to the southeast, has grown quite tall, and you can easily inspect the trunks. Companion plants include iris, columbines, and hostas.

South, back toward the house, a water garden flanks a small creek. Its denizens include the umbrella plant (*Cyperus alternifolius*), native ferns, and darlingtonias. On a damp rock wall above the creek are more ferns and the native *Synthyris stellata*.

The northeast corner of the property has a nature trail through a collection of natives including red huckleberry (*Vaccinium parvifolium*), thimbleberry (*Rubus parviflorus*), and red elderberry (*Sambucus racemosa*). Just across the bridge from the house, in a hardy fern garden of both natives and exotics, with a variety of colors and leaf forms, the most striking is the maroon and silvery-green Japanese painted fern (*Athyrium nipponicum* 'Pictum').

Edna Holmes Garden

Lewis and Clark College
0615 SW Palatine Hill Road

❦

Seasons of interest: All

Directions: From Interstate 5 take the Terwilliger Boulevard exit (no. 297). Travel south on Terwilliger approximately two miles. Just past the Lewis and Clark Law School, proceed straight ahead on Palater, and then turn right, following signs to Lewis and Clark College, on Palatine Hill Road. At the college, turn left at Gate 4 and park near the administration building. The garden extends eastward from the rear of the building.

The garden is built on terraces, and the steps between levels are frequently cobblestone or somewhat rough larger stones, so touring it requires sure footing. Many of the walkways are grass, so they are likely to be muddy if the weather has been wet.

Public transit: Take Tri-Met bus 39-Lewis and Clark to Palatine Hill Road and Riverside Street, opposite Gate 4.

Labels: None

Background: Edna Holmes was the wife of M. Lloyd Frank from 1915 to 1932. Mr. Frank was a member of the family which then had an interest in the Meier & Frank department store. He was the home furnishings buyer for the store, and a connoisseur who wanted something special for his home. He hired Herman Brookman, a New York architect, to design a house and garden. (Brookman stayed in Portland for decades thereafter. He also designed Temple Beth Israel in Northwest Portland and Menucha, originally an estate and now a conference center, in Corbett.) Brookman was a perfectionist who believed that he should design everything: windows, light fixtures, weathervanes, etc. The resulting house and garden reward inspection of detail.

The manor house, slate roofed and built in brick in English modern style, was completed in 1926. Brookman designed the gardens but did not, as he had the house, oversee their construction. When the gardens were completed in 1929 they included a large cutting garden, and the original plant lists are heavy with dianthus, lilies, delphiniums, tulips, and narcissus. Along the east side were a conservatory and a Japanese garden. The garden staff, under direction of a man from Kew Gardens, ranged up to twenty-eight. The entire estate, named Fir Acres, received much attention in the architectural press and the local community.

Fir Acres did not remain a manicured showplace for long. Mr. Frank left Portland in 1931, the Franks divorced in 1932, and Mrs. Frank left the estate in 1935. Most of the gardeners also left; the one who remained could not keep the gardens from becoming overgrown. In 1942 Albany College acquired the estate, moved its campus there, and became Lewis and Clark College. A college uses land differently from a wealthy family. Cutting gardens and the like, requiring much attention but not the sort college students would give them, did not survive intact.

In 1962, the Columbus Day Storm broke all the glass in the conservatory. It was rebuilt with mostly opaque walls and roof, and became an art building. The sixties also brought the rediscovery of the nearby Japanese garden, which had long lain buried under blackberry vines. The deodar cedars that had begun to overwhelm the largest terrace were removed. Volunteers restored the rose garden and obtained its certification as a test garden, but parts were later turfed over and it reverted to being a display garden.

In the mid 1990s, the remains of the conservatory and most of the Japanese garden were removed during construction of three major buildings along the north side of the garden.

What to see: The garden is a long, lovely sweep of green displaying an interesting use of terracing and playing with perspective. The hardscaping is worth at least as much attention as the plant material.

The vista from the terrace on the east side of the house stretches down through the gardens (designed with straight lines angled slightly outward, to counter the illusion of narrowing that parallel lines present in perspective; stonework and bricks incorporate the angle) to the bowling green and its flagpole. From the stone terrace immediately east of the manor house, where a climbing hydrangea (*Hydrangea anomala*) hugs the south end of the east wall, wander down the sloping lawn to a terrace of multicolored stone. Notice the light fixtures atop the pergola just below you.

Steps lead down to the next level, where wisteria covers the pergola shading a small lion fountain. Another fountain with ornamental fish tops a series of small pools leading down to the reflecting pool. To the east, steps angle around stone gazebos. Beyond the gazebos, stone steps flanked with Japanese maples (*Acer palmatum*) lead down to the largest terrace, a lawn now frequently used for informal football games and edged with azaleas, rhododendrons, honeysuckles, and other shrubs.

Yet more cobblestones, flanked by Japanese maples, lead to the steps down to the swimming pool. Andromeda scents the steps in early spring. Below the pool, stop and look back up the hill toward the manor house; notice the pattern of red Japanese maples, stonework, and evergreens. Below the lowest terrace (walk to the wall and look over) is the rose garden—a surprise or reward for those who have walked that far. It's a collection of hybrid teas and floribundas. The trees to the left, behind the last row of roses, are a fig and a harlequin glorybower (*Clerodendrum trichotomum*).

Fulton Display Garden

Fulton Park Community Center
68 S.W. Miles

Seasons of interest: Summer, early fall

Directions: From Interstate 5 in Portland, take the Terwilliger Boulevard exit (no. 297). Proceed east on Barbur Boulevard. At the first traffic light past Terwilliger, angle right onto Miles Street. Turn right at the driveway on your right, into the community center's parking lot. The garden is down a short road northwest of the lot.

Public transit: Take Tri-Met bus 1-Vermont, 12-Barbur Boulevard or 38-Boones Ferry Road to Barbur and Miles.

Labels: Plants in the children's garden may have labels. A brochure available from a box on the main signboard includes a diagram of all the plantings.

Background: The garden was started in 1990 to display plant and design possibilities for home gardeners. It is a joint effort of Portland Parks and Recreation, Metro, and the Friends of Portland Community Gardens.

What to see: In this small garden, the plantings change every year to provide new ideas for home gardeners. In 1997, the displays included an herb garden; a selection of drought-tolerant plants; a garden to attract beneficial insects; a mixed border; a garden of salad greens; and a children's garden, planted and cared for by children attending gardening classes at the community center. Along the perimeter is a Metro composting display.

The Jenkins Estate

Grabhorn Road (P.O. Box 5868)
Aloha, OR 97006
(503) 642-3855

Seasons of interest: All

Directions: From Beaverton, take Farmington Road (Highway 10) to Grabhorn Road (near 209th), which intersects just west of the sign for the community of Hazeldale; turn left on Grabhorn Road and continue three-tenths of a mile. The Jenkins Estate is on the right, well marked by signs.

Call before visiting, as the garden and buildings are frequently rented for private gatherings. If you're particularly interested in herbs, visit on Monday, when knowledgeable volunteers work in that garden. If you'd like to talk to members of the Tualatin Valley Rhododendron Society, visit on Thursday.

The house (which has none of the original furnishings, but has been spared remodeling and thus has much of the original interior except in one bathroom) can be seen by appointment.

Public transit: Take Tri-Met bus 88 to 198th and Farmington Road.

Weddings: The garden can be rented. Call for information.

Special events: The Tualatin Valley Chapter of the American Rhododendron Society holds a show each April. The garden clubs of Pioneer District 13 hold a Festival of Flowers in June.

Labels: Some. A brochure with trail map is available.

Background: The Jenkins Estate was developed at the beginning of World War I. Mrs. Jenkins was born Belle Ainsworth, the youngest child of Captain John

Ainsworth, a steamboat captain, railroad builder, and founder of one of the forerunners of the United States National Bank. Ralph Jenkins was a school teacher. The couple's main interest was horses, but they also planted and maintained extensive gardens. Mr. Jenkins died in 1957, and Mrs. Jenkins in 1963. A real estate developer acquired the estate, but it was then too far from urban services to make development profitable.

Tualatin Hills Park and Recreation District, which had long been interested in the estate, purchased it in 1976 and decided to gradually restore the buildings and gardens. One challenge was determining what was grown where and when. The Jenkinses gardened for half a century, but didn't leave planting lists and plans. Restoration of the perennial border proceeded with reference to photographs and educated guesses. Another obstacle to restoration was posed by the maturing of trees over the last eighty years, changing growing conditions in some areas of the garden. Some of the original plantings, which were suitable for sun and adequate moisture, cannot now be duplicated in the shade and competition of mature trees; decades ago, for instance, wallflowers flourished behind the primroses along the Primrose Path, but can no longer survive there. Restoration also required the graceful removal of what had grown up and invaded the gardens. The rockery was shorn of its covering of blackberries and relieved of the hegemony of lily-of-the-valley (*Convallaria majalis*). The battle to keep dwarf periwinkle (*Vinca minor*) out of the paths continues.

The perennial beds and herb garden are maintained with the assistance of the garden clubs of Pioneer District #13. The Tualatin Valley Chapter of the American Rhododendron Society planted the rhododendron garden in 1982 and 1989 and continues to maintain it.

What to see: The estate covers a dozen acres, with many subsidiary gardens: woodland, wildflower, perennial, rhododendron, rose, rock, and herb.

West of the house is the stable. A new garden stepping up the hill from the patio on the south side has two Japanese maples (*Acer palmatum*), a Japanese stewartia (*Stewartia pseudocamellia*), tulips and daffodils, variegated weigela (*Weigela florida* 'Variegata') and variegated andromeda (*Pieris japonica* 'Variegata'). On the west side of the main house is a small rock garden. Beyond the northwest corner of the house is a group of Japanese maples in an intriguing variety of foliage colors. (This is the most photographed spot in the garden.) Along the front (north side) of the house are rhododendrons, evergreen azaleas, and daphnes. Along the east side are a lacecap and a climbing hydrangea (*Hydrangea macrophylla* var. *normalis* and *H. anomala*).

Behind the house is a woodland wildflower garden. Hundreds of erythroniums are kept company by wild delphiniums, shooting stars, grape hyacinths, Johnny jump-ups, English daisies, and yellow violets. The path from the house ends at the pumphouse. The bank of blue *Hydrangea macrophylla* along its north wall dates from the Jenkinses' day. Beyond the pumphouse is the main rock garden, arrayed around a fish pond and home to seventy-five-year-old Japanese maples, primroses, bridal wreath spiraea (*Spiraea prunifolia* 'Plena'), western azalea (*Rhododendron occidentale*), forget-me-nots, and red and pink pasqueflowers.

Across a rock-lined path, the perennial border curves around the southern and western side of the rockery. It is edged with daffodils, and contains winter aconite (*Eranthis hyemalis*), dogtooth violets (*Erythronium* spp.), dodecatheons, and trilliums. The eastern extension of the path between the rockery and the perennial border is known as the Primrose Path. Behind an edging of purple primroses (*Primula japonica* 'Wanda') are primroses in various colors, astilbes, candelabra primroses, and hostas.

The small open Tea House, a favorite setting for weddings, is fittingly surrounded by *Exochorda* x *macrantha* 'The Bride' and by Oregon grape (*Mahonia nervosa*). Near a stump behind the Tea House are a couple of pungent Mexican orange plants (*Choisya ternata*) in a bed of violets and mitella.

In the perennial garden northeast of the Tea House, the only survivors of the original garden are peonies and daylilies. Asiatic lilies—one of Mrs. Jenkins's favorite flowers—have been planted there, along with old-fashioned delphiniums, colchicums, cornflowers (*Centaurea cyanus*), leopard's bane (*Doronicum*), false dragonhead (*Physostegia virginiana*), violets, and other old-fashioned flowers. From the path west of the perennial garden, the Rhododendron Path leads north from a small pool near a mountain laurel. Large old plants of 'Pink Pearl' and an unidentified lavender rhododendron tower on either side. These plants have suffered from years of neglect and are unlabeled; the principal rhododendron gardens are elsewhere, and are described below. At the north end of the path are foxgloves, hydrangeas, magnolias, and tree and other peonies.

Paralleling the Rhododendron Path to the east is the Moss Path. It is not particularly mossier than other areas but is a delight in early spring when violets, trilliums, and dwarf periwinkle bloom under mature deodar cedars (*Cedrus deodara*), pines, and weeping spruces. The path was formerly lined with perennial borders; the only survivors from the original garden are mock oranges. From the south end of the Moss Path another path leads east to the restored greenhouse (not open to the public), used for growing cuttings of shrubs that are past their prime. South of the greenhouse lilacs brought from elsewhere on the estate rim one side of a new perennial and annual bed. Delphiniums line the other side of the bed and decorate the middle.

Return to the main house. An unpaved road lined with elms leads east to a farmhouse, built about 1870 and now being restored. Northeast of the farmhouse an herb garden of four beds around a sundial set in a bed of Roman chamomile (*Chamaemelum nobile*) displays industrial, fragrant, decorative, and culinary herbs. To the south is a raised bed with Braille labels, and further south up by a shed is a shade herb garden. To the east of the main herb garden is a display of scented-leaf geraniums.

North of the herb garden a pergola supports climbing roses including 'Harison's Yellow,' 'Mme. Alfred Carriere' and 'Zepherine Drouhin.' To the west are old garden roses, mostly introduced before 1910, including a Gallica, 'Hansa,' and 'Honorine de Brabant.' To the east is a display of edible flowers. Further east on the hillside an old orchard has several varieties of pears and apples. While you're here, enjoy the view of the Tualatin Valley; the growth of conifers north of the main house has obscured the view from there.

Return to the main house again. Between the house and the parking lot is a one-and-a-half acre rhododendron garden. Its thousand plants include almost six hundred species and varieties, with something in bloom from late January into July. The specialty—in the garden's southeast corner—is native American rhododendrons, including forty different forms of the native *Rhododendron macrophyllum*.

Harold Eastman Memorial Rose Garden

5th and Grant
Hillsboro

Seasons of interest: Spring, summer, fall

Directions: Highway 8, the Tualatin (TV) Highway, is Oak Street eastbound and Baseline Street westbound in downtown Hillsboro. Turn north on 6th. Proceed six blocks; turn left on Grant, and left on 5th.

Public transit: Tri-Met buses 57-Forest Grove and 58-Sunset stop at 5th and Washington, a few blocks south of the garden. Westside Light Rail is scheduled to open in September of 1998, and a stop is planned between 7th and 8th on Washington Street.

Labels: Most of the roses are labeled.

Background: Harold Eastman was a past president of the Tualatin Valley Rose Society and active in other community groups. In the late 1980s he served on the mayor's task force for beautifying Hillsboro and got donations from the community to supplement city funds to get the traffic island at 5th and Grant, already planted to roses, but faring poorly, replanted. After he died, his widow donated roses from his garden. The garden is maintained by the City of Hillsboro, except for the roses, which are cared for by the Tualatin Valley Rose Society.

What to see: This small, fragrant garden is planted in a traffic triangle. Although it has dozens of roses—hybrid teas, climbers, floribundas and polyanthas—it also has interest earlier in the season from flowering trees, andromedas, and bulbs.

Washington Park, Portland

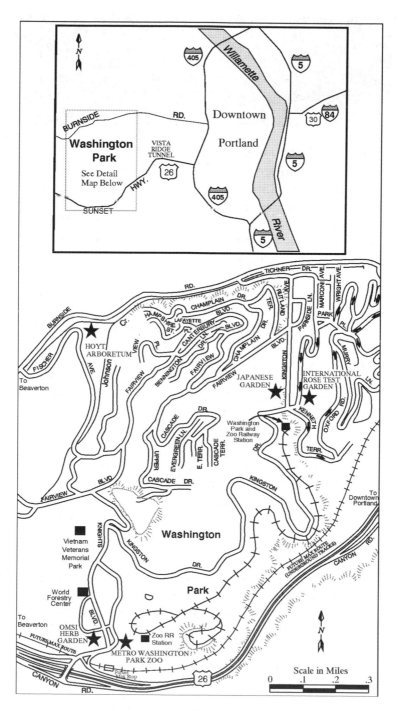

International Rose Test Garden

400 S.W. Kingston Avenue
(503) 823-3636

Seasons of interest: Spring, summer, fall

Directions: From downtown, proceed west on Taylor to 15th; turn left on 15th. From Interstate 405 northbound, take the Salmon exit (no. 2A), bear left, at the top of the ramp continue across Salmon on 14th, turn left on Taylor and left on 15th. From Interstate 405 southbound, take the Couch-Burnside exit (no. 2A), and at the top of the ramp continue south on 15th until it ends at a T intersection. From 15th, turn right on Salmon. Where Salmon reaches a T intersection, turn right on King and then immediately left on Park. At the end of Park, turn right on Lewis and Clark Circle and follow the signs to the rose garden.

From eastbound West Burnside Street or from Northwest 23rd Avenue, turn south onto Vista (where 23rd would be, south of Burnside) and then right onto Park at the first traffic light, and follow the directions from Park given above.

The garden is generally open during daylight hours, but parts may be closed for watering or spraying, and the entire garden may be closed late on summer afternoons when a concert is to be held in the amphitheater.

The terraced gardens have some steep slopes and stone steps.

Public transit: Tri-Met bus 63-Washington Park.

Weddings: You may obtain a permit from the Portland Park Bureau ((503) 823-2525) for either the Shakespearean or Gold Award garden. Each accommodates up to one hundred people, standing. The Gold Award Garden has a small covered area and electricity. These are popular wedding sites; obtain a permit early in the calendar year of the wedding. No weddings are scheduled during the

Rose Festival, which runs for most of June. Alcoholic beverages and food are not allowed unless they are part of the wedding ceremony.

Labels: All roses are labeled; other plants are not.

Background: The Rose Test Garden is not just a test garden, although that's how it started. Its history is part of the story of how Portland became the City of Roses.

At the turn of the century, Portland prepared to celebrate the centennial of the Lewis and Clark Expedition with an exposition. Although the theme of the exposition was the trek, its purpose was to build Portland into a major metropolis by showcasing the natural resources in the surrounding area, its potential for trade with countries across the Pacific, and its desirability as a place to live. Frederick V. Holman, a local lawyer, addressed livability by campaigning to make Portland the Rose City. He wrote newspaper articles and helped organize the Rose Mission Club to get Portlanders to plant their parking strips with roses—particularly the pink 'Madame Caroline Testout,' which became the city's unofficial signature rose. He continued the campaign even after the exposition closed. Mayor Harry Lane had urged, on the exposition's final day in the fall of 1905, that Portland stay in the limelight by hosting an annual rose carnival. Portlanders responded by organizing the first Rose Festival in 1907.

At the urging of the Rose Festival Association, the city started in 1908 to promote Washington's Birthday (February 22) as Rose Planting Day, to show that Portland's mild climate allowed rose planting even in winter. On Rose Planting Day in 1910, the city planted 215 roses from various countries in Washington (then City) Park, probably near Burnside Street. In 1911 the city planted roses in the park squares in Ladd's Addition, and in 1912 it planted ten thousand roses in Peninsula Park.

At least one Portlander thought that the city needed
one more rose garden, to spread the Rose City's fame as a
wonderful city in which to live and to spur the rose-
growing business in the area. Jesse A. Currey was a
businessman who had come to Portland for a hunting trip
in 1904 and liked it so much that he stayed. He saw roses
as not just plants but a potent positive advertising symbol
and a civilizing influence on the working class that grew
them. He urged the development of a rose test garden in
Portland, and got the American Rose Society to sanction
it. An American Rose Society official suggested planting
the garden on a terrace in Washington Park.

Despite World War I, European growers sent four
dozen plants. The gardens were planted around Armistice
Day, 1918, on a terrace that later became the rose garden
parking lot. The City of Portland, using a judging system
devised by Currey, awarded its first Gold Medals in 1919.

In the late 1920s, the rose garden began to grow. In 1927
the Royal Rosarians, a group of civic boosters, started a
garden with one rose for each member. In 1929, the test
garden moved down the hill to the lowest terrace and, in
1932, a huge influx of roses for testing forced expansion of
the garden. The All-America Rose Selections organization
chose the garden as one of its testing locations in 1938,
and the garden developed display beds. During World
War II part of the garden became a vegetable patch to
provide food for animals in the nearby city zoo, but after
the war attention returned to flowers. The Shakespearean
Garden was dedicated in the spring of 1946, and the
Queen's Walk was developed in the early 1950s.

As the garden sought to recover from a freeze in
December 1964 that killed thousands of plants, the Royal
Rosarian garden was redeveloped. Not large enough to
allow a bush for each of the ever-growing number of
Royal Rosarians, it was redesigned to showcase those
chosen by the organization's prime ministers. The terrace

just below the Royal Rosarian garden had long been a
rosebush nursery and a catchall for compost and old and
Gold Award roses. In 1970, with prodding and help from
the Portland Rose Society, it officially became the Gold
Award Garden, showcase for winners of Portland's top
rose prize. It now displays all except five of the roses that
have won Portland's Gold Award since its inception in
1919. Plants of 'Mrs. George C. Thomas' (1921), 'Feu
Pernet-Duchet' (1936), 'Golden State' (1937), 'Sterling'
(1938), and 'Charlotte E. Van Dedem' (1938) could not be
found, despite a worldwide search, when the garden was
reworked in 1990. More than one-third of the Gold Award
roses are no longer commercially available, but Portland
Rose Society members grow them and supply
replacements as needed.

The top terrace received several gifts in the 1970s from
the family of Frank E. Beach, a Portland businessman and
civic leader credited by some with naming Portland the
Rose City. His son donated a fountain in his father's
honor, and the son in turn was honored by his family
with an information kiosk and raised beds for miniature
roses.

In 1990, the garden started its collection of breeder
David Austin's English roses—hybrids with the
appearance and fragrance of old roses, and the color
range and long blooming period of modern roses—along
the tennis courts above the parking lot.

In 1996 the garden began a new award program.
"Portland's Best Rose" honors new or recently introduced
roses in five categories: hybrid tea, floribunda,
grandiflora, landscape, and miniature; and an all-around
favorite. One hundred judges, some from the rose world
and some from the general public, make their selection at
a garden party held the day after the Rose Festival's
Grand Floral Parade, in mid-June.

To the north of the rose garden, the area within the loop of Rose Garden Boulevard was planted to camellias and rhododendrons in 1940. In 1993, the inner row of camellias was replaced with a mixed border.

Construction of a visitors' center is planned for 1999.

What to see: This is a spectacular, polished rose garden. Its thousands of roses include some for every interest: new, old, in-between, hybrid teas, climbers, shrubs, and miniatures. It's on a terraced hillside with—weather permitting—a marvelous view of Portland's downtown and east side, and of Mount Hood.

You can enter by any of three stone stairways descending through the border of firs and rhododendrons between the parking lot and the main gardens. At the bottom of the center stairway, nine raised beds of miniature roses surround an information kiosk listing locations of the roses in the main garden. Two terraces down the hill, miniatures are tested for the American Rose Society, and six classes of roses—miniatures, hybrid teas, grandifloras, floribundas, landscape roses, and climbers—are tested for All-America Rose Selections (AARS). The current year's and next year's AARS winners, chosen well in advance, are also on display. The surrounding terraces and slopes are filled with modern roses chosen to encourage rose growing. They are commercially available and appropriate for the home gardener: they have a long blooming period, preferably May to Thanksgiving; disease resistance; hardiness; fragrance; and good color.

The stairway at the south end of the parking lot leads to the Royal Rosarian Garden. Along the sidewalk are the favorites of decades of Prime Ministers of Rosaria. The rose named on each sidewalk plaque is that under which the prime minister was knighted as a Royal Rosarian. (There were no prime ministers during the war years of

1917 and 1918.) The rose next to the plaque might not be the named rose; some varieties are no longer available, so similar roses have been substituted. Along the south edge are species and hybrid forms of *Rosa rugosa*. Here also lives one of the garden's Portland roses, 'Jacques Cartier.' (Portland roses are not those grown in, awarded prizes by, or otherwise associated with the City of Portland. A Portland rose is one of a group of roses of uncertain heritage named for the Second Duchess of Portland, an eighteenth-century promoter of rose growing. Adding complexity, within the group of Portland roses is one called both 'The Portland Rose' and 'Duchess of Portland.' It can be seen east of tennis court number 5.) Other older roses, including 'Madame Caroline Testout,' and the pink single 'Dainty Bess' are displayed in beds in the interior of the garden.

Immediately below the Royal Rosarian Garden is the Gold Award Garden, a living history of the rose trade since World War I. Just downhill from the Gold Award Garden is the Shakespearean Garden, a pleasant enclosed garden whose box-edged beds are filled with perennials, bulbs, and annuals, and roses named for Shakespearean characters.

The Queen's Walk stretches along the east end of the garden, between the Shakespearean Garden and the amphitheater. Every Queen of Rosaria has a plaque; the apparent gaps are for years when there was no queen (although Flora was actually queen in 1908 rather than 1907) or, in 1918 and 1926, no Rose Festival. The roses next to the walk have nothing to do with the queens.

Down the north set of stone steps from the parking lot, and curving around the grassy amphitheater, are more terraces and slopes filled with modern roses.

Away from the main garden, on the slope west of the parking lot and east of the southernmost pair of tennis courts, are most of the garden's old garden roses, spring-blooming forebears of modern roses. Many, as their names attest, were developed in France. South of the steps to the tennis courts are the Gallicas, including 'La Belle Sultane' and 'D'Aguesseau.' Half a dozen Bourbons range along the east edge of tennis court 5; the border continues with English roses, including 'Fisherman's Friend,' 'The Countryman,' and the single yellow 'Wild Flower.' North of the white pine and east of tennis court number 5 are the Damasks, Albas, and 'The Portland Rose.' South of the white pine the centifolias include 'Fantin Latour' and 'Juno.' On the southwestern corner of the southernmost tennis court are moss roses. South of the tennis courts is a circle of beds of modern roses. The middle and north sets of courts are surrounded on three sides by modern roses.

On either side of the garden office door are early spring bulbs, and the rose over the door is the climber 'Royal Sunset.' Tucked in behind the restrooms, along with hostas and impatiens, are yet more, mostly older roses, including 'Louise Odier' and 'Madame Isaac Pereire,' both Bourbons; 'Moonlight' and 'Francesca,' hybrid musks from the first quarter of the twentieth century; and 'Souvenir de Dr. Jarmin,' a hybrid perpetual.

If you're in the mood to see something other than roses, return to the middle terrace and follow the walkway north, down the steps. Cross Rose Garden Boulevard. Just inside the ring of camellias (which nicely show foliage variations in such close ranks) a mixed border includes irises, daylilies, hostas, hydrangeas, daisies, and yarrows. A grass walk, lined with azaleas and rhododendrons, continues north almost to Park Street.

The Japanese Garden

Washington Park
(503) 223-1321

ॐ

Seasons of interest: All

Directions: From Interstate 405 northbound in Portland, take the Salmon exit (no. 2A). Bear left and at the top of the ramp continue across Salmon on 14th, turn left on Taylor and left on 15th. From Interstate 405 southbound, take the Couch-Burnside exit (no. 2A), and at the top of the ramp continue south on 15th. From downtown, go west on Taylor, then left on 15th.

From 15th, turn right on Salmon and proceed to the T intersection. Turn right on King, and then immediately left on Park. At the end of Park, turn right on Lewis and Clark Circle and follow the signs to the garden.

If you are elderly or disabled, you can drive up the hill and park near the garden's entrance. If you are neither, park by the tennis courts above the International Rose Test Garden and either walk or take the free shuttle bus up the hill.

The garden is open every day except Thanksgiving, Christmas, and New Year's Day, from 10 a.m. to 6 p.m. April 1 to May 31 and September 1 to 30, from 9 a.m. to 8 p.m. June 1 through August 31, and from 10 a.m. to 4 p.m. the rest of the year. Admission is charged. Some paths are rough or steep, and the water features are not fenced.

Public transit: Tri-Met bus 63-Washington Park.

Weddings: The garden is not available for weddings.

Special events: In May the garden has a Children's Day celebration and bonsai exhibition; in June, ikebana demonstrations and exhibitions of roses and iris; in July, Tanabata (the Star Festival); in August, Obon (the Spirit Festival); in October, another bonsai exhibition and a chrysanthemum show.

Labels: None, but Phyllis Reynold's booklet "Plant Material in the Japanese Garden," and Bruce Hamilton's book *Human Nature,* a history and guide to the garden, are both available for purchase in the service center.

Background: Mutterings about building a Japanese garden in Portland started in the early 1950s. A Japanese landscape architect visiting in 1953 proposed a garden for the north peninsula in Crystal Springs Lake, in southeast Portland. The Park Bureau suggested sites in George Himes Park in southwest Portland and Overlook Park in north Portland. Retired park superintendent C. Paul Keyser noted that the fourth green of the West Hills Golf Course had a spring, and perhaps a Japanese garden could be built there as part of the new zoo that was planned for the site.

None of those places was felicitous, but the old zoo site was suitable. It was a knoll, known as Round Top, on an east-facing hillside. Its shade and dampness were bad for animals, but fine for a garden that emphasized foliage more than flowers. By late 1960 the old zoo had been leveled and the Japan Society was eager to build a garden that would be a tourist attraction and an understandable cultural link with Japan. The society hired P.T. Tono, a professor of landscape architecture at a Japanese university, and had a plan in hand for a garden on Round Top by the spring of 1961.

The zoo site had to be modified. In preparation for the flat garden, the top of the knoll—where the zoo's monkey house had stood—was bulldozed down several feet. Down from the knoll to the west, the upper pond was dug where the pheasant house had been. The bear grotto had been tucked into the hillside rising to the west across the zoo road. Tono thought the grotto's rocks so ugly that he buried most of them behind the waterfall of the lower pond. (He found rocks worthy of being seen and directed the placement of each one.) The former site of an eagle cage became the sand and stone garden.

The garden got off to a slow start because Portland was in the midst of a wave of tearing down and rebuilding. While the other projects diverted time, money, and energy from the Japanese Garden, some of them provided materials. The remodeling of Civic Auditorium yielded dozens of granite steps. The wisteria arbor was built over cobblestones, recycled from old city streets. A maple tree rescued from the path of the new Interstate 405 became the first plant in the flat garden. The rhododendrons from the half of Coolidge Square that disappeared in excavation for the freeway were also rescued for the garden. Starting with full-grown plants gave the garden a more mature look, and was in keeping with Japanese tradition.

The garden opened to the public for a preview in September 1965, although nothing was complete except the restroom, a relic of zoo days, that had been reroofed and hidden behind a bamboo and cedar fence to appear more Japanesque. Fortunately, the public was so taken with its first sight of the garden that gifts came flowing in; cherry trees, bronze cranes, and money for the moon bridge, the wisteria arbor, the tea house, and Japanese irises for the lower pond.

With the completion of the pavilion in the spring of 1980, all the planned major garden features had been built. But the Japanese garden is no more static than any other. What had been a moss garden in the early 1970s was redesigned into the natural garden in the mid 1970s when some of the more delicate mosses could not be kept alive even with advanced garden technology. A couple of years later, the teahouse gardens were relandscaped to add paths, maple trees, cobblestone walls, and water features. Gifts arrived and had to be put someplace; the fountain that Sapporo gave in 1988 for the silver anniversary of the garden was installed near the pavilion.

Between 1985 and 1995, the garden finally got rid of the last two buildings remaining from the zoo. Outside the entrance, the old zoo commissary—which had been used as a garden shed—got replaced by a more Japanesque structure. And the zoo restrooms were finally replaced by a modern service center housing restrooms and a shop.

What to see: This is an all-season garden. When the leaves are off the deciduous trees, you can see views hidden in summer, and can also admire the tortuous branches of the maple trees. There are enough evergreens that the garden is never colorless, although it is most colorful in spring, when the azaleas, rhododendrons, cherry trees, and irises bloom.

Give yourself several hours to see the garden. It is not designed to be rushed or marched through. No single path will take you to everything, and it takes time to cover all the paths, stop at the many viewpoints, and notice details. The tour directions below don't cover every path and feature; they are intended to give you a general introduction to the garden.

Japanese maples and holly, andromedas, camellias, azaleas and rhododendrons, moss and ferns are used repeatedly, throughout most of the garden. But plants are only a part of a Japanese garden, and some areas of the garden have very few. Certain materials and decorative items are also used repeatedly. There are more than a dozen different lanterns. Bamboo is used in myriad ways for fencing, screening, and other decoration. Tiles are used as expected on roofs, but also on edge in gutters, to screen sprinkler heads, and to provide decorative accents in walkways. Stone ranges from coarse sand through river rocks to boulders; cut stones show up in walkways, as bridges, in walls, and in gutters. Water is present in basins, streams, and ponds, and suggested by river rock and raked gravel.

Much of the interest in a Japanese garden comes from seeing plants and other features from various viewpoints. Features visible at one point are obscured by rocks or plants from another viewpoint. This introduces an element of mystery, as you are encouraged to proceed to see what is hidden. It also makes the garden seem much larger than it truly is, because you never see the whole thing at once. The garden also seems larger than it actually is because tantalizing bits and pieces lie outside its main gate. You are introduced to the garden in the parking lot, with clipped pines and flowering cherries. The peninsula of land between the parking lot and the road up to the garden has been planted to azaleas, rhododendrons, and maple trees. The stone steps turn into a tiny waterfall in a hard rain.

Proceed up the road a few dozen feet to the antique gate, set in plantings of rhododendrons, evergreen azaleas, hostas, and small maples to get you in the mood for the garden proper, and to encourage you up the rather steep path to the main gate, unless you decide to walk back to the parking lot and take the shuttle bus.

The main gate is typical of the gates to a Japanese feudal lord's home. Inside, at the base of the steps, turn right onto the wide aggregate path. Where it swings around to the left, in front of the service center, bear right, down the hill and parallel to the garden's outer stucco wall. Along the hillside to your right are hundreds of azaleas, pruned into rounded shapes to suggest large smooth stones or hills.

At the bottom of the hill a small roofed gate leads into the tea garden. As you enter the tea garden and approach the teahouse, which is supposed to suggest a hermit's cabin, you are to leave your worldly cares behind, and prepare yourself for a wilderness or rustic setting. A curved bamboo fence (known, because of its shape, as a sleeve gate) blocks you from going into the inner tea garden, but you can see most of it from behind the fence. To see it from another angle, return to the walk outside the gate and turn right. At the end of the wall, turn right into the outer tea garden, and right again at the end of the bamboo fence.

After you have seen the inner garden, continue south on the path, toward the sound of the waterfall. The path changes to granite slabs as you leave the outer tea garden, and reaches a T. Turn right, and continue on the slab path toward the wooden bridge. At the near end of the bridge, stepping stones lead up to the right to a viewpoint. You can look to the right and see most of the pond and the wooden bridge, but not the waterfall feeding the pond—although you can certainly hear it.

Return to the path, and the start of the wooden bridge. The right angles at which its planks meet serve two functions: to keep demons from following you, because they can travel only in straight lines, and to slow you down, so you look at what's there. The Japanese iris (*Iris ensata*) in the pond bloom in late June. When you reach the end of the bridge and are back on the main walkway, you can see the waterfall. Walk back along the main aggregate path toward the teahouse. Cross the stream and continue up the gravel path.

Turn and cross the moon bridge, to your right. The metal finials are lotus blossoms, symbolic of enlightenment; many of the lanterns in the garden have similar ornaments. Just past the moon bridge, stepping stones to the left lead along the edge of the pond.

Continue uphill on the gravel path. On the right at the top of the hill, a stone pagoda lantern sits across a lawn in front of evergreen hedging. The lantern, a gift from Portland's sister city Sapporo, has five stories (representing earth, water, fire, wind, and sky) and nine rings (representing Buddhism's nine heavens). It is topped with a lotus blossom representing the Buddha. Continue to the right. The gravel path comes to a junction where a bamboo fence screens the view of Kingston Drive beyond. Take the lefthand path, which leads to the natural garden. Bear left, through the gate. The path steps down the hill next to the stream. Frequently, a Japanese garden will suggest mountains by providing winding paths like those in the mountains. At the pond, set with hostas, ferns, azaleas, and maples, you can look across to a tiny lantern on a promontory to the right in a miniaturized landscape. Continue to the benches. Granite slabs stepping up to and across the stream provide another viewpoint; looking back up the stream, you can see another small waterfall, and a maple tree on a mossy promontory.

Continue straight ahead at a junction where a pathway leads down the hill to the right, and at the next junction bear left on a path leading to the sand and stone garden. Such gardens have their roots in Zen philosophy, which stresses simplification and abstraction to encourage meditation. While there are Zen influences elsewhere in Japanese gardens, sand and stone gardens are the most simplified and abstract. You don't walk through this garden; you stand at the edge and look at it. The only plants are tiny groundcovers, so that you are not distracted from the sand, stone, wall, and tiles. The sand symbolizes the sea. The seven smaller stones symbolize tiger cubs, whose mother threw them into the sea to test their courage. The large stone symbolizes the Buddha, who jumped among the starving cubs to allow them to eat him, thus showing his love for all creatures. The benches here are granite, in keeping with the sand and stone theme, rather than wooden as elsewhere in the garden.

As you leave the sand and stone garden, a path to the natural garden takes off to the left. Take the flight of steps to the right, past camellias (members of the tea family), maples, and Japanese holly (*Ilex crenata*), leading to a viewpoint from which the pines, pond, and stream in the natural garden can be seen from above.

Continue up the steps to the aggregate walkway around the flat garden. Turn right, and on the east side of the pavilion walk to the wall at the edge of the granite and gravel expanse, and look over the hedge. If the leaves are off the trees, below the bamboo hedge you can see tennis courts and the rose gardens (which to the garden's original designer, Professor Tono, looked like rice paddies). Further east are the skyscrapers of downtown Portland; Portland's east side stretching out to knobs of hills; the farther foothills; and then, if it's clear enough, Mount Hood (which Tono likened to Mount Fuji).

Continue along the north side of the pavilion. On your left, dark, smooth rocks are arranged to look like a pond. Just beyond, a path to the left leads to the west side of the pavilion. The flat garden is designed to be seen from the pavilion porch. Raked gravel surrounds gourd and saucer shapes planted with ruby dianthus (*Dianthus* 'Tiny Rubies'). The shapes symbolize either cheer (as in the sake one would pour from the gourd into the saucer) or, on a deeper level, happiness (the gourd) and enlightenment or human perfection (the circle). The gravel represents water. In wintertime, some of the pine trees may be dressed in bamboo and rope tents as protection from breakage by snow and ice.

Down the steps at the west end of the pavilion, beyond the weeping cherry (*Prunus subhirtella* 'Pendula') is the Iyo stone, large and green with interesting wavy patterns. Such stones are prized in Japan. This one is a memorial to Philip Englehart, first president of the Japanese Garden

Society of Oregon (which built the garden). Continue past it to the main aggregate walk, and turn right. Along your right are trees and shrubs edging the flat garden; many of the trees have been pruned and trained to partially reveal and partially obscure the view beyond. Just before you reach the service center, the wisteria arbor is to the left. It frames the view of the pagoda lantern beyond. On the other side of the main walk, a gravel path leads through the shrubbery and trees edging the flat garden. Look left (northeast) from the junction of the path and main walk; you can see the entrance gate through the pine tree. Take the gravel path back to the northwest corner of the pavilion past pines, azaleas, and camellias.

From the pavilion, take the main walk left to the entrance gate. Just across the main walk at the junction is a young cherry tree with beautiful dark red bark (*Prunus serrulata*). Since its flowers are not particularly pretty, *P. subhirtella* 'Autumnalis' has been grafted to the top of its trunk. As you continue along the main walk, notice the tea viburnum (*Viburnum setigerum*) growing up through a bamboo framework on the left, and the shrubs and trees set off by the bamboo and board fence to the right. Farther along on the right the upright little wooden structure, looking something like a lighthouse, is a miniature Japanese fire house, and it hides an American fire hydrant.

Hoyt Arboretum

4000 S.W. Fairview Boulevard
Portland, OR 97221
(503) 228-8733

⁂

Seasons of interest: All

Directions: From Highway 26 west of downtown Portland, take the Zoo/Arboretum exit (the first exit west of Sylvan, and the first exit east of the tunnel); continue north on Knights Boulevard, between the parking lots. From the International Rose Test Garden or the Japanese Garden, take Kingston Drive; at its T intersection with Knights Boulevard, turn right. Where Knights Boulevard meets Fairview at a T intersection, turn right; the arboretum's visitor center is approximately one-tenth of a mile on the right; parking is on the left.

You can also reach the arboretum on foot on the Wildwood Trail, which crosses the arboretum twice.

Maps are available at the visitor center. Guided tours are run each Saturday and Sunday, April through October, and may be specially scheduled at other times.

Aside from one paved path with gentle grades, the dirt and gravel paths can be steep.

Public transit: Tri-Met bus 63-Washington Park. The arboretum is north of westside light rail's zoo station, scheduled to open in September 1998.

Special events: Classes may cover such topics as pruning, bird walks, bamboo identification, wildflowers, edible and medicinal plants, and wreath making. Call for a schedule.

Weddings: Several sites are available, including the Wedding Meadow, planted with white-flowering trees and shrubs. Call Portland Parks, (503) 623-2525, for reservations and permits.

Labels: Most plants are labeled.

Background: Hoyt's rugged terrain suggests that its paths be taken at a strolling pace rather than a brisk walk. Portland's civic arboretum itself started slowly and got underway in fits and starts.

At the turn of the century, Portland's park commission recommended that the area that is now the International Rose Test Garden be developed into an arboretum and botanical garden. The idea for an arboretum came to nothing and was put aside for a decade, until the city tried to acquire the amusement park on Council Crest. The *Oregon Journal* newspaper was certain that it would be more of a pleasure than a chore to establish an arboretum there that could be a tourist attraction as well as a botanical resource for high school and college students. But the bond issue for acquiring the park failed then and again two years later. (The city finally acquired Council Crest in the mid 1930s, but it became a regular park rather than an arboretum.)

Park Superintendent Emanuel Mische wasn't waiting for a bond issue. He thought rich people would like to fund such a long-lasting tribute as an arboretum, but none volunteered. He started a fruticetum—a collection of shrubs—emphasizing Northwest flora at the city's nursery in east Portland. He also sought federal help; he tried to get the Plant Introduction Bureau of the Department of Agriculture to establish a substation—but to no avail.

When the issue was raised again, in the mid 1920s, the impetus came not from the park bureau but from the Chamber of Commerce. Its Forestry Committee wanted the city to have an arboretum to showcase the gymnosperms, a class of plants including the conifers that fueled the city's timber-based prosperity.

By now the city also had an appropriate site. The hillside above Washington Park had been logged in the

1880s. It was too rugged—with four major ridges and three deep draws—for settlement, so the county used it as a poor farm until 1910. After an abortive attempt to sell it for private development, the county tried to sell the land to the city, but finally donated it in 1922, so long as the city used it "for park, recreational, and educational purposes." In gratitude, the city named the huge new park in honor of county commissioner Ralph Hoyt. The city's first improvement on the property was a golf course at the south end.

During Forestry Week in April 1928, the city approved the establishment of an arboretum on eighty acres of Hoyt Park. Park Superintendent C. Paul Keyser approached Mische about designing the arboretum. During his tenure in Portland Mische had designed Sellwood, Peninsula, Kenilworth, Laurelhurst, and Mt. Tabor parks, as well as Ladd's Circle and Squares, and he was an excellent horticulturist. Mische wanted the job, but his proposal was far too expensive for the city. Keyser regretfully declined and hired John Duncan, superintendent of Spokane's parks, who had trained at Harvard's Arnold Arboretum.

Duncan drew up a plan in August 1930, and work started that fall. Most of the effort—of eighteen men, five horses, and a mule—went into building roads and bridges, but also included planting fifty-five pines of three species. The next year, plantings branched out into firs, cedars, larches, spruces, sequoias, and hemlocks.

The Depression and several cold winters made further development sporadic. The supervisor and the laborers were all either on local relief or employed through one of the alphabet works agencies—WPA (Works Progress Administration), NYA (National Youth Administration), and CWA (Civil Works Administration)—and might be pulled away from the arboretum to work on trees on

other city property, the golf course, the Wilson River
Highway being built between Portland and Tillamook,
city streets, or crop harvesting.

In 1933 the arboretum got its first gift, and its first non-
gymnosperm collection, when the Portland Garden Club
planted magnolias on two acres. Watering and
maintenance were too irregular to keep the collection
healthy. By the time the club tired of making
replacements, in 1942, the arboretum had grown to
include eighty genera.

Occasionally severe weather trimmed the collections.
In 1950, ten days of temperatures around zero degrees
Fahrenheit between mid January and early February
destroyed subtropical hardwoods and many pines and
cypresses. In the 1962 Columbus Day Storm, fifty-three
gymnosperms got uprooted, broken off, or demolished by
falling trees, and cleaning up after the storm took more
than a year. But the destruction had a beneficial side. A
few months before, the city had started clearing out an
area of Douglas firs at the south end of the arboretum.
People had complained, as they did almost any time the
city tried to clear some of the second-growth Douglas firs
that had covered much of the arboretum, although the
city explained time and again that removal was necessary,
because a single species does not make an arboretum. The
destruction caused by the storm made this clearing easier
to achieve.

The arboretum was initially designed as an informal
park with woodland trails for hiking and riding, but in
1978, long before the Americans with Disabilities Act, a
barrier-free trail—hard-surfaced and wide enough for
wheelchairs—was built.

The arboretum got its first formal planting in the late
1980s, with the construction of the Vietnam Veterans'
Memorial. The memorial was placed in a natural
amphitheater at the south end of the arboretum to be near

the state's busiest parking lot for tourist attractions—
serving the Metro Washington Park Zoo, the Oregon
Museum of Science and Industry (OMSI), and the World
Forestry Center—so that it would, it was hoped, be
visited by many of those tourists.

The arboretum recently remodeled its visitors' center to
provide a sheltered courtyard for palms, podocarps, and
potted plants. (Podocarps are members of the family
Podocarpiacaea, tender evergreens, and include the
genera *Podocarpus* and *Dacrydium*).

What to see: The arboretum ranges over 180 acres of
rugged terrain. There is lots to see, although you have to
work a bit to see it. Don't expect the trees to be set in
close-clipped lawns; Hoyt isn't manicured. But it is well
organized and, along with the taxonomic groupings, has a
flowering tree trail. There's something in bloom most of
the year.

The arboretum may have the largest collection of
species conifers in the country; approximately two
hundred of its eight hundred and fifty taxa are conifers.
Most of the conifers are west of Fairview Boulevard and
range from the common to the exotic, such as the Chinese
(*Larix potaninii*) and Polish larches (*L. decidua* var. *polonica*)
on the Hemlock Trail, just a few feet off the end of the Fir
Trail and southwest of the picnic shelter. Three special
collections west of Fairview are not limited to conifers.
Bamboos grow along the Creek Trail. In the Wedding
Meadow, at the end of Bray Lane, white-flowering plants
include fragrant snowbell (*Styrax obassia*), clerodendrons,
a dove tree (*Davidia involucrata*), a Chinese dogwood
(*Cornus kousa* var. *chinensis*) and a Japanese stewartia
(*Stewartia pseudocamellia*). The Bristlecone Pine Trail, a
gently sloped hard-surfaced path accessible to the
handicapped, winds through areas representing
temperate forests all over the world: a snow gum

(*Eucalyptus niphophila*) from Australia; European beeches
(*Fagus sylvatica*) and white birches (*Betula pendula*); orange
ball trees (*Buddleia globosa*) and monkey puzzle trees
(*Araucaria araucana*) from Chile; Modoc cypress (*Cupressus
bakeri*), madrone (*Arbutus menziesii*) and a grove of Pacific
dogwoods (*Cornus nuttallii*) from North America.

On the east side of Fairview, the oak collection includes
tan (*Lithocarpus densiflorus*), swamp (*Quercus bicolor*),
white (*Q. alba*), shingle (*Q. imbricaria*) and water oaks (*Q.
nigra*). To the east the winter garden blossoms in January
and February with witch hazels, hellebores, winter
aconite (*Eranthis hyemalis*), lacebark pine (*Pinus bungeana*),
Cornus sericea, and the flowering cherry *Prunus subhirtella*
'Autumnalis.'

Southwest of the winter garden, the Beech Trail passes
hop trees (*Ptelea trifoliata*) from Texas, weeping beeches
(*Fagus sylvatica* 'Pendula'), and tricolored beeches (*F. s.*
'Tricolor'). Across Upper Cascade Drive to the east are
two magnificent copper beeches (*F. s.* 'Atropurpurea').

Also east of Upper Cascade Drive, the magnolia
collection is at its best from mid-March to mid-April.
Along the path south of the magnolias are several large
California bay trees (*Umbellularia californica*), a sassafras
(*Sassafras albidum*) grove, and a Japanese spice tree
(*Lindera obtusiloba*).

South across Upper Cascade Drive, near the white
reservoir, the parrottias and yellowwoods (*Cladrastis* spp.)
provide fall color. Other representatives of the pea family
include honey locusts (*Gleditsia triacanthos*), laburnums,
redbuds, and an Amur chokecherry (*Maackia amurensis*).

Southeast of the reservoir the flowering fruit trees
include several cherries and half a dozen crabapples. To
the south, along the Rose Trail, the Chinese pistachio
(*Pistacia chinensis*) turns bright orange in the fall, and the
birds gather in the mountain ash trees—European (*Sorbus*

aucuparia), Moravian (*S. a.* 'Edulis'),
and American (*S. americana*)—to eat
their fruit. Nearby are several London
plane trees (*Platanus* x *acerifolia*), rarely
seen so far from paving.

Take the Hawthorn Trail to the
maple collection, which includes a
Cretan maple (*Acer sempervirens*), *A.*
palmatum cultivars in several hues, and
the three-foot mound of *A. circinatum*
'Little Gem.' Norway maple (*Acer platanoides*) cultivars
include 'Globe' and 'Olmsted.' To the west, birches are
south of the path, hornbeam maples (*A. carpinifolium*) to
the north. Poplars and ashes are further west. Then the
Maple Trail crosses Knights Boulevard, which loops
around a grouping of styrax, sour gums (*Nyssa sylvatica*),
poplars, and persimmons.

Down the hill to the south, past willows, black
walnuts, and franklinias, the Vietnam Veterans' Memorial
has a witch hazel collection at roadside, dogwoods along
the back sweep, and representatives of the rose family
(spiraea and Bradford pear [*Pyrus calleryana* 'Bradford'])
up the middle.

On your return to the visitors' center, stop and examine
the three dozen hollies on the hillside to the south of the
center.

❧

Metro Washington Park Zoo

4001 S.W. Canyon Lane
Portland, OR 97201
(503) 226-1561

ॐ

Seasons of Interest: All

Directions: From Highway 26 west of downtown take the Zoo-Arboretum exit (the first exit west of Sylvan, and the first exit east of the tunnel). Proceed north; the zoo is on your right. The parking lots are north of the entrance.

From the International Rose Test Garden or the Japanese Garden, follow Kingston Drive. Where it Ts at Knights Boulevard, turn left; the zoo is down the hill on your left.

The zoo is open every day of the year except Christmas, but its open hours vary by season. There is an admission charge.

Public transit: Tri-Met bus 63-Washington Park. The zoo will also be served by westside light rail, scheduled to open in September 1998.

Labels: Mainly in the Cascades exhibit and the bamboo garden. A brochure identifies many of the specimen trees.

Background: Gardening at the zoo is not for the faint of heart. For one thing, the zoo changes far more than most gardens. The zoo was originally built by the City of Portland in the late 1950s, when plain concrete animal enclosures seemed to solve zoo sanitation problems. Construction ran far over budget, so little money was left for landscaping.

In the intervening decades, attitudes, techniques, and styles in animal exhibition have changed. Metro took over the zoo from the city in 1976 and was able to raise far more money for zoo construction. Five directors had their own visions of what they wanted the zoo to look like. Old exhibits were remodeled, closed, or razed; new exhibits

were built and, in the fashion current for at least the last
two decades, they were not the taxonomic exhibits of the
original zoo (e.g., ten different felines in one clump of
moated areas and cages), but ecosystem exhibits (e.g.,
Alaska Tundra, a series of natural-habitat-style enclosures
and interpretive areas) that seek to give the visitor a feel
for the area portrayed, including plant as well as animal
life. Some of the areas present special challenges. The
smoked glass and the lushness of plants in the center of
the Vollum aviary allow little light to reach the back wall.
The swamp in the Africa Rain Forest requires plants that
can survive low light, restricted even more by vertical
flaps that shut for the rainstorm, and drenching by that
storm every thirty minutes all day.

The zoo is an intensely public place; about a million
people visit every year. Zoo visitors have become more
sophisticated but also more unruly. The zoo has to look
good all year long and withstand the pressure of all those
people, some of whom won't leave the plants alone. It
also has to be safe for both visitors and animals; the
exhibits must be kept clear of trees that could blow over
and provide an escape route, and also of toxic plants.
Animals in captivity might eat plants they wouldn't touch
in the wild.

Visitors aren't always happy with what they see. The
feline cages and the bear exhibits were part of the original
zoo construction and ran heavily to concrete. People
complained about the plain concrete snow leopard cage,
on a highly visible and noisy corner. The zoo's solution:
jackhammering out much of the concrete floor, leaving a
few paths for the keepers and the animals, and adding
plants, including grass. The grass survives because it is
planted under river rock, which protects the crown; even
if the leopards beat down the tips of the grass, it will
grow back. A water feature provides the pleasant sound
of splashing water. In recent years, plants have also been

used to mask concrete walls and to replace some of the
concrete in the floor of several of the bear enclosures.
These projects are hard work; the concrete must be
removed, and the dirt brought in, by hand.

Animals get to know every square inch of their
enclosures. They notice—and may destroy—anything
new. Zoo gardeners plant three times as many plants as
they hope will survive, start with fairly large specimens,
and do what they can to protect the plants in a manner
that won't endanger the animals. Instead of stakes or
fencing, a new plant may be buttressed by rocks which
are in turn surrounded by prickly barberries.

Once the animals get accustomed to a plant they'll
usually leave it alone. But animals die and are replaced by
others of their own species, which—animals being what
they are—have different personalities, and thus different
ways of dealing with the plants in their exhibits. One
species may be replaced by another. The jaguars didn't
bother the plants in their cage much, and the plants got so
lush they had to be pruned so the animals could be seen.
Then a zoo enrichment program added interest to the
jaguars' lives by hiding food for them to find. They
became so active that they destroyed the plant material
and it had to be replaced. The next denizens of that cage
were the cougars, and they kept the plants pruned. In the
Africa exhibit, some trees were planted just outside the
animal enclosure; the animals couldn't reach the trees
which, ungrazed, shaded out the grass below.

Gardening at the zoo is a series of experiments. One
experiment that seems to be working is installing hanging
logs and perches in the feline cages. With the animals off
the ground more, the plants do better and the visitors can
see the animals more clearly and from different angles.

The weeping pines (*Pinus strobus* 'Pendula') masking
the wall of the elephant museum were chosen because
they won't grow up into the flight paths of the birds of

prey (which demonstrate their flight, during special shows, by swooping from above the museum down to the amphitheater stage to the west), and they harmonize with the lilies, weeping hemlock, and purple nandina (*Nandina domestica* 'Nana') also planted on that slope. The plants are meant to blend in, rather than stand out; the zoo isn't a display garden. It also sometimes sacrifices authenticity for other values. The real tundra doesn't have trees, but Alaska Tundra uses them for screening. For aesthetic reasons, Africa's grass isn't as scruffy as the real thing.

In the 1990s, tax limitation measures necessitated cuts in staff and closure of some exhibits. The zoo gardeners shifted away from labor-intensive annuals toward perennials and moved plants out of closed exhibits into the rest of the zoo.

What to see: The zoo is a challenging place to garden: the animals can't be exposed to toxic plants; the exhibits and their surroundings should give the look and feel of the animals' native territory; and the plants have to withstand the press of people and animals, and look good all year long. Despite these limitations, the zoo has been attractively gardened with an astonishing range of plant material. It is also home to several specialty gardens.

Just outside the entrance, note the giraffe-shaped weeping sequoia (*Sequoiadendron giganteum* 'Pendulum') towering over the bus shelter. Inside the zoo, the island in front of the Warren Iliff Sculpture Court has a European mountain ash (*Sorbus aucuparia*) at its west end and a European larch (*Larix decidua*) to the east, across from the lions.

Continue past the cat enclosures and turn north; take the walkway above the railroad tracks and turn right into Cascades. On the outside of the first curve to the left is a collection of huckleberries. Further along, on the left, in Cascade Meadow, an interpretive sign identifies some of the plants.

Returning to Zoo Street, just west of the railroad trestle and north of the polar bear exhibit is a magnificent red oak (*Quercus rubra*), considerably older than the zoo. In front of the polar bear exhibit are willows (*Salix purpurea*) and wildflowers. Across from the polar bears, outside the chimp play yard, are silk trees (*Albizia julibrissin*) and bigleaf magnolia (*Magnolia macrophylla*). On the north side of the primate house is a bamboo garden.

From the primate building, head northeast to the elephant museum. North of the lawn in front, in the picnic plaza, are raised beds with dahlias, evergreen azaleas, cotoneaster, and coral bark maples (*Acer palmatum* 'Sango kaku'). The bed separating the picnic plaza from the lawn includes perennial grasses and spiderwort (*Tradescantia virginiana*) in three colors. Just west of the museum is a Himalayan white pine (*Pinus wallichiana*); across the walk is a bed with a Hinoki cypress (*Chamaecyparis obtusa*), imperial bloodgrass (*Imperata cylindrica* 'Rubra') and other ornamental grasses. Across the walk from the museum's main entrance are small maples, a Chinese witch hazel (*Hamamelis mollis*), and rhododendrons. Continue along the museum to the walk to the elephant overlook. To the right are azaleas, small maples, bamboos, and other grasses. At the elephant overlook are three katsura trees (*Cercidiphyllum japonicum*), and at the back of the knoll above are more rhododendrons and azaleas.

Return to the front of the elephant museum, and go
south to the front yard of the elephant house. Here
eastern Asia is evoked by *Magnolia macrophylla* and *M.
gigantea*, *Fatsia japonica*, palms, yucca, figs, mulberries,
ginkgos, gunnera, arbutus, paperbark maples (*Acer
griseum*), kniphofias, and bergenias. The thorny tree near
the shelter at the south end is a *Kalopanax*.

Proceed west past the concert stage, noting the
organically maintained lawn. Beyond the stage is the
entrance to Alaska Tundra, carpeted with wildflowers
including lupines, clovers, snow-in-summer (*Cerastium
tomentosum*), daisies, and pinks. There are also kalmia,
mountain hemlocks (*Tsuga mertensiana*), and alpine firs
(*Abies lasiocarpa*). Between the entrance and exit of the
exhibit is a Metro composting demonstration.

Across from the Tundra exhibit is the Africa exhibit.
Look for bananas on the banana plants in the Vollum
Aviary. In front of the black rhino pen is a Russian olive
(*Eleagnus angustifolia*), attractively pruned so that it
doesn't obscure your view of the animals. Farther along,
the trees in the zebra exhibit—zelkova (*Zelkova serrata*)
and honey locust (*Gleditsia triacanthos*)—were chosen for
their evocation of the savanna. Along the perimeter are
silk trees (*Albizia julibrissin*) and more Russian olives.

In the Africa Rain Forest, the effect is achieved with
lush plantings of a wide variety of plants. Along with
bamboos, *Fatsia japonica*, and snow gum (*Eucalyptus
niphophila*) are roses, thimbleberry (*Rubus parviflorus*),
hostas, mahonia, sweet woodruff (*Galium odoratum*), and
photinia. In the low light and humid atmosphere of the
swamp building are a mahogany tree (*Swietenia
macrophylla*), bromeliads, and orchids.

A return trail to the entrance opened in the fall of 1997.
It is to be lined with gardens replicating Oregon botanical
habitats, to give ideas for planting backyard wildlife
habitats. Planting is planned for spring 1998. The forest

shade garden will include plants from groundcovers up
through trees, living under the canopy of Douglas firs.
The edge garden, transitional between the forest and sun
gardens, will include Oregon grape, willows and other
natives. The sun garden will be planted with perennials
as well as a pesticide-free lawn and shrubs such as
cinquefoil, barberry, and blueberry. Across a pond, the
wetland garden will include ashes, willows, and
dogwoods. The wild meadow is to be planted with
wildflowers, dogwood, cotoneaster, and other plants
providing food for wildlife. At the top of the path, the
butterfly garden is to include honeysuckle and, of course,
butterfly bushes.

Seasons of interest: Summer, early fall

Directions: From Highway 26 west of downtown take the Zoo-Arboretum exit, the first west of Sylvan, and the first east of the tunnel. Passing the zoo entrance on your right, the parking lot for OMSI's Education Resource Center is to your left. The garden is just west of the south end of the parking lot, outside the large blue and green structure.

From the Rose Garden or the Japanese Garden follow Kingston Drive to its T intersection; turn left; proceed down the hill to the OMSI parking lot on your right.

The garden is open all hours.

Public transit: Tri-Met bus 63-Washington Park. The garden will also be served by the zoo's westside light rail station, scheduled to open in September 1998.

Labels: Most plants are labeled.

Background: The garden was built and is maintained by the Oregon Herb Society as a community service project. It was originally planted in 1959, on an interior patio of what was then the new Oregon Museum of Science and Industry. (The building became the Education Resource Center when OMSI moved its museum elsewhere in 1992.) It originally displayed one hundred medicinal herbs. The garden was moved to its present location in 1973, and now includes nonmedicinal herbs.

What to see: The garden is planted in raised brick beds around a fountain (which, because of vandalism, is no longer operative). The plants include fennel (*Foeniculum vulgare*), sages, lavenders, rosemary, a few roses, and Joe Pye weed (*Eupatorium maculatum*). In the bed along the north side of the geodesic dome are angelica (*Angelica archangelica*) and several hardy geraniums.

Northern Willamette Valley

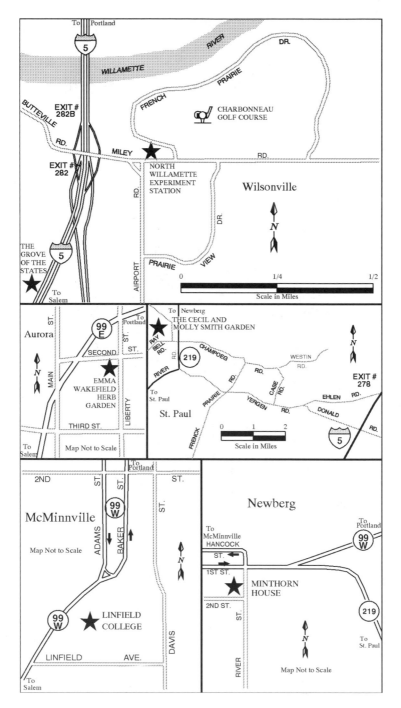

To Portland

5

WILLAMETTE | RIVER

BUTTEVILLE

EXIT # 282B

PRAIRIE

FRENCH

DR.

CHARBONNEAU
GOLF COURSE

RD.

MILEY

EXIT # 282

NORTH
WILLAMETTE
EXPERIMENT
STATION

Wilsonville

N

THE
GROVE
OF THE
STATES

5

To
Salem

AIRPORT RD.

PRAIRIE

VIEW DR.

0   1/4   1/2

Scale in Miles

Aurora

99 E

ST.

To
Portland

SECOND

ST.

N

MAIN

EMMA
WAKEFIELD
HERB
GARDEN

LIBERTY

THIRD ST.

To
Salem

Map Not to Scale

To Newberg
THE CECIL AND
MOLLY SMITH GARDEN

RAY
BELL
RD.

219

RIVER RD.

CHAMPOEG RD.

RD.

WESTIN
RD.

N

EXIT # 278

PRAIRIE RD.

CASE RD.

YERGEN RD.

EHLEN RD.

DONALD RD.

5

RD.

To
St. Paul

St. Paul

FRENCK

0   1   2

Scale in Miles

2ND

ST.

ST.

To
Portland

ST.

McMinnville

99 W

Map Not to Scale

ADAMS

BAKER

ST.

N

99 W

LINFIELD
COLLEGE

DAVIS

LINFIELD   AVE.

To
Salem

Newberg

To
McMinnville

HANCOCK ST.

1ST ST.

2ND ST.

ST.

MINTHORN
HOUSE

To
Portland

99 W

219

To
St. Paul

N

RIVER ST.

Map Not to Scale

114

Emma Wakefield Herb Garden

2nd and Liberty
Aurora
(503) 678-5754 (Aurora Colony Museum)

❧

Seasons of interest: Late spring, summer, and early fall

Directions: From Highway 99E northbound turn right onto Liberty; southbound, turn left onto 2nd. The herb garden is behind the buildings of the Aurora Colony Museum on the south side of Liberty. You need not pay the admission charge to the museum if you are just going to look at the garden. The museum hours (and therefore the hours the garden may be seen) are 10 a.m. to 4:30 p.m., Wednesday through Saturday, and 1 p.m. to 4:30 p.m. on Sunday during April, May, October, and November. In June, July, and August the hours are 10 a.m. to 4:30 p.m. Tuesday through Saturday and 1 p.m. to 4:30 p.m. on Sunday.

Labels: Most plants are labeled with common and botanical names and descriptions of pioneer and modern uses.

Background: The garden was originally planted in 1974, with herbs from Old Economy, Pennsylvania, whence many of the Aurora Colony's first settlers came. The colony was a nondenominational Christian commune.

Emma Wakefield was a school teacher from Portland, Maine. She taught school in St. Helens and Damascus before settling in Canby in 1943. After she retired from teaching, she worked in the Canby Library. She started gardening in the 1940s with four or five herbs. By 1974, when she helped found the Willamette Valley Herb Society, she had more than one hundred herbs in her collection, and fifty volumes on herbs in her library. Wakefield was a member of the Canby Garden Club, and each year she hosted an herb picnic for the club. She returned to Maine in 1978, leaving her books on herbs with the Canby Library. She died in 1981 at age ninety-three. She was the first person not a member of the Aurora Colony to be honored by having an element named after her.

The Northwest Herbal Society takes care of the garden.

What to see: This well-tended herb garden is square, edged in wood, and divided into four smaller squares by brick walkways.

Each smaller square has its own emphasis: traditional, fragrant, medicinal, and culinary. The center sundial in the traditional bed is surrounded by four mints (spear, orange, pepper, and woolly apple), several thymes, and calendulas. The medicinal bed includes marshmallow (*Althaea officinalis*), common valerian (*Valeriana officinalis*), mugwort (*Artemisia lactiflora*), elecampane (*Inula helenium*), and germander (*Teucrium* sp.). Among the culinary herbs are sweet cicely (*Myrrhis odorata*), French tarragon (*Artemisia dracunculus*) and winter savory (*Satureja montana*). The fragrant herbs include southernwood (*Artemisia abrotanum*), orris root (*Iris* x *germanica* 'Florentina'), dianthus, and English lavender (*Lavandula angustifolia*).

North Willamette Experiment Station

15210 N.E. Miley Road
Aurora, OR 97002-9543
(503) 678-1264

Seasons of interest: All

Directions: From Interstate 5 south of Portland, take exit 282B and proceed east about one mile. The station is open to the public from 8:00 a.m. to 4:30 p.m. weekdays, excluding holidays.

There are no organized tours. You must check in at the visitors' center when you arrive, to avoid stumbling into a recently sprayed area or similar problems. The station primarily serves commercial growers, and the visitors' center does not answer home gardening or landscaping questions. The greenhouse is not open to the public.

Labels: Most plants are labeled.

Background: The North Willamette Station, a branch of the Oregon Agricultural Experiment Station headquartered at Oregon State University in Corvallis, was established on two adjoining farms in the late 1950s. One of its emphases is ornamentals, reflecting the fact that the northern Willamette Valley has a large and growing ornamental horticulture trade. Greenhouse and nursery plants are Oregon's largest crop, and Oregon is the third leading nursery state in the country.

What to see: Because the emphasis is on plants grown for the horticultural trade, many are cultivars rather than species.

In the parking lot, a couple of Kousa dogwoods (*Cornus kousa*) and other trees tower over groundcovers, most of which have labels that helpfully provide the year each was planted. North of the parking lot, back toward

Miley Road and between the two driveways, the most garden-like area displays conifers and small ornamentals. This is a good place to compare cultivars within species; among the collections are dwarf boxwoods, *Cryptomeria japonica*, Hinoki cypress (*Chamaecyparis obtusa*), hibiscuses, hollies, evergreen azaleas, and camellias.

The main collection is of shade trees, mostly stretching west from the west driveway, some of them flowering, of all shapes, sizes, ages up to thirty years, and colors. Since this is an experiment station, geared toward agriculture, the trees are planted in straight rows on fairly level ground, like other crops.

Most of the dogwoods line the west driveway. Other flowering trees, mainly redbuds and flowering cherries, are further west. Among the other collections are beeches, elms, birches, and eucalyptuses. The maples include a trio of red maples (*Acer rubrum* 'Red Sunset,' 'Bowhall,' and 'Autumn Flame'). If you're pondering the purchase of a zelkova (*Zelkova serrata*), a huge one planted in 1966 may give you second thoughts. Less common trees include evodias, persimmons, pawpaws, and hawthorns.

Magnolias can be found along the west driveway and in a separate bed south of the grapes in the station's northwest corner. Between the magnolia bed and the station office are andromedas, rhododendrons, and azaleas.

The Grove of the States

Southbound Baldock Rest Area, Interstate 5
Wilsonville

❧

Seasons of interest: All

Directions: From Interstate 5 southbound at Wilsonville, exit to the rest area. The grove is at the north end.

Background: In the summer of 1967, Oregon hosted the annual meeting of the National Association of Attorneys General. Robert Y. Thornton, then Oregon's attorney general, sought some permanent, appropriate commemoration of the occasion. After considering and rejecting construction of a fountain, Thornton came up with the idea of planting a grove with the official tree of every state and other jurisdiction (Guam, the Virgin Islands, and Puerto Rico) represented at the conference. Six of the official trees would not have survived in Oregon's climate, so substitutes were chosen.

The conference was held at the Portland Hilton. Some attorneys general brought their state trees with them, walking through the hotel lobby with the trees on their shoulders like rifles. Some had sent their trees ahead. The bulk of the trees, however, were tracked down, acquired, and donated by the Oregon Association of Nurserymen.

Labels: All, by common name

What to see: The Grove of the States provides a partial respite from the Douglas firs gloomily dominating the remainder of the rest area. (There are a few Douglas firs in the grove; it is Oregon's state tree, and some existing specimens were left standing when the grove was planted.) Many of the trees have grown huge in thirty years, and therefore are difficult to appreciate in the crowded conditions.

A sign at the entrance to the grove identifies the location of the tree representing each state, commonwealth, and territory. The yellow poplars (*Liriodendron tulipifera*) representing Kentucky, Tennessee, and Indiana are usually known here as tulip trees. The trees representing the thirteen original colonies cluster at the entrance to the grove, and include the most exotic plant—South Carolina's palm (*Sabal palmetto*). Other trees rarely seen in Oregon include Illinois's bur oak (*Quercus macrocarpa*) and Ohio's buckeye (*Aesculus* sp.).

The conifers also provide good variety. New Mexico's piñon pine (*Pinus edulis*) is handily planted next to Nevada's singleleaf piñon pine (*P. monophylla*) for easy comparison, and other pines include Minnesota's red (*P. resinosa*) and Alabama's longleaf southern (*P. palustris*).

The Cecil and Molly Smith Garden

5065 Ray Bell Road
St. Paul
(503) 771-8386 (Portland Chapter,
American Rhododendron Society)

❧

Season of Interest: Spring

Directions: From Interstate 5, take the Donald/Aurora exit (no. 278). Follow signs to Champoeg State Park. Continue on Champoeg Road, turning right at the T intersection at the Robert Newell House. At State Highway 219, cross the highway; two-tenths of a mile further, where Champoeg Road curves north, continue straight ahead on Ray Bell Road six-tenths of a mile. The parking lot is past the house on the right.

The garden is open to the public only by appointment or on the first and third Saturdays in March, April, and May. There is an admission charge for all except American Rhododendron Society members. For group tours, call (503) 623-6311 or (503) 590-2505.

Special events: Plant sales, of rhododendrons and companion plants propagated from the garden, are held on the open garden days.

Labels: None, but knowledgeable people staff the garden on open days and can identify plants.

Background: The garden was begun by the Smiths in the early 1950s. Mr. Smith, who grew up a few miles away, purposely chose a site shaded by mature second-growth Douglas firs and easing down a north-facing slope near the Willamette River. He did not just collect rhododendrons; he also hybridized them, and took great care in preparing the sort of soil they needed. His love of local wildflowers influenced his choices of companion plants.

Although he pruned with an ax to get rid of plants he didn't want, he left many stumps and fallen trees, treating them as design elements and planting surfaces in his landscape. The method has its risks; sometimes plants have to be rescued when their supporting log or stump rots away.

When Mr. Smith retired to a smaller garden, the Portland chapter of the American Rhododendron Society acquired this one, and continues to maintain and develop it.

What to see: This woodland garden is known better internationally than locally for its collection of rhododendrons, put together with the zeal of a plantsman and the eye of an artist.

At the garden entrance, west of the house, a recently developed area features spring bulbs and deciduous small trees and shrubs. Head toward the house and down the hill to see the more mature part of the garden.

The garden well illustrates the immense variety within the genus *Rhododendron* in plant habit, color of blossom, size of plant, and size and shape of leaf. Large, mature, open rhododendrons include *R. calophytum* and 'Loderi King George.' There are rhododendrons with heart-shaped leaves (*R. williamsianum*) and with rounded oval leaves (*R. orbiculare*). *R. forrestii* var. *repens* sprawls along the ground and a fallen log. The northeast ell of the house shelters *R. radicans*, a mound of tiny leaves one foot high and two feet in diameter, and three tiny *R. keiskei* 'Yaku Fairy.'

Along the north side of the garden are species rhododendrons with huge, leathery leaves including *R. eximium* (better known as *R. falconeri* subsp. *eximium*) and *R. montroseanum*. Along the east side are the large reds 'Taurus,' 'C. B. Van Nes,' and 'Double Winner,' and smaller reds 'Matador' and 'Elizabeth.' Not far from the

slightly fragrant *R. yakushimanum* x
calophytum, sporting pinkish white
flowers with a magenta splotch, is the
more fragrant *R. bodinieri,* whose pale
pink flowers have an orange splotch.

Mr. Smith collected and bred
rhododendrons with indumentum, a
tawny, fuzzy growth on the underside
of leaves. Among those in the garden
are the white-flowered 'Sir Charles
Lemon' and one of Mr. Smith's own
hybrids, 'Cinnamon Bear.'

The genius of the garden is not
simply in its display of a great variety
of rhododendrons, but also in its
delightful array of companion plants. In
early March trilliums, forsythia, violets,
snowdrops, pink and white hellebores, and standard and
cyclamen-form narcissus are in bloom, along with several
small cyclamens, including *Cyclamen purpurascens* and *C.
hederifolium* 'Album.' By mid-April, accents are provided
by primroses; red, white, and pink trilliums; bloodroot
(*Sanguinaria canadensis*); hoop-petticoat daffodils
(*Narcissus bulbocodium*); and white and blue anemones.

The trees include a canopy of Douglas firs and also the
Japanese umbrella pine (*Sciadopitys verticillata*), a twenty-
foot cone on the western edge of the garden with whorls
of long white-ribbed needles, and a small *Cunninghamia
lanceolata,* an unusual broad-needled conifer.

Minthorn House

115 S. River Street
Newberg, 97132
(503) 538-6629

❧

Seasons of interest: Spring, summer, fall

Directions: From Highway 99W just east of downtown and just west of the bridge between the commercial strip and downtown, turn south on River Street and proceed one block; the house, on the northwest corner of the intersection, is well marked.

An admission fee is charged for the house, which is open Wednesday through Sunday, 1 p.m. to 4 p.m., but not for the grounds, which are visible from the sidewalk.

Labels: None

Background: Henry John Minthorn, who built the house in 1881, was Herbert Hoover's uncle. After Hoover was orphaned he came to Newberg and lived with his uncle Henry and aunt Laura from 1884 to 1889, from the age of ten through fifteen. He came from Iowa, and had not tasted pears until he came to Oregon. He ate so many from a tree in the Minthorns' yard the first two days he was there that it was years before he ate any more.

The house and grounds have long been owned by the Colonial Dames, descendants of early colonists, who are active in preserving historical records and sites. In the early 1950s one of their number, Elizabeth Lord of the Salem landscape architecture firm of Lord and Schryver, agreed to do the landscaping gratis. She planned simple plantings in the yard, echoing the late Victorian period when the house was built and Hoover lived there.

Lord did not, for practical reasons, reproduce the yard exactly as it was in Hoover's day; the flowers he remembered growing along the walk to the house would have impeded mowing. The lot to the north had not been part of the Minthorn property when Hoover lived there, but the Colonial Dames had acquired it and it was incorporated in Lord's design. Her research showed that very few broad-leaved evergreens were available in the Victorian era, so she decried the laurel hedge at the northern edge of the property, now screening the convenience store, as inauthentic.

Hoover attended the formal opening of the house and garden on August 10, 1955, his eighty-first birthday, and was a bit astonished by how colorful the garden was. Dr. Burt Brown Barker, an Oregon historian and longtime friend, wrote Lord shortly thereafter that the former president was "most surprised and pleased with the garden." Barker also asked that the house and garden be kept in perennially good shape the next year because Hoover, on his customary but as yet unscheduled fishing trip to Oregon, would probably want to slip over to the house unannounced and tour it alone.

What to see: This is an old-fashioned yard of the late Victorian style, with lots of lawn and many deciduous shrubs. Among them are viburnums, hydrangeas, peonies, and weigelas. Some of the lilacs and the pear tree in the middle of the yard may date from Hoover's day. Other fruit includes apple trees in the north lot, rhubarb (*Rheum* x *hybridum*) next to the shed, a quince (*Cydonia oblonga*) next to the side gate, and a 'Flame' crabapple (*Malus* 'Flame') southeast of the house. Bulb beds skirt the front of the house. Along the back wall are bleeding hearts and forget-me-nots. The herb garden along the back fence includes epimediums and angelica (*Angelica archangelica*).

Linfield College

Highway 99W
McMinnville

Seasons of interest: All

Directions: The college is on the southwest edge of town. Highway 99W (Baker Street), the main road through McMinnville, runs along the college's northwest edge, past its main entrance.

Labels: None

Background: Linfield was founded in McMinnville in 1855, and moved to its present site in 1881. The planting of a wide variety of trees dates to the tenure of Dr. James A. MacNab, a biology professor, and Arthur Fairhill, groundskeeper, in the late 1920s and early 1930s. The rhododendron garden north of the president's house was planted in the early 1940s, when the house was being built. The dogwoods in the grove west of Campbell Hall were planted in honor of the May Queen. Planting began in 1943, when the McMinnville Garden Club donated a tree each year for the current queen, and additional trees in honor of the queens from the beginning of the May festival in 1904. In the 1960s, the tradition was changed to planting a rhododendron on the northeast side of the main drive. The celebration of May Day on campus ceased in the early 1970s. When many native oaks fell in the Columbus Day Storm of 1962, they were replaced by non-natives.

What to see: Linfield is a beautiful old campus, with a wide collection of trees and shrubs to complement its white-trimmed brick buildings. The trees include a much lower proportion of conifers than is usual.

The main entrance road skirts a circle of lawn which is home to a magnificent Oregon white oak (*Quercus garryana*), the oldest tree on campus. Also near the lawn is an umbrella-shaped Cedar of Lebanon (*Cedrus libani*) and, along the northeast side, streamside collections of hybrid rhododendrons and native plants. A grove of dogwoods stretches east from Pioneer Hall to Campbell Hall. Southeast of Campbell Hall is a small garden of conifers and flowering shrubs.

Head back toward the buildings along the entrance road. Rhododendrons line the walk west of Haley Center and Walker Hall. Further west, the trees in the quadrangle behind Melrose Hall include Japanese maples (*Acer palmatum*) tucked around the entrance to Murdock Hall; tamaracks (*Larix occidentalis*); several giant sequoias (*Sequoiadendron giganteum*); and a yellowwood (*Cladastris lutea*). Small rosebeds sit at the northwest corner of the soccer field south of Linfield Avenue, past Dillin Commons.

Salem–Dallas Area

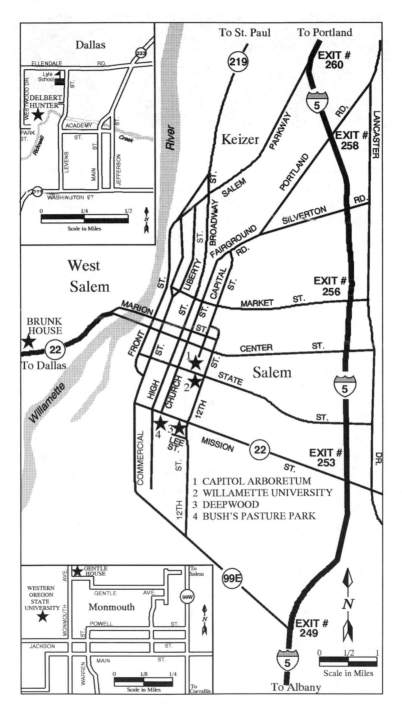

To St. Paul

To Portland

Dallas

EXIT #
260

ELLENDALE RD.

Lyle School

DELBERT HUNTER

PARK ST.

ACADEMY ST.

Rickreall Creek

LEVENS

MAIN

JEFFERSON

WASHINGTON ST

Scale in Miles
0   1/4   1/2

River

Keizer

219

5

EXIT #
258

LANCASTER

PARKWAY

PORTLAND

RD.

SALEM

SILVERTON

RD.

West
Salem

BROADWAY ST.

LIBERTY ST.

FAIRGROUND RD.

CAPITAL ST.

MARKET ST.

EXIT #
256

BRUNK
HOUSE

MARION

FRONT ST.

ST.

ST.

ST.

CENTER ST.

22

To Dallas

HIGH ST.

CHURCH ST.

1

2

STATE ST.

Salem

5

Willamette

12TH

ST.

COMMERCIAL ST.

4

3

LEE ST.

MISSION ST.

22

EXIT #
253

12TH ST.

1 CAPITOL ARBORETUM
2 WILLAMETTE UNIVERSITY
3 DEEPWOOD
4 BUSH'S PASTURE PARK

DR.

GENTLE HOUSE

WESTERN
OREGON
STATE
UNIVERSITY

MONMOUTH AVE.

GENTLE AVE.

To
Salem

99W

99E

Monmouth

POWELL ST.

N

JACKSON

ST.

MAIN ST.

WARREN

Scale in Miles
0   1/8   1/4

To
Corvallis

EXIT #
249

5

N

Scale in Miles
0   1/2   1

To Albany

129

Capitol Arboretum

Surrounding the Capitol
Salem

✣⳪

Seasons of interest: All

Directions: From Interstate 5 south of Salem, take the Highway 22 exit (no. 253) and proceed west; from the north, take the Salem Parkway exit (no. 260). Follow signs to the capitol or look for the gold pioneer on its dome. Public parking is available at meters along State Street south of the capitol, Waverly Street east of the capitol, and the mall north of the capitol, including the Chemeketa Street underground parking garage.

Labels: Few. You can obtain a free map of the grounds with a key identifying some of the trees at the information desk inside the capitol.

Background: The area around the capitol—bounded by Waverly, State, Cottage and Court streets—is two parks. To the east is Capitol Park; to the west is Willson Park.

Willson Park is named for H.W. Willson, who arrived in Oregon in 1837 as a missionary. In 1843 he was elected second treasurer of the provisional government, in 1846 he platted Salem, and in 1853 he and his wife gave the park land to the city. Willson Park was still just a flat expanse in 1870. In 1873, a capitol was built at its east end. Citizen outcry prompted the planting of trees in the park in the spring of 1878. By 1894, many of the trees in the north end of the park were clipped as topiary.

After the capitol burned in 1935, some trees were transplanted to make way for its replacement, built slightly west of the old site and perpendicular to the former alignment. In 1962, the Columbus Day storm wrought much destruction. Three years later, the state acquired ownership of Willson Park and set about resuscitating it.

Many of the trees, statues, and fountains in the arboretum are gifts to the state. Local garden societies maintain the rose and fuchsia beds.

What to see: To the east of the capitol is Capitol Park, mainly given to lawn, trees, and statuary. To the west is the more formal Willson Park, with fountains and flower beds.

The Douglas fir (*Pseudotsuga menziesii*) has been Oregon's state tree since 1939. (College basketball fans will recall that in the same year the University of Oregon's Tall Firs won the first NCAA basketball title.) But if the capitol has a signature tree it's not the fir but the Camperdown elm (*Ulmus glabra* 'Camperdownii'), which flanks the east and west entrances and appears here and there around the grounds (and, across Waverly Street, guards the entrance to the parking lot between the Justice Building and the Supreme Court Building).

Starting on the capitol steps, behind Sacajawea (who doesn't have her name carved in marble, but she's the woman leading Lewis and Clark, who do), and proceeding east into Capitol Park, you pass a southern magnolia (*Magnolia grandiflora*). You can see, out in the parking strip near the intersection of Court and Summer streets, a big American elm (*Ulmus americana*), and to the east a ginkgo (*Ginkgo biloba*). Rhododendrons and camellias line the north wall of the capitol.

Continue east. Fragments of columns of the old capitol rest under two large old black walnuts (*Juglans nigra*) and an American linden (*Tilia americana*). The statue of the Circuit Rider is surrounded by rhododendrons. A massive tulip tree (*Liriodendron tulipifera*) anchors the northeast corner of the park. Turn south along Waverly; halfway down the block a shagbark hickory (*Carya ovata*) shades an old-fashioned weigela that blooms pink in May.

Along State Street, the capitol wings are flanked by a line of 'Chanticleer' pears (*Pyrus calleryana* 'Chanticleer'); behind the boxwood hedge atop the wall are flowering cherries. Farther west, the bed of approximately two hundred and fifty fuchsias blooms from late July until frost. The huge trees in the parking strip are sycamores (*Platanus* sp.). Near the corner of State and Cottage are an arborvitae (*Thuja occidentalis*) with wonderful loopy branches and a huge blue Atlas cedar (*Cedrus atlantica* 'Glauca'). Along Cottage Street are formal groves of Japanese flowering crabapples (*Malus* sp.) and European hornbeams (*Carpinus betulus*).

The flowering cherries at the west end of the elliptical sidewalk are *Prunus subhirtella* 'Autumnalis'; those on the east end are *P. yedoensis*.

In the north half of Willson Park are a small grove of red horsechestnuts (*Aesculus* x *carnea*) and a cluster of saucer magnolias (*Magnolia* x *soulangiana*). Along Court Street, across from the end of Winter Street, is a bed of several hundred roses—hybrid teas, grandifloras, floribundas, and English roses. Further east along Court Street, tucked into the northeast corner of Willson Park, is a small border with hostas, bergenias, scilla, and cannas.

Return to the west side of the capitol steps. The southern magnolia (*Magnolia grandiflora*) just to the west is the companion of the one where your expedition began.

✿

Seasons of interest: All

Directions: From Interstate 5, take the Highway 22 exit (no. 253) and proceed westbound into Salem. Highway 22 becomes Mission Street.

To drive to the Martha Springer Botanical Area, take the 12th Street exit, get into the left lane, and turn left into a parking lot across 12th from the big brick Thomas Kay Woolen Mill. The Botanical Area is just south of the parking lot, across the mill race. To visit the university's other two gardens, walk north on 12th Street and turn left on State Street. The Sesquicentennial Rose Garden is on State Street in front of Eaton Hall and across the street from the east wing of the capitol. Continue west on State Street; the Germaine Fuller Japanese Garden is behind the Art Building, which sits at the southeast corner of State and Winter streets.

To drive to the Germaine Fuller Japanese Garden and Sesquicentennial Rose Garden, take the Willamette University ramp from Mission Street. Across 12th Avenue, Mission becomes Bellevue. Continue two-tenths of a mile to Winter Street, and turn right. Winter Street ends at State Street; park along Winter Street or State Street. The Japanese garden is behind the Art Building at the corner of Winter and State; the rose garden is east a few hundred feet along State Street.

A one-page history and explanation of the Japanese garden is available in the Art Building.

Labels: The plants in the Martha Springer garden and the roses are labeled; those in the Japanese garden are not.

133

Background: Willamette University, the oldest college west of the Mississippi, was founded in 1842, but its special gardens are quite new.

In the early 1980s, a group that sought to develop a botanical garden on campus succeeded in defeating an attempt to turn a rail spur on a narrow strip between the mill race and the athletic complex into a parking lot. The project got funded several years later as part of the 1985-86 construction of the Mark O. Hatfield Library nearby. (Former Senator Hatfield attended Willamette University, graduating in 1943. He later taught political science and served as dean of students here while beginning his career in public office.) The garden, first planted in 1986, honors the late Martha Springer, a botanist and beloved professor emerita of biology, who had hoped to establish an arboretum on campus.

In 1991, Germaine L. Fuller, Professor of Asian Art History, designed and built the Japanese garden with students in her art history class. The garden was named in her honor after her death in 1994. Shade resulting from construction just south of the garden in 1996 may occasion changes in the plant material.

When the university prepared to celebrate its sesquicentennial in 1992, it planned a garden for which people could buy roses. Each rose would have a plaque identifying the rose, the donor, and the honoree. The initial plan was to start with one hundred and fifty roses, and then add one a year. After the first were planted, people clamored to buy roses, and by January of 1996 almost three hundred roses had been planted.

The garden also contains a nod to history. Jason Lee founded Willamette University (his statue is across State Street from the university, in Capitol Park, because he was an important figure in Oregon's early days; he also established permanent settlements, churches, and other schools). When he married Anna Maria Pittman in 1837, she was given a rose as a wedding present. One each of the three varieties claimed to have been given to her ('Quatre Saisons,' 'Provence,' and *Rosa damascena* 'Semperflorens') was planted in the garden.

What to see: The campus is pleasant, particularly in spring, when the rhododendrons, heather, bulbs, andromeda, and camellias around its buildings and along the mill race are in bloom. Even more pleasant are three special campus gardens. None is particularly big, but each is full of interesting plants or features: distilled essences of gardens, you might say.

The Germaine Fuller Japanese Garden is about two thousand square feet. From Winter Street, enter through a covered gate. On your left, in the northwest corner, is a rustic Mountain Viewing Shelter and in front of it is a flat sand and stone garden. On your right in the moss garden, a camellia, bamboo, and pines are arranged around the Mountain Stone group of rocks. The path crosses a dry stream bed, planted with iris and azaleas near the path and maples farther away. Another rock group, of petrified wood symbolizing the paradisiacal Islands of the Immortals, is arranged near the northeast corner; near the southeast corner is a stone lantern. A secondary path winds through the north half of the garden. The garden fence is wood and bamboo in a variety of patterns.

The Sesquicentennial Rose Garden is a fan shape, to show the entire rose color spectrum from white, to yellow, to orange, and so on. (The vagaries of catalog illustrations kept the scheme from being followed with precision.) The roses cover the entire spectrum of rose types: hybrid teas, floribundas, grandifloras, shrubs, miniatures, polyanthas, climbers, old garden roses, and English roses. Near the northwest corner of the garden are several bushes of the 'Mark Hatfield' rose.

The Martha Springer Botanical Area encourages town and gown to learn about native, unusual, and popular garden plants. Its kiosk describes it as "a place for leisure learning." You can certainly enjoy it at a leisurely pace, but it is a very ambitious garden, with lots of plants and information packed pleasantly into a small space.

Southwest Oregon natives on the berm along 12th Street include hoary manzanita (*Arctostaphylos canescens*), western blue flax (*Linum perenne* var. *lewisii*), and 'Diamond Lake' rock penstemon (*Penstemon davidsonii* 'Diamond Lake'). Oregon regional plantings continue across the grass path. In front of the building's east wall are Willamette Valley natives such as goldenrod (*Solidago canadensis*) and *Geranium oreganum*. Around the corner of the building Cascade natives include grand fir (*Abies grandis*), fringecup (*Tellima grandiflora*), and starflower (*Trientalis* sp.). An open, rocky clearing displays *Penstemon cardwellii*, bear grass (*Xerophyllum tenax*), and *Sedum oreganum*. Further west, and wrapping into the ell of the building, a Coast Range area harbors tree lupine (*Lupinus arboreus*), Pacific Coast red elderberry (*Sambucus racemosa*), and coast silktassel (*Garrya elliptica*).

Beyond the ell, in front of the windows above the swimming pool, is a garden of culinary and fragrant herbs. The next bed, labeled the language of flowers, invites you to think of your own messages rather than telling you what the flowers—including roses, columbines, and white bellflower (*Campanula persicifolia* 'Alba')—have traditionally meant. Beyond a patch of columbines the cutting garden is meant to inspire you to plant your own, not to bring your secateurs and help yourself. Stretching to the west end of the building is a gold garden, with grasses, conifers, and shrubs as well as flowers ranging from cream through yellow to pale orange. Varieties include a single-flowered *Kerria japonica*,

the locally developed Trost dwarf birch (*Betula pendula*
'Trost's Dwarf') looking like a pale little Japanese maple,
an orange-gold Rheingold arborvitae (*Thuja occidentalis*
'Rheingold') and several variegated hollies.

Down the other side of the garden, along the millrace,
the plant material in a pink and blue mixed border
includes pussytoes (*Antennaria dioica*), iris, roses, and a
very blue R. H. Montgomery spruce (*Picea pungens* 'R. H.
Montgomery'). Halfway along, the border is interrupted
for a small rock garden of dwarf conifers and flowers
including *Lewisia cotyledon*.

The beds down the center of the garden start at the
west end with a bird and butterfly garden. The first two
raised beds contain plants that attract moths, followed by
beds containing plants used for medicines, fibers, and
dyes. After cereal and vegetable plant displays, the rest of
the beds contain plants from a variety of families selected
to show the diversity within each: grasses and sedges;
borages and mints; and the rose, mustard, violet and
mallow, buttercup, iris, and heath families.

Deepwood

1116 Mission Street S.E.
Salem, OR 97302
(503) 363-1825

Seasons of interest: All

Directions: From Interstate 5, take the Highway 22 exit
(no. 253) and proceed westbound into Salem; Highway 22
becomes Mission Street. After you scale the overpass
above the railroad tracks and return to ground level, turn
left at the first traffic signal, onto 12th Avenue. Proceed
one block, turn right onto Lee Street, and then into
Deepwood's parking lot.

The gardens are open from dawn to dusk; the
greenhouse is open from 9 a.m. to 4 p.m. The house, for
which admission is charged, is open 12 noon to 4:30 p.m.
May to September, every day except Saturday, and 1:00
p.m. to 4:00 p.m. October to April on Mondays,
Wednesdays, Fridays, and Sundays.

Labels: None

Weddings: The gardens accommodate up to one hundred
and fifty people. The house may be rented on Saturdays,
or evenings after 6 p.m.

Background: The house, built in 1893-94, was designed
by William Christmas Knighton, among whose many
other works are the Oregon Supreme Court building a
few blocks north, designed during his 1913-17 stint as
state architect; North Salem High School; and, in
Portland, the Seward—now Governor—Hotel and the
Charles F. Berg building. The gardens (except, possibly,
the entrance garden) and the name came later.

Clifford and Alice Brown became the third owners of
Deepwood in 1925. Mrs. Brown, widowed two years later,
was the moving force behind the development of the
gardens. In 1929 she hired the landscape architecture firm

of Lord and Schryver. Elizabeth Lord and Edith Schryver, who had just hung out their shingle—and who lived just a few blocks down Mission Street—comprised the first female landscape design firm in Oregon. They designed the Scroll Garden in the southwest corner, the Tea Garden in the southeast corner, and the Great Room garden between the house and the Tea Garden. Years later Schryver remembered the commission as difficult, because the garden was then separated from the house by a driveway.

Mrs. Brown, while quite appreciative of their efforts—in one letter, enclosing a payment, she praised Lord's "inspiration and artistic comprehension" and Schryver's "sensitive and delicate little touch"—did not just sign checks. She made her own addition to the Great Room in the form of a reflecting pool (later planted to ivy). She apparently designed the Shade Garden next to the tennis court. She was fond of garden ornament, and had two gazebos—a wooden one that originally decorated the spring house, and a metal one from the Lewis and Clark Exposition. The column fragment in the Shade Garden is from the old state capitol, which burned in 1935. The fence in the Scroll Garden, a gift from Mrs. Brown's sister, originally decorated the top of the Davis Building in Portland. At the west end of the same garden is a platform originally built for a Chinese jar Lord and Schryver brought back from the Orient; Mrs. Brown later moved the jar inside to prevent vandalism.

It was also Mrs. Brown who named the estate, in 1935. An ancient yew tree with a hole in its trunk inspired her to name the tree and the estate after a children's book, *The Hollow Tree and Deepwoods Book*, by Albert Bigelow Paine. (The tree died in the 1980s and has been removed.)

When Mrs. Brown remarried in 1945, the wedding took place in the Scroll Garden. Her groom, Keith Powell, was

the widower of the daughter of the second owners; his
first wife had grown up at Deepwood.

The couple moved out of Deepwood in 1968, and the
Friends of Deepwood came up with enough money to
buy 2.29 acres of the five-acre estate. It was placed on the
National Register of Historic Places in 1974. The gardens
were restored in 1980 and 1981, but not as to specific
plants; Lord and Schryver kept no lists, as the plants were
to change each year, and many were no longer available.
The volunteer Deepwood Gardeners soon began assisting
in maintaining the gardens, and developed the border
outside the laurel hedge, paralleling 12th Avenue, in the
mid 1980s, and the other garden areas outside the main
hedge.

What to see: Inside the hedge are the formal gardens first
planned and planted more than half a century ago.
Outside the hedge are an impressive perennial border and
informal plantings around a greenhouse.

The path from the parking lot leads to the south end of
the formal gardens, a series of garden rooms inside the
hedge. The Tea Garden, in the southeast corner, is the
most floriferous. Attractive stone planters hold geraniums
and pansies; other plants include hostas, irises, meadow
rue, and a double reddish-purple
columbine with white edges. The
next garden room to the north has
a box-edged lawn; beyond the
low hedges are irises, poppies,
roses, dicentras, and peonies.
Running along the west side of
those two gardens is a sidewalk
over which arch holly, lilacs,
clematis, and grapes.

West of the walk is the
Great Room, with sculpted

box entrances at the north and south ends and a wrought-iron gazebo at the south end. To the west of the gazebo, a walk winds downhill under an ivy-covered trellis to the Scroll Garden, named for the shape of its boxwood hedges. Another box-edged path leads along the west side of the gardened area, ending in a lawn below the sunroom. To the west are the moldering tennis court and wooden gazebo; ahead is a fragment of a column from the old state capitol.

Circle around the north end of the house, and venture outside the hedge. Along the east side of the hedge is a magnificent border, in bloom from March to September in waves of color: lavenders and purples set off with yellows at the north end grade to yellows, then pinks, whites, oranges—contrasting with a purple smoke tree (*Cotinus coggygria*)—more yellows, reds, and pinks, and ending in blues at the south end.

Continue around the south end of the hedge. To the northwest of the greenhouse, beyond the restrooms, is a nature trail. On the northern end of the west side of the greenhouse are hot-colored flowers; around the north and east sides, cooler colors prevail. Inside the greenhouse tender plants include cactuses, bamboos, and ferns.

The flowers continue along the east edge of the parking lot to the south end where, south of the greenhouse, are a small rock garden, a small herb garden, and a home composting demonstration center.

Bush's Pasture Park

600 Mission S.E.
Salem, OR 97302

❧

Seasons of interest: Spring, summer, fall

Directions: From Interstate 5 north of Salem, take the Salem Parkway exit (no. 260) and continue south on Commercial Street to Mission, and turn left on Mission. From the south, take the Highway 22 exit (no. 253) westbound; Highway 22 becomes Mission Street. Turn south onto High Street, proceed two blocks, and turn left into the marked driveway.

Labels: All of the roses are labeled, but few of the other plants are.

Weddings: The rose garden will accommodate up to one hundred people. Call (503) 588-6256 for reservations.

Background: Bush House was built by Asahel Bush II, a Salem banker, in 1877-78. Sally Bush, daughter of the builder and chatelaine of the house (her mother died before the house was built) until her own death in 1946, was an avid gardener. The house and grounds became a city park in 1953, following the death of her brother.

Elizabeth Lord and Edith Schryver, landscape architects who designed the gardens at Deepwood, a few blocks east of Bush House, and many other private houses, lived across Mission Street from the Bushes. They helped Miss Bush place and plant flowering and fruiting crabapples in the area northwest of the rose garden, near High Street. They were apparently just being neighborly; there doesn't seem to have been any commission, or any plan committed to paper.

The extensive rose garden west of the house was planted after the property became a city park. Miss Bush had planted rose bushes near the house but they almost disappeared after her death. The modern roses were first planted in 1955. Lord and Schryver did the preliminary layout for the beds to the west, which contain old and species roses from the collection of Mae M. Tartar, donated in the late 1950s. Tartar's collection was of varieties brought to Oregon by wagon train.

The conservatory, built in 1882, had several brushes with extinction during its first century. When the city developed the park in the 1950s, several plans proposed replacing it with parking or gardens. It was condemned in the late 1970s, and plans were made to replace it with classroom space. But it was reprieved and restored, and continues into its second century.

The official name of the park was stipulated by the Bush family in the deed transferring the property to the city. The pasture surrounding the house was home to Oregon white oaks, some more than five hundred years old, and a collection of wildflowers. The city converted the pasture to lawn with an irrigation system.

What to see: The park is not designated as an arboretum, but has some interesting trees. Less common than the

Oregon white oaks (*Quercus garryana*) near Mission Street is the American persimmon (*Diospyros virginiana*) near the northeast corner of the house. Contrast the cutleaf birch (*Betula pendula* 'Gracilis'), between the garden shed and the roses, with the European beech (*Fagus sylvatica*) by the porte-cochère.

Flowering trees include dogwoods, cherries, sweet bay and southern magnolias (*Magnolia virginiana* and *M. grandiflora*, respectively), quince, and crabapples. Among the flowering shrubs are *Enkianthus campanulatus*, beautybush (*Kolkwitzia amabilis*), white and pink weigelas, mock orange (*Philadelphus* sp.) and Persian lilac (*Syringa* x *persica*).

The rose garden, west and southwest of the house, contains approximately two thousand rosebushes of more than one hundred and twenty varieties. At the north end, the four small beds in a semicircle framing a white bench under a trellis contain roses that were grown around the house before the rose garden was built. Nearby, in the northwest corner and to the west, are many old garden roses, including an oddity, 'The Green Rose' (*Rosa chinensis* 'Viridiflora'), grown for curiosity and not for looks. The rest of the roses are modern.

The beds south of the house and near the port-cochère are planted to bulbs in the spring and annuals in the summer.

Inside the conservatory are many begonias and cactuses, a Crown of Thorns (*Euphorbia milii*), several bougainvilleas, a lime tree, and ferns. Just outside the door is a small herb garden. The low espalier to the north supports four kinds of apples (Golden Delicious, Yellow Transparent, Winesap, and Red Delicious). In formal beds to the south are box topiary, *Kerria japonica*, a few roses, delphiniums, and poppies.

Brunk House

5705 Salem-Dallas Highway N.W.
Salem

Seasons of interest: Spring, summer

Directions: From Interstate 5 southbound, take the Salem Parkway exit (no. 260); from Interstate 5 northbound, take the Highway 22 exit (no. 253). Proceed through Salem, following signs to Dallas. Brunk House is on the north side of Highway 22, approximately five miles west of Salem. The house is open in summer (June 15 through September 1) from 1 p.m. to 4 p.m., daily except Wednesdays and Thursdays.

Labels: Some plants are labeled.

Background: Brunk House was built by the Brunk family in 1861. They lived there until 1974, when it became the property of the Polk County Historical Society, which maintains the house and the acre surrounding it as a museum.

The grounds are planted to reflect the period 1895-1920. The society is not attempting a precise reproduction of the grounds as they were then, but many of the flowers around the house (including the lilacs) have been in place for years. One of the turn-of-the-century features is a "walking garden"—a collection of plants you walk on. The vegetable garden has been in the same location since at least the early 1930s.

The rose garden, planted in the late 1980s, features old roses gathered from all over the Willamette Valley. The Monmouth Garden Club planted the rose and herb gardens. The dahlia garden was added in the 1990s.

What to see: From the parking area, the first obvious gardens are the dahlias and the rose garden, in the front lawn to the south. Each holds several dozen varieties. The roses are all older varieties; the dahlias are a mix of old and new. The vegetable garden, full of squash, beans, corn and potatoes, is intended to be an old-fashioned garden.

Toward the house, the sidewalk passes a walking garden of tiny, tough groundcovers: Blue Star (*Laurentia fluviatilis*); Irish and Scottish mosses (*Sagina subulata* and *S. s.* 'Aurea'); Roman chamomile (*Chamaemelum nobile*); a dianthus, and a thyme. To the north is a flower garden, with yarrows, globe amaranth (*Gomphrena globosa*) and calendulas.

The sidewalk continues around the house past columbines, clematis, lupines, iris, forget-me-nots, lilacs and wisteria, to the herb garden behind the house. The herbs include several mints, thymes and lavenders.

Delbert Hunter
Arboretum and Botanic Garden and Japanese Garden
City Park
Dallas

※

Seasons of interest: All

Directions: From Highway 22 west of Salem, follow signs to Dallas, turning south on Highway 223. When 223 veers left toward the city center, proceed straight on Ellendale Road. Turn left on Levens Street (Lyle Elementary School is on the southeast corner); proceed .15 mile, turn right on Brandsvold at the entrance to the Dallas City Park, and proceed through the park to its south end; the Japanese Garden is on the left, with a parking lot just beyond it. Or go one block further on Ellendale and turn left on Westwood; at the end of Westwood, turn left on Park, proceed one block; the arboretum is on the right, parking is on the left. The Japanese Garden is one-tenth of a mile north of the arboretum.

Labels: Most of the plants in the Arboretum and Botanic Garden are labeled, but none in the Japanese garden are.

Background: The Japanese garden was designed by Art Higasha and Delbert Hunter, and built by the Dallas Rotary Club in the 1960s.

In 1978 the City of Dallas set aside five acres at the south end of the park for Oregon native plants. The park board, crew, and volunteers got the arboretum started, building trails and installing an irrigation system. The Friends of the Delbert Hunter Arboretum and Botanic Garden organized in 1983, and proceeded to plan and plant the area with examples of Oregon plant habitats. The arboretum is named for a charter member of the park board who served as its chairman for decades.

What to see: The small Japanese garden is furnished with
an interesting modern metal lantern and a half moon
bridge over a stream which is dry in summer. Trails wind
around a small pond and among clipped evergreens,
rhododendrons, ferns and other plants.

The arboretum is arranged along a long loop trail, with
several cross-trails and an inner loop. Inside the entrance,
to the left, is the classroom building. Just beyond the
building a mound displays plants of the Eastern Oregon
steppes, including squaw currant (*Ribes cereum*), gray
rabbitbrush (*Chrysothamnus nauseosus*), desert buckwheat
(*Eriogonum* sp.), and western blue flax (*Linum perenne* var.
lewisii). Straight ahead from the entrance is a pool with a
waterfall, fringed with wetlands plants. Just east of the
pond, the leaves of a lobe-leaved red alder (*Alnus rubra*
var. *pinnatisecta*) appear oaky rather than aldery. A
hackberry (*Celtis reticulata*) from the Snake River area and
a golden western currant (*Ribes aureum*) grow along the
dike of LaCreole Creek—or Rickreall Creek, according to
your sympathies (according to Lewis A. McArthur, in
Oregon Geographic Names, the proper name of this creek is
more disputed than almost any other geographic name in
Oregon. Disagreements regard whether the original
name was LaCreole (from the French for native, because
an Indian drowned near the site of Dallas) or Rickreall,
and whether Rickreall is a corruption of LaCreole, from
the Chinook jargon "hyak chuck" meaning "swift water,"
or from an Indian name for a locality near the stream). To
the right are several birches and varieties of *Prunus,* and a
wildflower meadow with many bulbs, wild hollyhock,
and Indian plum (*Oemleria cerasiformis*).

The trail continues along the east side of the arboretum
past hardwoods and conifers; the arboretum has
specimens of almost all the native pines and a good
selection of western oaks. At the south end, in the
southwestern Oregon section are azaleas, blueblossom

(*Ceanothus thrysiflorus*), mountain silktassel (*Garrya fremontii*), and *Iris innominata*. On the west side of the arboretum a dogwood (*Cornus nuttalii*) and vine maple (*Acer circinatum*) trail provides color in fall and spring. Farthest to the west is a fern trail.

Back at the entrance, up the hill on the west side a display of native groundcovers includes western leucothoe (*Leucothoe davisiae*) and alum root (*Heuchera micrantha*).

Western Oregon State University
and Gentle House
North Monmouth Avenue
Monmouth

ॐ

Seasons of interest: Spring, summer, fall

Directions: Monmouth is on Highway 99W, north of Corvallis and south of Rickreall. If you're coming from the north and like pastoral scenery, Highway 99W south of McMinnville is well worth forgoing the freeway. If you're approaching on Interstate 5 from the north, take the Salem Parkway exit (no. 260); from the south, take the Highway 22 exit (no. 253). Proceed west on Highway 22 to Highway 99W, and turn left. In Monmouth, follow signs to the college; the main street through campus is Monmouth Avenue.

Visitors may park free on campus, but you'll have to obtain a permit. From Monmouth Avenue turn west just north of Arbuthnot Hall and opposite Campus Estates; wind around to the Safety Services building, where parking permits are issued.

Gentle House is just north of the northern edge of campus. The house and grounds are sometimes rented to private parties, so call Western Foundation's Institutional Advancement Office ((503) 838-8281) before visiting. If you want a tour of the house, arrange it through the Foundation.

The garden of Jensen Arctic Museum is, at this writing, at the corner of Church Street and Stadium Drive, although there are plans to move it to the plot between campus and Gentle House. Church Street runs west from Monmouth Avenue, just north of Todd Hall.

Weddings: Gentle House and its grounds may be rented for weddings. The outdoor capacity is four to five hundred people. Call Western Foundation's Institutional Advancement Office, (503) 838-8281, for rates and availability.

Labels: None

Background: The Western Oregon State University campus dates to 1856. Early landscaping used a very limited range of plant material and suffered much destruction from the Columbus Day Storm, so most of the plantings of interest are relatively young.

Gentle House, built about 1880, sits near the southwest corner of the J. B. Smith Donation Land Claim north of campus. It changed hands several times before the Gentle family bought it with one hundred and sixty acres in 1914. They ran an orchard and a dairy farm. The father, Thomas Gentle, was a professor of education who came to Monmouth to revive the college's elementary teacher training program.

The grounds around the house already had a few trees and camellias, but the Gentles had a landscape architecture student from what is now Oregon State University draw up a plan in 1917. It included many of the shrubs growing along the north side of the lawn and around the house.

Professor Gentle's son Morris planted the catalpa trees. His daughter Catherine replaced fir trees when they died and brought shooting stars (*Dodecatheon* sp.) from the woods to plant around the maples in the front yard. She gardened until 1980. She died in 1981, and willed the house and 3.7 acres to the Western Foundation for "genteel entertaining."

The Western Foundation built an extension on the back of the house for entertaining and conferences and made a museum of the family's life in the 1920s and 1930s in the upstairs rooms. In keeping with the museum's focus, the Polk County Master Gardeners landscaped around the extension with plants commonly used in those decades. Many of the plants around the rest of the house are also from the Gentle era, except the rhododendrons in front. The gazebo, a gift of the Monmouth Garden Club, is not original. The Gentle family looked out from the house to the crescent-shaped garden behind the gazebo, but many of the plants there now are new.

Friends of Gentle House, organized in 1987, helps care for the house and the garden.

What to see: The main show on campus, with most of the color, stretches along Monmouth Avenue. The bulbs of early spring are supplanted by annuals in late spring, planned to peak at commencement in June. 'Redspire' ornamental pears (*Pyrus calleryana* 'Redspire') along Monmouth Avenue have pink-tinged leaves in spring, and provide fall color along with katsura trees, zelkovas, and flowering cherries.

Back from the street, closer to the buildings, are azaleas, andromedas and rhododendrons. There's a row of camellias along the north wall of the administration building and several magnolias behind it.

At the south end of campus, on the west side of Monmouth Avenue just north of Jackson Street, is the Natural Science building. In front is a small all-season garden of a pond surrounded by pines, andromedas, rhododendrons, and maples.

There are three very small rose beds. One is behind and one is on the south side of the Cottage, which sits back from Monmouth Avenue but is easy to find from the sign. The third is on the west side of the student center.

In front of the Jensen Arctic Museum is a tiny collection of tundra natives, including kinnikinnick (*Arctostaphylos uva-ursi*) and a weeping Alaska cedar (*Chamaecyparis nootkatensis* 'Pendula'). An Arctic rose lives by the front porch, and across the driveway an Alaskan flower garden displays western columbine (*Aquilegia formosa*) and lupine (*Lupinus* sp.).

At Gentle House, start at the south side (toward campus) of the new east wing of the house. Along the ramp at the southeast corner of the house are daffodils and peonies. Along the rest of the south side are tulips, lilies, daisies, rose campion (*Lychnis coronaria*), forget-me-nots, and sweet sultan (*Centaurea moschata*). The plantings along the south side of the main house include a moss rose, rose of Sharon (*Hibiscus syriacus*), spiraea, abelia, and bulbs. Across the lawn, a crescent-shaped garden behind the gazebo is planted with lady's mantle (*Alchemilla mollis*), astilbe, Jupiter's beard (*Centranthus ruber*), several phlox, iris, hyacinths, tulips, oriental poppies (*Papaver orientale*) and the rose 'Grand Duchesse Charlotte.'

Along the north side of the house, a big old leatherleaf viburnum (*Viburnum rhytidophyllum*) hovers over coral bells (*Heuchera* sp.), lily of the valley (*Convallaria majalis*), and *Kerria japonica*. The round tulip bed nearby was formerly a lily pond. Further from the house a wildflower garden includes *Viola glabella*, trilliums, mock orange and camas (*Camassia*). The rose garden along the fence includes some old bushes and some replacements; an extension to the east, adding climbers, is planned. Beyond the roses a honeysuckle and other old plantings include pasqueflower (*Anemone pulsatilla*), laurel, and a big daffodil bed bracing the corner.

The black walnut trees beyond the house each have a skirt of bulbs—daffodils, wood hyacinths, fall crocuses—and violets. Along the north and east sides of the new addition are herbs, quince, clematis, violets, butterfly bush, dead nettle and columbines.

Corvallis–Albany Area

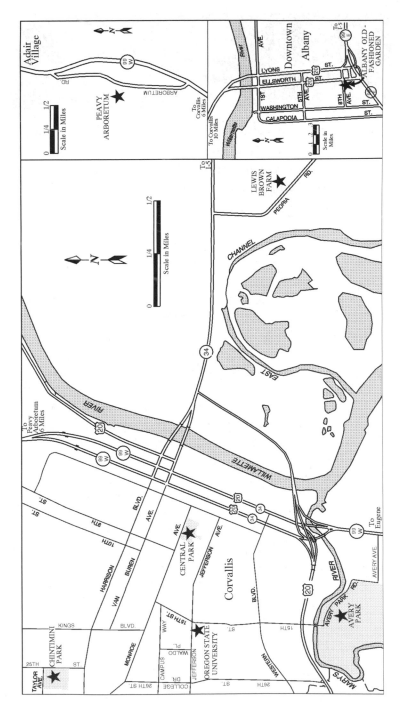

Albany Olde–Fashioned Garden

8th and Ellsworth

Seasons of interest: Spring and summer

Directions: The garden is easily accessible from Highway 20, which is Ellsworth eastbound and Lyons westbound. The garden is on 8th, at the Ellsworth end of the block.

Labels: None, but there is a map.

Background: The garden is a living museum, in keeping with its site in a historic district. The garden was built with city funds and funds donated by the Albany Historic Tour Committee, which offers annual tours of historic houses. An information center includes displays about the history of Albany and its three historic districts.

What to see: This garden illustrates how to make much of what you have to work with. It packs a lot of interesting plant material nicely into a small space around a gazebo and benches.

The fourteen Victorian roses include one species rose (*Rosa foetida*) and thirteen different old garden roses. They have a short blooming period, generally mid-May to early June. The rest of the garden, although still old fashioned, extends the blooming period with annuals and perennials, including red and pink lupines, several clematis and dianthus, delphiniums, snapdragons, bleeding hearts, a lilac, a mock orange, and herbs. The strip down the center of the parking lot is planted with sweet gums, daylilies, and bearded iris.

Peavy Arboretum

Peavy Arboretum Road
Corvallis

Seasons of interest: All

Directions: Peavy Arboretum Road loops off Highway 99W north of Corvallis. From the north, turn right onto Peavy Arboretum Road just south of Adair Village. From the south, turn left onto Peavy Arboretum Road approximately six miles north of Corvallis. The road and the arboretum are well marked.

The arboretum is open from 8 a.m. to sunset.

Weddings: Reservations for weddings are made through Oregon State University's MU business office, (541) 737-2650. Up to one hundred people can be accommodated, and tables, chairs, and a kitchen are available.

Labels: Some plants are labeled.

Background: The arboretum, covering eighty acres acquired in 1925, is named for George Peavy, then first dean of the School of Forestry (1910-32) and later president (1932-39) of what was then Oregon State Agricultural College.

During the Depression the arboretum was the site of the Civilian Conservation Corps' Camp Arboretum. The CCC built Peavy Lodge and did some clearing. A chin-up bar from Camp Arboretum days can be seen along the nature trail.

What to see: This arboretum is rather rustic. It focuses on woody plants of the Pacific Northwest, but still has exotic trees acquired before the decision was made to limit the collection.

Inside the entrance, the road bearing west leads to the McDonald Forest. Other roads branch off to the northwest. Just inside the entrance, before you reach the first junction, north of the road are new raised beds of grasses, sagebrush, and other plants native to the juniper and ponderosa pine forests of Central Oregon. (Plantings representing nine other Oregon ecological zones are planned elsewhere in the arboretum.) To the northwest, a nature trail winds among familiar natives over a carpet of spring wildflowers.

West of the first junction, the mixed species include a Western white pine (*Pinus monticola*) and a katsura (*Cercidiphyllum japonicum*). Southwest of the junction are *Prunus* species, including western chokecherry (*P. virginiana*), American wild plum (*P. americana*) and bitter cherry (*P. emarginata*).

Past the second junction, the pines south of the road to the McDonald Forest include maritime (*Pinus pinaster*), Scotch (*P. sylvestris*), and lodgepole (*P. contorta* var. *latifolia*). North of the road, near the pond, is sticky manzanita (*Arctostaphylos viscida*); further west, among the firs are a Johnson (*Abies grandis* 'Johnson')—a local variety, from Scappoose—and a California red (*A. magnifica*). The cypresses include Monterey (*Cupressus macrocarpa*) and Baker (*C. bakeri*).

Chintimini Park

25th and Taylor
Corvallis

Seasons of interest: Summer, fall

Directions: In downtown, from Highway 99W (3rd Street northbound, 4th Street southbound) proceed west on Harrison; turn right on 25th and proceed three blocks to Taylor.

Labels: None

Background: The roses were planted by senior citizens, who first met at St. Mary's Church across the street, and then in a converted fire station in the southwest corner of the park.

What to see: This is a curiosity: dozens of climbing roses hugging Chintimini's ballfield fences along the 25th and Taylor sides.

Oregon State University

15th and Jefferson
Corvallis

✣✿

Seasons of interest: Spring, summer, fall

Directions: Highway 99W through downtown is 3rd Avenue northbound and 4th Avenue southbound. From either street, turn west onto Jefferson Avenue. Just beyond 15th on Jefferson is an entrance kiosk where you can obtain a visitor's parking permit and directions to visitors' parking lots. Or you can proceed west on Jefferson two blocks, turn right on Waldo, and park in the pay lot immediately on your left. The Memorial Union is just west of the pay lot.

Labels: None. Descriptions, locations, and cultural information about many campus plants are available at several Horticulture Department class websites:

http://www.bcc.orst.edu/hortpm/226hweb.htm
http://www.bcc.orst.edu/hortpm/227hweb.htm
http://www.bcc.orst.edu/hortpm/228hweb.htm

Background: The institution now known as Oregon State University moved west from downtown Corvallis in the late 1880s. The citizens of Benton County, anxious to keep the state agricultural college in Corvallis, donated Benton Hall and a thirty-five-acre triangle of land. The campus soon came under the care of George Coote, an English immigrant of 1877 who had farmed before being hired by the college in 1890. He took on everything having to do with plants: care of campus ornamentals, production of fruits and vegetables for the dorms, maintenance of recreational greenswards, and assistance with horticultural experiments. He planted shrubs and trees, maintained greenhouses and forcing houses, and tended a hay field. He worked his way up to head of the department of horticulture, retiring six months before his death at the age of sixty-six in 1908.

Toward the end of his tenure the Olmsted Brothers
landscape architecture firm from Massachusetts, which
had been consulted in the development of Portland's park
system and the design of the 1905 Lewis and Clark
Exposition, was hired to give advice on campus
development. Over the next few years John Olmsted
made several visits. His 1909 recommendations included
keeping the broad meadow between Benton Hall and
downtown Corvallis free of trees to maintain the view
and to allow occasional military drills and parades;
developing a quadrangle system of building; and
restraining planting. He counseled that the formal plan of
the campus should not be obscured in fussy details, but
limited to grass and trees. He suggested that the college
develop a separate arboretum and a shrub garden.

Although the Olmsted report assumed that the college
would not grow beyond two thousand students—and by
1915 the college enrollment was over four thousand—it
guided campus development until 1925. Then, with the
building of the Memorial Union and the acquisition of
more campus lands to the west, another planner was
brought in. A. D. Taylor, from Cincinnati, thought that the
campus looked barren. He suggested planting trees in
rows along the streets, and as specimens or occasional
groups in the quadrangles or around the buildings.
Olmsted had recommended against obscuring the
architecture of campus buildings; Taylor counseled that
trees could emphasize the nice portions of buildings—
interesting façades and entrances—and screen the less
attractive parts. He suggested that the campus look be
unified by mainly planting trees similar to the American
elm. Variety would be provided by specimen evergreens
and beeches; building lines would be softened with mass
plantings of flowering trees.

Taylor suggested a formal rose garden north of
Campus Way and west of College Drive, but the garden

actually planted as a National Youth Administration project in 1940 and 1941 included other species. The garden included a Tudor maze in dwarf boxwood, hundreds of iris and peonies, and seventy-five roses. These soon disappeared, probably because of the shift in priorities compelled by World War II.

After the war, the emphasis in landscaping shifted again as Don Martell, a former OSU landscaping student, became the campus landscape architect and head of the Campus Planning Committee. He wanted campus to look less formal. The student population soon surged, and he was able to plant a new residential quadrangle with meandering paths and informal plantings. The Columbus Day Storm, which destroyed fifty-five trees and damaged forty-three others, presented him with another planting opportunity. Martell also thought the campus grounds should be more colorful, so that it would be obvious when spring had arrived. He planted dozens of rhododendrons, azaleas, and flowering trees. Some of the rhododendrons were donated by the United States Department of Agriculture. Some had names, but most were culls from hybridizing programs at the Oregon Agricultural Experiment Station. The culls weren't necessarily bad plants; it's relatively easy to breed a rhododendron that is a nice plant—it's much more difficult to come up with one that is superlative, and will earn a spot in the rhododendron trade. The azaleas were also the result of local breeding programs.

In the 1970s, the campus landscape suffered from pestilence and poverty. A Dutch elm disease scare led to a proposal to save some of the elms by replacing every other one with a disease-resistant species, and thereby slowing the spread of the disease. Before the scheme could get very far the campus community protested loudly enough to stop it. But a campus austerity program,

halting summer watering, managed to last long enough—
three years in the mid 1970s—to kill hundreds of plants.

In the mid 1990s, a windstorm caused the loss of thirty
trees, and many trees and shrubs were moved or removed
because of remodeling projects. The library was extended
two hundred feet north into its quadrangle, and other
remodeling took place on its west wall. The hybrid azalea
collection was moved to the west side of the social science
building, giving the plants the same exposure they had
had at the library. Smaller plants on the north side were
moved; the trees were sold.

It is not uncommon for azaleas and rhododendrons to
be moved; their shallow, fibrous root balls make them
good candidates for transplanting. Some trees can be
moved, such those in front of the library and a small
Cunninghamia, moved in front of the Memorial Union.
Others may simply have to be cut down or chance the
stresses of construction work. A huge elm, unusual for its
spreading branch structure, was too big to move from its
home along Waldo Place; it was left in the hope that it
would survive the remodeling of the library. Sometimes
work can be arranged to spare trees; a large Douglas fir
survived the recent remodeling of Fairbanks Hall when
digging around the foundation was done by hand rather
than backhoe. Such measures aren't always successful.
The *Cunninghamia* died, and the elm—surrounded by
more paving than originally planned—may not survive.

What to see: The central campus puts on a colorful show
in spring—both early, with flowering trees and some
flowering shrubs, and late, with rhododendrons and
azaleas—and a wide variety of trees provides interest at
other times of the year.

Start on the main, north steps of the Memorial Union
(MU). The quad is home to magnolias, flowering cherries,
and a dogwood. The larger tree west of the west steps on

the north side is an Amur cork tree
(*Phellodendron amurense*). Continue
west and cross the street. The big
Douglas fir tree (*Pseudotsuga
menziesii*) southeast of the
entrance to Fairbanks Hall has
survived such indignities in its
twelve decades as use as a
clothesline post when the hall was
a dorm (hence the large callus ten
feet up) and loss of its top in the
Columbus Day Storm (it grew a new
one).

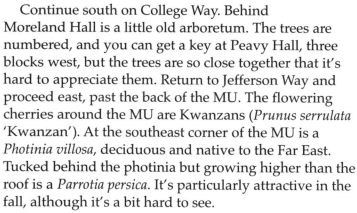

Continue south on College Way. Behind
Moreland Hall is a little old arboretum. The trees are
numbered, and you can get a key at Peavy Hall, three
blocks west, but the trees are so close together that it's
hard to appreciate them. Return to Jefferson Way and
proceed east, past the back of the MU. The flowering
cherries around the MU are Kwanzans (*Prunus serrulata*
'Kwanzan'). At the southeast corner of the MU is a
Photinia villosa, deciduous and native to the Far East.
Tucked behind the photinia but growing higher than the
roof is a *Parrotia persica*. It's particularly attractive in the
fall, although it's a bit hard to see.

Continue east on Jefferson, and turn right between
Waldo and Snell halls. Waldo's east side is planted with
camellias and rhododendrons, and the flowering crabs
between Waldo and Snell are *Malus* 'Ruby Red.' To the
south are more flowering shrubs and trees along Snell
and the MU East.

Return to Jefferson Street and proceed east to 15th.
Several hundred roses dress up the west side of a huge
parking lot from half a block south of Jefferson to
Washington Street. North of Jefferson on 15th a large lawn
is ringed with flowering cherries, and elms march by

twos toward downtown. Walk up the hill to the west
toward Benton Hall (the one with the clock tower).
Partway up is a pair of empress trees (*Paulownia
tomentosa*), and over to your right the white oak (*Quercus
alba*)—grown from a cutting of a tree on the National Mall
in Washington, D. C.—is a memorial to the students who
were killed at Beijing's Tienamen Square in 1989. Further
up the hill, just south of the walk, is a *Pinus wallichiana*
The dawn redwood (*Metasequoia glyptostroboides*) north of
the walk was planted in the late 1940s, and the Atlas
cedar (*Cedrus atlantica*) at the northeast corner of Benton
Hall around 1890. (According to legend, the dawn
redwood originally had a companion that got cut down
early in life, when it lost its needles one fall, by a
groundskeeper unaccustomed to deciduous conifers. A
similar legend is that, when Portland's city nursery
started growing dawn redwoods, most of the first batch
got thrown out when they first lost their needles.) The
birch trees southeast of Benton Hall were staked a
hundred years ago, so some branches grow at odd low
angles, and some have rooted.

Proceed north from Benton Hall to Campus Way, and
turn left. Angle past the front of Shepard; the photinia
blooms in the spring, and the deep red smoke tree
(*Cotinus coggygria*) blooms in the summer. Continue
north, past Gleeson's loading dock. South of the dock is
Viburnum plicatum var. *tomentosum*; north of the dock is
the rhododendron 'Loderi King George.' Around the
north side of Gleeson is another 'Loderi King George,'
next to the rhododendron 'Sappho.' On the west side of
Gleeson, the fragrant snowbell (*Styrax obassia*) has an
interesting trunk with exfoliating bark, and is surrounded
by fragrant azaleas. Proceed west, between Bexell and
Weniger. On the north side of Bexell, note the huge leaves
on the umbrella tree (*Magnolia tripetala*), and the two big
pin oaks (*Quercus palustris*). Turn south; the tree at the

south end of Bexell's west side is a *Sophora japonica*. One of its common names is Chinese scholar tree.

Turn right on Campus Way and continue past College Drive. On your left, north of Gilmore Hall, is a small Nordmann fir (*Abies nordmanniana*). Return to College Drive and continue south past the big beds of rhododendrons and deciduous and evergreen azaleas in front of the Women's Building.

Cross College Drive to the west side of the MU quad. Along the south side of Milam Hall, toward the west end two mountain silver-bell trees (*Halesia carolina* var. *monticola*) bloom in early May. Farther east a white fir that actually is quite blue (*Abies concolor* 'Candicans') sets off the blooms on the dwarf periwinkle (*Vinca minor*) at its base. Near the southeast corner of Milam is a harlequin glorybower (*Clerodendrum trichotomum*), producing fragrant blossoms in late summer and red calyxes surrounding blue fruit later in the year.

Head southeast to the Agriculture Building. The yellowwood (*Cladrastis lutea*) on the west side is the only one on campus. The big tree with skinny leaves about three inches long is a willow oak (*Quercus phellos*). Go west; the little tree that blooms with white flowers in summer is a franklinia (*Franklinia alatamaha*), native to the southeastern United States, but extinct in the wild.

Central Park

9th and Monroe
Corvallis

Seasons of interest: Spring, summer, fall

Directions: Highway 99W through downtown is 3rd Avenue northbound and 4th Avenue southbound. From either street turn west onto Harrison, then left on 9th and left on Monroe. Park along Monroe.

Labels: Some plants in the west end of the park are labeled in both Braille and Roman letters

Background: Central Park is on the site of the old Corvallis High School, which burned in 1946. In 1925 A.D. Taylor, a landscape architect hired by the city to address public development, had noted the value of the site for a future city park.

In the mid 1960s, thirty garden and service clubs designed and planted the rose garden on the eastern half of the site. The roses were planted in arc-shaped beds along a circle of sidewalk. The varieties were chosen for color, low maintenance needs, and ability to withstand the pressure of public life. The beds, originally planted in double rows, are gradually being replanted to single rows to ease maintenance.

Local master gardeners maintain a small perennial garden that they planted in the early 1990s.

What to see: Central Park is home to a rose garden and a mixed border. It also has a display of plants with Braille legends.

The rose beds are in a large circle, bordered on the outside by a sidewalk, in the eastern half of the park. The roses, all of which are modern, are planted in color blocks.

The mixed border is in the southeast corner of the park. Although it is at its best in May and June, usually something is in bloom. Shrubs include butterfly bush and variegated elderberry. Other plants include herbs, hardy geraniums, ornamental grasses, peonies, several species of iris, and shrub roses.

The western half of the park is home to many flowering shrubs, including azaleas and rhododendrons. Some of the plants along the outside of the sidewalk circle are labeled with descriptions in Braille; they include forsythia, *Cotoneaster lacteus*, and cutleaf weeping birch (*Betula pendula* 'Dalecarlica').

Avery Park

Avery Avenue and Avery Park Drive
Corvallis

ॐ

Seasons of interest: Spring, summer, fall

Directions: Avery Park has a rhododendron garden and a rose garden.

To get to the rhododendron garden, from Highway 99W south of downtown, one block south of the railroad tracks, turn west on Avery Avenue; continue across Allen Street to the end of the road.

To get to the rose garden, from Highway 99W south of downtown turn west on Avery Avenue; turn right on Avery Park Drive and proceed half a mile to the drive's curve to the north. West of downtown, from Highways 20 and 34, turn south onto Avery Park Drive; proceed into the park one-tenth of a mile, to the drive's curve to the east. The rose garden is on the south side of the road, with parking areas to the north and west.

Labels: All of the roses and very few of the rhododendrons are labeled.

Background: Joseph C. Avery was one of the founders of Corvallis, and he coined its name. He helped develop what is now Oregon State University, and donated the land for Avery Park.

A.D. Taylor, a landscape architect who served as consultant to the city and university, recommended in late 1925 that the city build an "important city park" in Avery Woods. The giant sequoias in the rose garden area were planted in 1942, and the roses were first planted in 1958. In 1995-96 the rose garden was renovated and the memorial garden—in which roses can be planted in someone's honor or memory—was begun. The care of the garden is a cooperative effort between the local rose society and the city.

The rhododendron garden was cooperatively developed by the Men's Garden Club and the city, beginning in 1975. In 1996 several dozen plants were added from the garden of the late Winston Hanke, a local hybridizer and founder of the Corvallis chapter of the American Rhododendron Society. After his death in 1992 the chapter faded, so the rhododendron garden no longer has a private group helping to keep it in trim.

What to see: The rose garden has approximately fifteen hundred bushes and emphasizes modern varieties. It is an All-America Rose Selections (AARS) display garden, with most of the winners of the past five years, and many from the past fifteen years, on display in the center and western portions of the garden. Miniatures are in the center part of the garden. Climbers are grown in the center part and, along with shrub roses, along the west and south edges of the western portion. A decorative iron fence, salvaged from the Avery estate, runs along the south side of the center portion. The eastern portion is still under development, but at this writing the memorial garden is edged with English and shrub roses.

A chart at the front of the garden keys each rose to its location on a map of the garden and lists its classification, color, AARS rating (if any), and the year it became an AARS winner.

In the rhododendron garden, several hundred bushes are planted along grassy paths sloping to the southwest from the road in a grove of firs dotted with hardwoods. Near the plaque memorializing Hanke, and just east of the sprawling 'Sappho,' are three 'Sunsprays' from his garden, given by his widow. To the west, across the path from 'Point Defiance,' hybridized in Seattle, are two 'Martian Kings,' hybridized by Hanke and also from his garden.

Another plaque memorializes James L. Overholser, late member of the Corvallis Park Board. To the southwest is 'Ring of Fire,' gold with an orange rim, and to the southeast is 'Barto White,' hybridized in Junction City. Just north of the azaleadendron with fragrant lavender blossoms blotched with gold is the pink-tinged white 'Pawhuska,' hybridized in Veneta.

Lewis–Brown Farm

33329 Peoria Road
Corvallis, OR 97330
(541) 737-5483

⁂

Seasons of interest: Spring, summer, fall

Directions: From Interstate 5, take exit no. 228 and proceed west approximately nine miles; from Highway 99W proceed east, and from Highway 99E proceed west, on Highway 34. Turn south on Peoria Road (at the first three-color traffic signal you come to from the freeway or Highway 99E). Proceed south 1.2 miles, and turn left. After a tenth of a mile, turn right. Park just past the U-shaped building.

Labels: The maples and many of the ornamental grasses are labeled.

Background: The farm has been operated by the Horticulture Department of the College of Agricultural Science of Oregon State University since about 1940. It is named for two past department heads. C.I. Lewis's tenure was from 1906 to 1919, and Dr. Walter S. Brown served from 1920 until his death in 1942.

Most of the farm is used for research projects for the United States Department of Agriculture and six departments and colleges (horticulture, crop science, botany and plant pathology, agricultural engineering, entomology, and forestry) at Oregon State. In 1980 a display of turf grasses was planted as part of a landscaping laboratory. In 1990 about fifty maples were planted along with flowering shrubs and perennials at the south end of the turf trials. The perennial border was planted in 1996.

What to see: The farm has gardens and lawns of interest in a small area across the road from its office building.

At the south end of the display an attractive planting of several dozen Japanese maples demonstrates the variety of growth habits, and of leaf colors and shapes, available within the species *Acer palmatum*. Just north of the maple area a long low mound displays twenty-one ornamental grasses. The next area north is turf trials of "ecology" lawns—mixtures of English daisies, yarrow, chamomile, and strawberry clover that require no fertilizer and only two or three mowings a summer.

The perennial border north of the turf trials includes salvias, penstemons, and veronicas. Beyond the border are more turf trials, rows of ornamental shrubs, and a display of about a dozen more ornamental grasses. Along the east fence, roses range to the north and flowering shrubs to the south.

Eugene

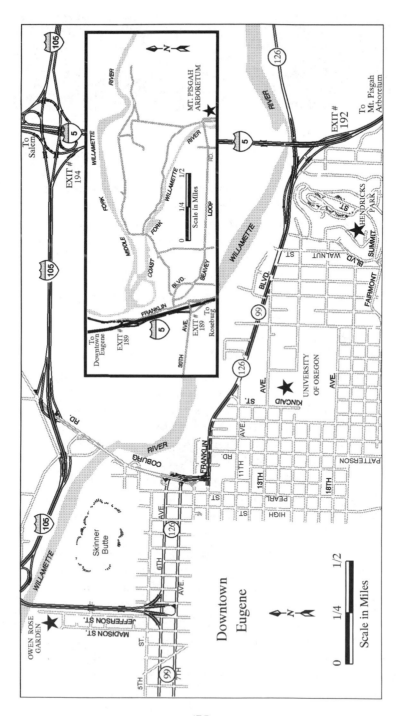

Owen Rose Garden

300 N. Jefferson Street

❧

Seasons of interest: Spring, summer, fall

Directions: From Interstate 5, take I-105 to Eugene. Where it ends, get in the right lane at the West Eugene exit. At the light at the end of the ramp, turn right on Madison Street. Turn right on 5th, go one block, and turn left on Jefferson. Continue north to the end of Jefferson Street.

The garden, just west of Skinner's Butte Park, can also be reached by the bike path along the south side of the Willamette River.

Labels: The roses are labeled; the other plants (except the cherry tree) are not.

Weddings: The garden is available, except in winter, for groups of up to fifty. Call Park Services, (541) 682-4800.

Background: In 1950, George and Enid Owen donated a parcel to be developed into a park. The Eugene Rose Society and individual donors gave the initial rose collection. The park has grown east and west beyond the bike paths and freeway built along its edges during the 1960s and '70s. In 1996, the garden began to extend its color range and season by planting several beds of perennials. There are plans to regroup the roses, and to plant a collection of shade-loving members of the rose family north of the bike path, along the river.

What to see: The rose garden now has more than four thousand rosebushes, of more than four hundred varieties. The roses start in the parking lot, which has more rosebushes, and a wider range of roses, than some rose gardens have in their entirety. The parking lot collection includes hybrid musks (to the east, against the freeway mound), hybrid teas, floribundas, and grandifloras, as well as rhododendrons.

The pergola between the parking lot and the garden proper is, of course, dressed with roses: *R. banksiae* 'Alba' and 'Lutea' on the parking lot side, and the *R. wichuraiana* rambler 'Albèric Barbier' on the garden side.

As you enter, to the left are two mounds recently planted to English roses and a wide range of perennials, including columbines, hostas, gunnera, rodgersia, oriental lilies, and artemisias. To the north, and stretching west and east, at the far edge of the lawn, are the main display beds, including AARS winners back to the 1950s. More musk roses are found at the base of the freeway mound. Beyond the freeway, rugosas line the south side of the bike path and a dozen albas line the north side.

The most magnificent plant in the entire garden is not a rose at all, but a one-hundred-and-fifty-year-old Black Tartarian cherry tree. The tree is huge, gnarled, and lovely. The remnant of an old orchard, it is the largest cherry tree in Oregon. It is, of course, ringed with roses: the floribunda 'Merci' next to the tree and the miniature 'Green Ice' in the outer ring.

University of Oregon

13th and Kincaid

Seasons of interest: All

Directions: From Interstate 5, take I-105 westbound (exit no. 194B) and follow signs to the University of Oregon. When you reach Franklin Boulevard (you'll be traveling eastbound, with three lanes of traffic in each direction), get in the right lane. If you're visiting on a weekday, proceed a little more than a mile and turn right on Agate, turn right on 13th, and inquire about parking at the kiosk in the center of the street. Park and walk to 13th and Kincaid. If you're visiting on a weekend or during a university vacation period, proceed just a few blocks on Franklin, turn right on Patterson; turn left on 13th; and, where 13th Ts at Kincaid, turn either right or left, and park at a meter along the street.

The University's Museum of Natural History, at 1680 E. 15th (just east of Agate Street), (541) 346-3024, open Wednesday-Sunday from noon to 5 p.m., at this writing has a permanent exhibit on campus trees.

Labels: None. You may wish to purchase Kenneth W. Knapp's *Trees of the Oregon Campus* or Mande May's *University of Oregon Atlas of Trees* at the University Bookstore, 13th and Kincaid. Both books divide campus into manageable sections relative to readily identifiable buildings and identify the trees with a helpful taxonomic indexing system. The university may eventually have similar information available on a web page.

Background: When the university was founded in the mid 1870s the only trees on campus were two Oregon white oaks (*Quercus garryana*) at its northern edge. They are northeast of Villard Hall, and have since been named the Condon Oaks in honor of Thomas Condon, early faculty member, eminent geologist, and tree lover.

Tree planting began early on. The graduating class of 1878 planted a tree at the June commencement exercises; other classes followed suit, or claimed extant trees, through 1900. Eight class trees survive, all in the vicinity of Villard Hall. One of the Condon Oaks was claimed as class tree by the class of 1897 and the other by the class of 1900. The latter choice may have irked the oak, which has grown to obscure all but an s and one and a half 0s on the class plaque. (In 1989, University Day was revived; the class of 1993 gave a bigleaf maple, planted between Deady and Villard.)

In the mid 1880s, the university's custodian was sent out to find trees to bring back and plant. He was not paid for them until two years later, when it could be determined how good a job he had done in transplanting.

Tree planting continued in a rather haphazard manner until the 1930s brought a surge in major building projects that spurred preparation of a campus plan. The landscape architect involved pointed out that the campus had an exceptional collection of trees. As a result, more order was imposed on tree planting, in order to improve the cohesiveness of the collection. Conifers already prevailed in Old Campus, where the Pioneer sculpture presides over a quadrangle north of 13th Avenue bordered by Fenton, Deady, and Villard halls on the west and Lawrence, Allen, and Friendly halls on the east. For contrast, the Women's Quadrangle south of 13th Avenue (bordered by Johnson, Hendricks, Susan Campbell, and Gerlinger halls and home to the sculpture of the Pioneer Mother) was to emphasize deciduous trees. To the west, in the early 1940s the lawn in front of the Knight Library was planted with pyramidal oaks in memory of the president of the class of 1939, who drowned in the Mill Race shortly after graduation.

Almost a hundred trees were lost in the Columbus Day Storm. The older Douglas firs in the double column west of Deady Hall survive from the late nineteenth century; most of the younger ones replaced casualties of the storm. The next major flurry of tree planting came in the late 1970s, when almost four hundred trees—carefully chosen to complement and expand the university's collection— were planted in honor of its centennial.

Until the campus expands, the collection generally cannot grow without compromising the open space that is an important part of campus design. But trees do succumb to the weather (besides the Columbus Day Storm, losses have been occasioned by less noteworthy windstorms, snow, and extreme cold), to vandals, and to disease, allowing opportunities for new plantings. When new buildings are planned, the university tries to either build around existing trees or move them to new locations. Construction traffic can be hard on trees, but great pains were taken to keep the dawn redwood (*Metasequoia glytostroboides*) at the northeast corner of Volcanology alive when new science buildings were built nearby. Professors in surrounding buildings, alerted to the danger, shooed away crane operators who got their equipment too close to the tree.

What to see: The campus, more than a century old, has a wide variety of mature trees; its collection has representatives of forty-five of the sixty-one botanical families that include temperate-climate trees.

From 13th and Kincaid, proceed east on 13th Avenue. Just inside the gates, the big tree to the north, in front of Chiles Hall, is a common catalpa (*Catalpa bignonioides*); to the south, along the north side of Condon Hall, are two big American plane trees (*Platanus occidentalis*). Further east, toward the west end of the courtyard in front of Gilbert Hall, is a yellow buckeye (*Aesculus octandra*), a gift from Ohio State University after it beat Oregon in the 1958 Rose Bowl. Proceed south between Chapman and Condon halls. Large pyramidal English oaks (*Quercus robur* 'Pyramidalis') march toward the Knight Library down the east and west sides of the lawn between the Art Museum and Prince Lucien Campbell Hall. To the east of the library, a huge copper beech (*Fagus sylvatica* 'Purpurea') and a California laurel (*Umbellularia californica*) with eight trunks send branches arching above the sidewalk. They are kept company by a very tall pin oak (*Quercus palustris*).

From Gerlinger Hall north to 13th Avenue, the emphasis is on deciduous trees. In the lawn northeast of Susan Campbell Hall, the two huge old trees are a giant sequoia (*Sequoiadendron giganteum*) and an eastern black walnut (*Juglans nigra).* Along the south side of Collier (the faculty club) are younger trees, including a northern Chinese paper birch (*Betula albo-sinensis* var. *septentrionalis*), a sweetbay magnolia (*Magnolia virginiana*), and a Japanese snowbell (*Styrax japonicus*). On the 13th Avenue side of Johnson Hall is a huge London plane tree (*Platanus* x *acerifolia*).

North across 13th Avenue, Old Campus is home to a reasonably large collection of conifers, and therefore is full of impostors: the obligatory Douglas firs (*Pseudotsuga menziesii*), five cultivars of Lawson false cypress (*Chamaecyparis lawsoniana*), and two of Sawara false cypress (*C. pisifera*). (The only true cypress in the central part of campus, a Cuyamaca cypress (*Cupressus arizonica*), lives south of 13th, in the Women's Quadrangle, behind Collier.) Old Campus has two true hemlocks, western (*Tsuga heterophylla*) and Canadian (*T. canadensis*). The pines and firs include the usual natives, a Nordmann fir (*Abies nordmanniana*) (in front of Friendly Hall) and a Sakhalin fir (*A. sachalinensis*) (north of Villard Hall). Between the Sakhalin fir and the Robinson Theater (the western addition to Villard) are two living fossils: a dawn redwood (*Metasequoia glyptostroboides*) and a ginkgo (*Ginkgo biloba*). Other deciduous trees—including magnolias, dogwoods, stewartias, and lindens—dot Old Campus, which is just as well when you consider the gloom of unrelieved conifers in a western Oregon winter.

Return to 13th Avenue and proceed east to University Street. The Douglas fir near the northeast corner of the Erb Memorial Union (EMU) is called a "moon tree" because it grew from seed that went to the moon. In the lawn south of the EMU, along with huge specimens of common trees like the bigleaf maple (*Acer macrophyllum*) and a coast redwood (*Sequoia sempervirens*) are a thirty-foot Spanish Fir (*Abies pinsapo*) in the center of the south side of the lawn and, just south of the bigleaf maple, a Kaki persimmon (*Diospyros kaki*).

Return to the north side of the EMU. Across 13th Avenue, the space between Volcanology and Willamette Hall is lovely in spring, with a red horsechestnut (*Aesculus* x *carnea*), rhododendrons, azaleas, small redbud trees, and, at the northeast corner of Volcanology, the feathery light green foliage of another dawn redwood.

If you want to visit the Museum of Natural History to see the exhibit on campus trees, continue east on 13th to Agate, turn right, continue on Agate Street to the next intersection, turn left, and proceed about three-quarters of a block; the museum is on your right.

The campus is home to hundreds of roses in small beds scattered among the classroom buildings and residence halls.

Hendricks Park

Summit Avenue
(541) 687-5324

❧

Season of interest: Spring

Directions: From Interstate 5 from the north, take the I-105 exit (no. 194B) and follow signs to the University of Oregon, which will bring you to the six-lane Franklin Boulevard. Turn right onto Walnut Street; continue to Fairmount, turn right, and turn left onto Summit.

From Interstate 5 from the south, take the Eugene exit (no. 192), to Franklin Boulevard. From Franklin turn left onto Orchard, left on 19th, and right onto Fairmount. From Fairmount, turn left onto Summit Avenue.

Labels: Most plants are labeled.

Weddings: Weddings are not allowed in the park.

Background: Hendricks Park was Eugene's first city park, begun in 1906 with a gift from Thomas and Martha Hendricks of forty-seven acres of ridgeline southeast of downtown. (Hendricks Hall on the University of Oregon campus is also named for Mr. Hendricks, a benefactor of the university.) The Eugene Chapter of the American Rhododendron Society began working with the Eugene Parks Department in 1951 to develop the rhododendron garden. Among the society's donations were plants obtained through worldwide correspondence, from plant expeditions in Asia and hybrids of those, and from the collection of James Barto. From the 1920s until his death in 1940, Barto, a carpenter, collected and hybridized many rhododendrons on his homestead near Junction City, helped by Rae Berry (see the Berry Botanic Garden, page 65) and his many children. By the time of his death, Barto's rhododendron collection was the largest in North America.

Almost all of the plants here have been donated. The garden honors Barto, its founders, and major contributors with named beds and walks. The first rhododendron planted in the garden, 'Rosemary Chipp,' was given by Marshall and Ruth Lyons, who donated three hundred other rhododendrons, including some they hybridized. They are honored by a bed at the entrance.

What to see: Although most of the rhododendrons are hybrids, the garden is also home to species rhododendrons, flowering trees, and companion plants.

If you park in the lot east across the road from the garden, you enter by a small perennial garden planted with *Salvia verticillata*, columbines, and the rose 'Henry Hudson.' At the pedestrian crossing further south, primroses, *Darmera peltata*, meadowfoam (*Limnathes douglasii*), Kenilworth ivy (*Cymbalaria muralis*) and *Sedum* 'Autumn Glory' are tucked in along a small stream.

The main entrance is on top of the ridge. South of the entrance is a large lawn shaded by Oregon white oaks (*Quercus garryana*); *Clematis montana* var. *rubens* drapes over the lowest limb of one of the oaks, which stands in a bed with white bleeding hearts, violets, bear's breech (*Acanthus mollis*), and rhododendrons 'Virginia Richards' and *Rhododendron fargesii* 'Barto Rose.' In a bed on the east side of the lawn, lady ferns (*Athyrium felix-femina*), several narcissus, and *Epimedium* x *youngianum* are among the companion plants of a local hybrid, 'Crater Lake,' and *Rhododendron gymnocarpum*.

Southwest of the lawn, species rhododendrons mix with other flowering plants and trees: a dove tree (*Davidia involucrata*) from Barto's garden, andromedas, primulas, viburnums, and stewartias. South of the lawn the Del James walk honors another local hybridizer. The rhododendrons *Rhododendron racemosum* 'Rock Rose' and

R. augustinii 'Tower Coat' are complemented by *Daphne genkwa* and *Primula veris* x *P.* 'Sunset Shades.'

East down the hill from the lawn are the beds of the Barto Walk and the Founders Walk. Rhododendrons, including a *R. niveum* hybrid with leaves at least nine inches long, are kept company by maples, including *Acer argutum.* Along the northeast corner are *Cornus nuttallii* 'Colrigo Giant,' beautybush (*Kolkwitzia amabilis*), and sourwood (*Oxydendrum arboreum*).

Deciduous and evergreen azaleas are found throughout the garden, but the largest group—waves of purple, orange, and yellow during blooming season—is at the bottom of the hill.

Mt. Pisgah Arboretum

34901 Frank Parrish Road (P. O. Box 5621)
Eugene, OR 97405
(541) 747-3817

Seasons of interest: All

Directions: From Interstate 5, take the 30th Avenue exit (no. 189). From the north, stay to the right at the top of the ramp and continue on the frontage road to the traffic light at 30th Avenue; turn left and proceed over the freeway one block; turn left at the blinking light, go one block and turn right. Approaching from the south, proceed straight ahead at the blinking light at the top of the ramp; proceed one block and turn right. Continue under the railroad bridge and take the first left. Proceed approximately two miles; follow signs for the arboretum. After crossing the one-lane bridge at the end of Seavey Loop Road, turn right on the gravel road, which leads to the entrance, parking lots, and visitor center. Tours can be arranged.

Labels: Many of the plants, except those already in place when the arboretum started, are labeled.

Weddings: The arboretum can be rented for gatherings of up to two hundred people. There is a covered area to which to retreat from the rain.

Background: The arboretum was founded in 1974. It is within the Buford Recreation Area, owned by Lane County, and is developed and maintained by the Friends of Mt. Pisgah Arboretum. Development is gradual; much of the land is still in the original grassy, oaky hillsides. The Friends started with native plants, but plan to obtain plants from around the world.

What to see: Spring is the arboretum's high season, with rhododendrons and wildflowers in bloom. The planted area is fairly small.

Rhododendron vernicosum, R. yakushimanum 'Mist
Maiden,' *R. ponticum* 'Variegatum,' and the tiny ground-
hugger *R. keleticum* are among the rhododendrons sharing
the mound in the middle of the drive with heathers, a
dawn redwood (*Metasequoia glyptostroboides*), a katsura
tree (*Cercidiphyllum japonicum*). and dogwoods. East of the
drive, among the trees planted in the late 1980s are blue
Atlas cedars (*Cedrus ullantica* 'Glaura'), honey locusts
(*Gleditsia* sp.), several pines, a Japanese maple (*Acer
palmatum*), and a bay tree (*Umbellularia californica*). South
of the visitor center, the Patricia Baker Wildflower Garden
(named in memory of a local patron of the arts who died
in 1983) nestles under Oregon white oaks (*Quercus
garryana*). Among the wildflowers are irises, trilliums,
shooting stars, and bleeding hearts. More wildflowers
grow in front of the visitor center.

Southern Oregon

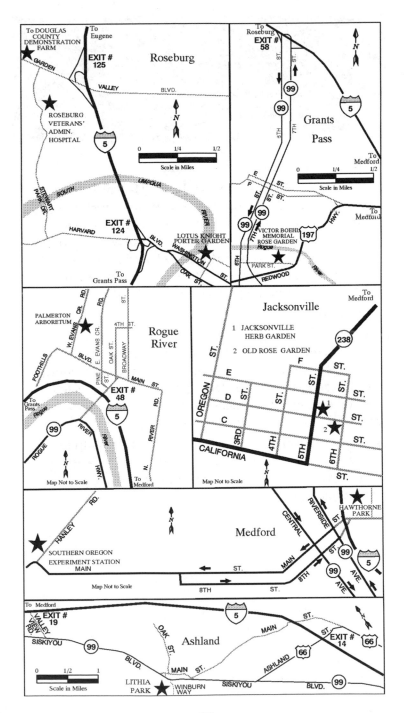

Lotus Knight Porter Garden

Riverside Park
Douglas and Washington Streets
Roseburg

Seasons of interest: Spring, summer

Directions: From Interstate 5 take the Harvard exit (no. 124) and proceed east, toward downtown, on Harvard, which will become Oak as you cross the bridge over the Umpqua River. Just past the Best Western Motel turn left on Douglas, cross Washington Street, and park north of the Chamber of Commerce. The garden stretches around the Chamber building and toward the bridge.

Labels: None

Background: The garden was built as a community project in memory of Porter who was, for many years before her death in 1968, society editor of the Roseburg *News-Review*, an avid gardener particularly interested in rhododendrons and azaleas, and a supporter of local activities.

What to see: This is a colorful spot in spring, with bulbs, flowering trees, hybrid rhododendrons, and evergreen and deciduous azaleas. A little summer color is provided by daylilies and roses.

Roseburg Veterans' Administration Hospital

Northwest Garden Valley Boulevard

❧

Seasons of interest: Summer, fall

Directions: From Interstate 5, take the Garden Valley Road exit (no. 125). Proceed west a few blocks, and turn left at the Veterans' Administration Hospital entrance. Continue south; the rose garden is just north of the parking area.

Labels: None

Background: The rose garden was built as part of a horticultural therapy program. At its peak it contained sixteen hundred rosebushes, plus herbs, bulbs, and a vegetable garden. Now few patients work in the garden, but there are still several hundred rose bushes.

Roseburg, incidentally, is named not for the flower but for Aaron Rose, an early settler.

What to see: The sidewalk along the roadway passes under trellises supporting the climbing roses 'Piñata' and 'Blaze.' To the south and west of the walk are large beds of modern roses in a large lawn that is also dotted with an interesting variety of trees: flowering crabapples, dogwoods, half a dozen different oaks, a goldenchain, and several maples, including a sycamore maple (*Acer pseudoplatanus*).

❧

Douglas County Demonstration Farm

Roseburg
(541) 440-4511 (Douglas County Extension Service)

❦

Seasons of interest: Summer, fall

Directions: The demonstration farm is approximately five miles west of Roseburg. Visits are by appointment except for open houses in July, August, and September. Call to obtain dates and directions.

Labels: Some plants are labeled

Background: The farm was established in 1965 as a cooperative venture among the Douglas County-OSU Extension Service, the Pitchford Boys Ranch (a facility for juvenile offenders), and the Douglas County Master Gardeners. The extension service and the master gardeners provide horticultural knowledge, planning, planting, and supervision of the juveniles, who do much of the gardening. In 1995, the farm became one of two trial sites in the West for the American Dahlia Society.

What to see: The big, well-kept flower and vegetable garden includes the current All-America selections. The master gardeners also maintain plots with changing gardening themes. A six-thousand-square-foot plot is devoted to dahlia trials. Breeders choose the varieties on display. The September open house is an opportunity to taste grapes grown by the master gardeners.

❦

Victor Boehl Memorial Rose Garden

Riverside Park
Grants Pass

Seasons of interest: Summer, fall

Directions: From Interstate 5, take exit 58, which will become 6th Street, the main street southbound through town. After you cross the bridge south of downtown, go to the second light (a very short distance beyond the first light) and turn left on Park Street. Cross 7th Street (the main street northbound) and continue on Park Street. The parking lot for the park is two-tenths of a mile on the left. The rose garden is north of the white gazebo.

Labels: None

Background: The garden was planted by the Rogue Valley Rose Society in 1966-67. It honors Victor Boehl (pronounced "bail"), 1901-1965. He was a charter member of the Rogue Valley Rose Society and an American Rose Society show judge active in the Northwest District. He was also involved in many other community and statewide activities including granges, the Oregon Health Service, the county planning commission, the Oregon Reclamation Congress, the Chamber of Commerce, and the Grants Pass Irrigation District.

What to see: There are four hundred modern roses in twelve beds, six on each side of the central lawn north of the gazebo.

Palmerton Arboretum

West Evans Creek Road
Rogue River

❧

Seasons of interest: All

Directions: Take the Rogue River exit (no. 48) from Interstate 5. Go north; cross the railroad tracks and turn left onto Pine Street. Then turn left onto Foothills Boulevard; proceed three-tenths of a mile, and turn right on West Evans Creek Road. The arboretum is approximately two-tenths of a mile on the right.

Weddings: Arrange through City Hall, (541) 582-4401.

Labels: A sign provides a map with the locations and names—both common and scientific—of the trees. Also, a brochure is available at the city museum at 1st and Broadway.

Background: The arboretum is named for Orrin Palmerton. He operated a private nursery on the site from the 1920s through the 1950s, planting trees for his own enjoyment. Shortly after he died in 1966, Jackson County purchased the property, built restrooms and a playground to equip it for its new use, and opened it as a park in 1970. It became a city park in 1995.

What to see: Although the arboretum is neither large nor crowded, it contains a good variety of trees. The cedars are well represented, with an Alaska yellow cedar (*Chamaecyparis nootkatensis*), golden deodar cedar (*Cedrus deodara* 'Aurea'), Atlas cedar (*C. atlantica*), blue Atlas cedar (*C. a.* 'Glauca') and western red cedar (*Thuja plicata*). Probably the most exotic evergreen, just north of the overlook in the southeast corner of the arboretum, is a China fir (*Cunninghamia lanceolata*).

The deciduous trees include an almond (*Prunus dulcis*) guarding the day use sign, a Marshall ash (*Fraxinus pennsylvanica* 'Marshall'), a tamarisk (*Tamarix* sp.), a black

194

locust (*Robinia pseudoacacia*), and a honey locust (*Gleditsia triacanthos*). Flowering trees include a Kwanzan cherry (*Prunus serrulata* 'Kwanzan'), a redbud (*Cercis* sp.), star and saucer magnolias (*M. stellata* and *M.* x *soulangeana*), and silk trees (*Albizia julibrissin*).

Among the shrubs are rhododendrons, camellias, roses, and butterfly bushes.

Jacksonville Herb Garden

6th and D Streets

Seasons of interest: Late spring, summer, early fall

Directions: From Highway 238 (California Street), turn north onto 6th. Turn left onto D Street. The garden is between 5th and 6th, tucked in behind the Children's Museum, which is next to the Jacksonville Museum of Southern Oregon History.

Labels: None

Background: The garden was developed as part of a living history exhibit.

What to see: This garden is tiny, even among herb gardens. It is home to several mints, chives, wormwood, fennel, yarrow, a lavender, a thyme, and several other herbs.

Old Rose Garden

5th and D streets
Jacksonville

Season of interest: Early summer

Directions: From California Street (Highway 238), turn north on 5th and proceed two blocks to D Street. The garden is on the north side of St. Andrews Traditional Episcopal Church.

Labels: Most plants are labeled.

Background: The Medford Rose Society planted approximately two hundred bushes in 1959 and 1960. Almost all are roses the pioneers might have brought with them or sent for, because Jacksonville is a historic town.

What to see: Although a bit unkempt, this little garden is full of interesting roses. The only hybrid tea you might see is the first one, 'La France,' bred in 1867. Damasks include 'Madame Hardy'; among the gallicas are 'Nestor' and 'Narcisse de Salvande.' Hybrid perpetuals include 'Charles Lefebvre,' 'Frau Karl Druschki,' and 'Cardinal de Richelieu.' The China rose 'Old Blush' is here, along with the tea rose 'Maman Cochet' and Bourbons 'Honorine de Brabant' and 'Mme. Ernest Calvat.' Newer rugosa hybrids include 'Carmenetta' and 'Agnes' from the 1920s.

Southern Oregon Experiment Station

and Claire Hanley Arboretum

569 Hanley Road
Medford, OR 97502
(541) 772-5165 (the Station)
(541) 776-7371 (Master Gardeners—
regarding the arboretum)

Seasons of interest: All

Directions: From downtown Medford proceed west on Main Street, which will change from a one-way to a two-way street. Approximately eight miles from town the road curves to the right and then, after a thousand feet, to the left. At the left-hand curve, turn right onto Hanley Road. Proceed about a quarter of a mile and turn left into the extension service driveway. If you miss that, go a bit farther and turn left into the Experiment Station parking lot.

The Experiment Station is mainly given to research, so don't go wandering around; check in with the receptionist if you want to see anything north of the building. The arboretum and display gardens are all east, south, and west of the building.

Labels: Some plants are labeled

Special events: In April the Master Gardeners hold a spring garden fair, at which they sell plants and garden furniture.

Background: Claire Hanley was a granddaughter of pioneers who came to the Jacksonville area in the 1850s to farm rather than prospect for gold, as did so many others. The Hanley farm included some of the best land in the area. Hanley participated in many civic activities including the Jackson County home extension service, the Southern Oregon Historical Society (of which she was president at her death in 1963), and garden clubs (she was once president of the Oregon Federation of Garden Clubs). She and her sisters, Mary and Martha, sold eighty acres of their portion of the family farm to the Southern Oregon Agricultural Experiment Station in 1957.

The arboretum was established in 1961 to display ornamental trees and shrubs. After Hanley's death the station dedicated the arboretum to her. Many of the trees were planted from 1963 to 1966 by the extension service and local garden clubs. The display gardens, including the fern, bulb, and Japanese gardens, were planted in the 1980s. The gardens around the extension service building were planted in the mid 1990s.

What to see: The arboretum is south of the Experiment Station building; there are display gardens in front of the building and behind it. Display gardens also ring the extension service building, which is behind the Experiment Station building.

The several dozen deciduous trees in the arboretum include half a dozen magnolias. The trees provide shade for several small specialty gardens. A Kobus magnolia (*M. kobus*) near the center anchors a fern garden planted along a dry stream bed. A dozen ferns are complemented by coral bells, cyclamen, oxalis, and violas. A shade garden nearby is home to hostas, astilbes, Asian lilies, and spring bulbs. Two more bulb beds are tucked under the magnolias along the southeast edge of the arboretum. West of the bulb beds, peonies grow in a garden of ornamental grasses. To the south, the Japanese flower garden includes several iris and azaleas under a lace-leaf maple (*Acer palmatum f. dissectum atropurpureum*), weeping cherry (*Prunus* sp.), and Japanese pagoda tree

(*Sophora japonica*). In the northwest corner, toward the zelkova tree (*Zelkova serrata*), are dozens of wildflowers.

Walk west, behind the Station, to the extension service building. At its southwest corner, common herbs grow in front of a satellite dish. Along the south side is a seasonal garden. Along the east side is a water-saving garden of grasses. The fruit trees and berries north of the building are used for teaching gardening techniques to master gardeners. Along the west side is an herb garden. Across the driveway to the southeast, in front of the plastic greenhouse, is a cottage garden.

Walk back toward the Experiment Station. Near its back wall, the Wanda Houser herb and rose garden, named for a retired head of the master gardeners, also includes peonies and several brooms. In front of the Station building is a small planting of ornamental grasses, a few herbs, and New Zealand flax (*Phormium tenax*). Out by Hanley Road are peonies, candytuft, and chrysanthemums.

Lithia Park

Winburn Way
Ashland

Seasons of interest: All

Directions: From Interstate 5 north of Ashland, take exit 19; proceed south on Valley View Road; turn left on Siskiyou Boulevard (Highway 99), and proceed into downtown, to the Plaza. From Interstate 5 south of Ashland, take exit 14; proceed into town on Ashland Street (Highway 66); then right on Siskiyou Boulevard (Highway 99), which becomes E. Main Street northbound; proceed past Pioneer and Oak; cross a bridge and immediately turn left, looping back toward downtown on N. Main; proceed one block to the Plaza.

Bear to the right; the road heading up the canyon, through the park, is Winburn Way. There is a parking lot on Winburn, one block south, on the right.

If you're on foot, the park is downhill behind the Elizabethan Theater.

Labels: None, but you can buy a guide, identifying many of the trees and shrubs and pointing out interesting features about them, at the kiosk in the Plaza.

Background: Lithia Park winds south up Ashland Creek's canyon. The Plaza, just outside the canyon, is where Ashland began in the 1850s. A flour mill sat at the mouth of the canyon.

The canyon has long been home to parks. In 1892, a local Chautauqua Association bought eight acres at the north end of the present park. In 1903, the Ladies Chautauqua Club hired a landscaper to plant lawns in the area between current sites of the lower pond and the playground. Five years later Ashland citizens, at the urging of the Women's Civic Improvement Club, voted overwhelmingly to convert to a park the mill site and the land bordering the creek all the way to the Forest Reserve (now Rogue River National Forest). Over the next few years the mill was torn down, the city bought another forty-five acres along the creek, the lower lake was built, and azaleas and rhododendrons were planted down the hill from the Chautauqua building (which decades later became the site of the Elizabethan theater).

In 1914 the city brought John McLaren, designer of San Francisco's Golden Gate Park, to Ashland to campaign for a bond issue for funds to bring lithia water (a local mineral water, high in lithium) to the park and to develop a spa. After the bond issue passed, the city hired McLaren to design the park grounds above the playground. During the next two years the city built and planted the upper pond, the Japanese garden, the plane tree groves, the main paths on either side of Ashland Creek, the madrone picnic area, the tennis courts, and the steps across from the tennis court landing to the original site of the rose garden.

McLaren designed the roadway so that the park could be enjoyed by car as well as on foot. He also designed registration and recreation buildings for an auto camp the city ran from 1915 to 1961 at the south end of the park. Among the features he planned that were never built were a sanitarium, a casino, a lawn bowling and handball court, a spring gazebo, a greenhouse nursery area, and an aviary. A few more of his designs—for a cottage, a teahouse, and two other gazebos—were built, but were later torn down.

The next major era of park development was the late 1930s, when WPA workers relandscaped the north park area, improved drainage, built pathways, and replaced a weed and bramble patch with a rose garden. Chet Corry, park superintendent from the late 1930s until the late 1960s, added many native plants along the creek. After he retired in 1968, he served as a consultant to design and supervise the remodeling of the swan pool below the theater into Meyer Memorial Lake, funded by family members of former Ashland residents A.C., Coral, and Yale Meyer.

The park suffered in the 1970s from a flood and the effects of years of heavy use—Ashland has hot summers, and Lithia Park is cooler than much of the rest of town. The park commission replanted and reuilt parts of the park, installed an irrigation system, and remodeled the Japanese garden in the early 1980s.

In the winter of 1996-97, Ashland Creek flooded again. The entrance area to the park—trees and shrubs as well as lawn, sand, and earth—was bulldozed into two large berms to keep the floodwaters from inundating downtown. That area is now being restored, and a wall is being built along Ashland Creek to channel future floods and prevent similar landscaping disasters.

What to see: There is something for almost every taste somewhere in the park.

Although the park does not claim to be an arboretum, it has a wide variety of interesting trees. The most formal plantings are two groves of London plane trees (*Platanus* x *acerifolia*); one at the lithia water spring (not a taste treat) and the other across the road and west, toward the Japanese garden.

Above the upper pond is a grove of more than four dozen maples. The grove is perhaps at its most attractive in late fall and winter, as several of the maples have striped bark. Among the species are *Acer davidii*, *A. capillipes*, *A. griseum*, *A. pensylvanicum*, *A. shirasawanum*, *A. sieboldianum*, and *A. pseudosieboldianum*.

The park has many plantings of rhododendrons and azaleas. Most are hybrids, but some species can be found north and east of the upper grove of plane trees. A collection of mostly 'Loderi' hybrid rhododendrons, planted with Kousa dogwoods (*Cornus kousa*), is south of the bandshell. Other flowering shrubs in the park include viburnums and andromedas.

The Japanese garden is south of the upper plane tree grove and bandstand, on the opposite side of the road from Ashland Creek. Its paths meander over hillocks and across a small stream with several pools. The plantings include several grasses, rhododendrons, azaleas, andromedas, *Epimedium* x *versicolor* 'Sulphureum,' Japanese maples, and dwarf conifers.

The rose garden, on the same side of the road as the Japanese garden but much closer to the parking lot, has eleven beds in a circle. Except for one bed—recently planted to *Rosa banksiae*—the beds hold uniform plantings of modern roses. The blossoms are mainly white, pink, and red.

The Coast

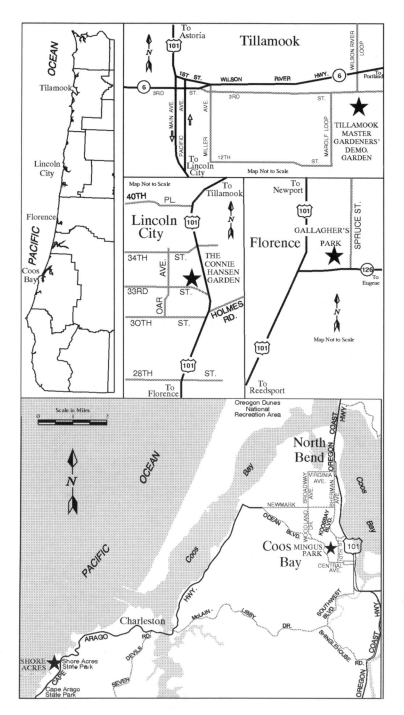

Tillamook Master Gardeners' Demonstration Garden

Tillamook County Fairgrounds

Seasons of interest: Late spring, summer

Directions: From Highway 101 in Tillamook, proceed east on 3rd Street. The county fairgrounds are on the right, just east of the cemetery on the left; the garden is inside the third gate from the west (the main gate). If approaching Tillamook on Highway 6, turn left on the Wilson River Loop (marked with a flashing yellow light); proceed one block, turn left, and turn right at the first gate.

The garden is planned to be at its best during the county fair in August, but is attractive from early June.

Labels: Some plants are labeled.

Background: The garden was established in 1987. The site was moved in 1989 to an area reclaimed from grass, gravel, and asphalt; the gardeners brought in soil, and tilled in sawdust and fertilizer. The garden was built by Master Gardeners to demonstrate varieties and cultural methods suitable to local conditions. Because of the cool coastal climate, the emphasis is on early or short-season varieties.

What to see: The Master Gardeners have packed a wide variety of plants into a small space, attractively demonstrating what can be grown in a coastal climate. Along with the expected flowers and vegetables suitable to the local climate, the garden includes turf trials, cane and blueberries, and a rock garden around a fish pond. Among the ornamentals are shade garden plants, rhododendrons and azaleas, dwarf conifers, a few roses, bulbs, and grasses.

The Connie Hansen Garden

1931 N.W. 33rd Street
Lincoln City
(541) 994-6338

❧

Seasons of interest: All

Directions: From Highway 101 near the north end of town turn west onto N.W. 34th Street, left on Oar Avenue, and left on 33rd Street. The garden is open 10 a.m. to 2 p.m., Tuesdays and Saturdays, or by appointment.

Labels: Few plants are labeled.

Special events: Two-day open garden and plant sale, Mother's Day weekend, and a Winter Garden Party, early December.

Weddings: Possibly, if very small (thirty-five or fewer people).

Background: Connie Hansen was a botanist and an assistant professor at the University of California, Berkeley. She belonged to many plant societies—Azalea, Rhododendron, Hardy Plant, Lily, Heather and Iris. She ran the seed exchange for the Iris Society, and introduced a French hybrid iris to the United States. She was an honorary member of the African Violet Society.

In 1973 at age sixty-five, after the death of her husband, she moved to Lincoln City and began this garden on nine city lots. She collected plants—particularly rhododendrons, candelabra primroses, hellebores, cyclamens, and heathers—and got rid of most of the lawn. She had help on the pruning and, in her later years, with the remaining lawn, but otherwise kept up the garden herself—working on it from dawn to dusk—until 1992. Her candelabra primroses appeared on the cover of *Sunset* for October 1984, and she wrote about the garden for the January/February 1992 issue of *Fine Gardening*.

She died the next year, at eighty-four, having already sold
the garden. The Connie Hansen Garden Conservancy
formed to save it.

With the help of a generous donor, the conservancy
bought the garden in 1994. Its members have done much
thinning and clearing. They discovered rhododendrons
along the north edge, hidden under a wall of blackberries,
and continue to find plants hidden under the sweet
woodruff, violets, and false lily of the valley that were
planted as groundcovers and took the opportunity, when
no one was looking, to become plantcovers as well.

The conservancy has moved plants from the southeast
corner of the property in order to build a small parking
lot. It plans to remodel the house into a horticultural
library and meeting place. Its goal is to show people that
despite the challenges of wind, lack of sun, drought, and
salt air, it is indeed possible to garden at the coast.

What to see: This is a coastal collector's garden;
thousands of plants are tucked attractively into a little
over an acre of ground, and that density helps protect the
plants from the ravages of coastal wind and rain. Much of
the garden is wet, with streams and a small pond, helping
to stretch the plant palette.

While at its most colorful in spring, with
rhododendrons, primroses, bulbs, and forget-me-nots in
bloom, the garden is interesting in every season of the
year, and in every direction. Japanese maples and
snowbells, dogwoods, and hydrangeas provide fall color;
in winter, cyclamen, witch hazels, hellebores, viburnums,
and shrub hypericum bloom. At any season the
composition of shapes and leaf textures is attractive. The
garden rewards both close inspection and glances from a
distance.

One of the first plants you're likely to see as you walk
down the driveway is the sixty-year-old Hinoki cypress

(*Chamaecyparis obtusa*) near the southwest corner of the house. Its open habit is so attractive you can understand why Hansen moved it from garden to garden—this is the third of her gardens it has graced.

The beds west of the house are long and sinuous, running along narrow grass paths. The second bed from the south is strictly for perennials; the others include shrubs and trees as well. The candelabra primroses have been collected near the west edge of the garden. Nearby, Exbury azaleas line the stream.

Species and hybrid rhododendrons—probably five or six hundred in all—are everywhere in the garden including, toward the center of the north side, a magnificent 'Taurus' and *R. davidsonianum* with lavender-pink flowers and attractive brown and white mottled bark. Closer to the house is 'Yellow Hammer,' a seven-foot plant with tiny leaves and small yellow blossoms.

A chocolate vine (*Akebia quinata*) grows up the drainpipe at the northeast corner of the house, and nearby a huge Sitka spruce (*Picea sitchensis*) towers over cyclamen. Toward the northeast corner of the garden is a bed of about two dozen Japanese iris (*I. ensata*), and further south is a bed of iris that includes Pacific Coast hybrids (and, possibly, Siberian iris (*I. sibirica*), the other type Hansen collected).

Other collections include columbines—mostly spurless or double, but some 'McKana' hybrids—astilbes, half a dozen magnolias, three stewartias, and weigelas.

Gallagher's Park

Highway 126 and Spruce Street
Florence

Season of interest: Spring

Directions: From Highway 101, turn onto Highway 126 and proceed two blocks. Turn north on Spruce Street, at the "Welcome to Florence" sign. Gallagher's Park wraps around the southwest side of the Florence police station.

Labels: Some plants are labeled.

Background: Gallagher's Park was donated to the city in 1911 by A.E. and Irene Gallagher, on the condition that it be improved and forever known as Gallagher's Park. The park already had native rhododendrons when the first hybrids were planted in the 1970s. Local rhododendron and flower clubs planted more rhododendrons in the mid 1990s.

What to see: The garden includes about a hundred rhododendrons.

At the front of the garden, in the Florence Garden Club Memorial Garden, most of the plants are smaller rhododendrons and evergreen azaleas. Behind this garden are mature natives and hybrids—including the reds 'Queen of Hearts' and 'Leo'—in plantings stretching west toward the creek. The rhododendron club has started planting large-leaved Himalayan species in the creek's ravine.

Mingus Park

10th Avenue
Coos Bay

❧

Seasons of interest: All

Directions: From Highway 101, follow signs to Ocean Beaches, which will get you to Central Avenue. Turn right on 10th. The main parking lot is half a block north on the right, across the street from the east end of the park. Or, drive further up 10th a few hundred feet, and turn left; park near the swimming pool.

Labels: A few of the plants in the arboretum are labeled; none of the plants in the Japanese garden are.

Background: There are two gardens in Mingus Park. The rhododendron garden and arboretum was planted by the Southwestern Chapter of the American Rhododendron Society several decades ago. The Choshi Garden was started in the late 1980s. Coos Bay and Choshi, Japan, became sister cities in 1983. A couple of years later a delegation from Coos Bay dedicated Coos Bay Park in Choshi, and Coos Bay's mayor announced that the city would dedicate a part of Mingus Park as Choshi Park. Conversion of an undeveloped part of Mingus Park, with a couple of streams running through it, into a Japanese garden began in 1989, and continued into the early 1990s. Murase Associates of Seattle designed the garden, which now covers half an acre. The work was done by volunteers, with assistance from city work crews and equipment. At this writing the final phase, a teahouse, is awaiting funding.

What to see: The rhododendron garden and arboretum is west of and up the hill from the swimming pool. Although planted first, it now seems like an afterthought. It has about a dozen native trees and plants (such as Douglas fir (*Pseudotsuga menziesii*) and Oregon Grape (*Mahonia nervosa*)), a few camellias, and several dozen old, rangy rhododendrons. It is somewhat unkempt.

The Japanese garden, young and ambitious, is colorful in spring, with flowering cherries, azaleas, and rhododendrons. Year-around interest is provided by the water and bridges, and the wide variety of evergreens. This garden begins at the red lacquered bridge at the west end of the lake, dividing the lake from a pond that stretches further west to a small, plain bridge. A wide pathway skirts the north side of the pond and the stream beyond it. The second, plain bridge provides a nice view of the red bridge reflected in the pool. From the second bridge, you can walk along the south side of the stream on a plank walkway, past bamboo and other grasses, maples, iris, and heavenly bamboo (*Nandina domestica*). The north stream bank is planted with iris and a variety of evergreens. At the end of the plank walk is an even smaller, plainer bridge over the stream. To the north of the bridge, across the broad path, a large pond fed by a waterfall contains a small island with a lantern. The pond is edged by iris, and on its east bank are rhododendrons and a weeping katsura tree (*Cercidiphyllum japonicum* 'Pendula').

Shore Acres

13080 Cape Arago Highway
Coos Bay, OR 97420
(541) 888-3732

Seasons of interest: All

Directions: From downtown Coos Bay, follow signs to State Parks. Shore Acres is approximately twelve miles southwest of Coos Bay. The gardens are open from 8:00 a.m. to sunset daily. Admission is charged.

Labels: Some of the plants are labeled.

Special events: The garden is decorated with thousands of lights from Thanksgiving through December.

Weddings: Call the park for information. Reservations are then made through the statewide park reservation system, 1-800-452-5687.

Background: Shore Acres began as the estate of Louis Simpson, a wealthy lumberman. Shortly after the turn of the century he began building a house, a formal garden and a Japanese-style garden (built for his pleasure, and not to strictly conform to Japanese gardening principles) on a shelf above a small inlet of the Pacific Ocean. The captains of his fleet brought him exotic plants from around the Pacific Rim. The house burned to the ground in 1921, and Mr. Simpson built a new mansion. By 1942, his fortunes had turned, and he could no longer afford to live and garden on a grand scale. He sold the estate to the State Parks Division. Shore Acres was used as an Army headquarters during World War II. After the war, the mansion was razed and the gardens were mothballed; the pond was filled, and the Japanese garden and many of the flower beds were turned into lawns.

The gardens were restored in the early 1970s. The formal gardens were recreated along the original outlines, and replanted in the spirit of the originals; the Japanese

garden was duplicated in both plantings and garden
ornaments. An All-America Rose Selections (AARS)
display garden was added. The only structure remaining
from Simpson's era is the gardener's cottage at the
northeast corner of the formal gardens. Plans are afoot to
build a replica of his first mansion that might house a
restaurant, bed and breakfast, and meeting center.

What to see: Shore Acres is many gardens: formal beds,
two rose gardens, a botanical garden of exotics
(particularly from the Pacific Rim) and common plants, a
collection of rhododendrons, and a Japanese-style garden.
Seasonal displays showcase spring bulbs, dahlias, roses,
and annuals. In a normal year, there is always something
in bloom.

The gardens start in the parking lot, where escallonia
(*Escallonia rubra*) (very tolerant of wind and sea air) and
pampas grass (*Cortaderia selloana*) from South America
line the south edge, and cistus (chosen in part because the
deer won't touch it) surrounds New Zealand flax
(*Phormium tenax*).

From the parking lot, enter the main gardens south
through a pergola displaying historical photos and
information about Shore Acres, and containing an
information center and gift shop run by the Friends of
Shore Acres. The line of Monterey cypress (*Cupressus
macrocarpa*) intersected by the pergola was planted by
Simpson.

The first gardens inside the entrance are rose gardens.
In front of the Monterey cypresses are rugosa roses, which
grow behind a selection of modern hybrids including
'Iceberg,' 'Summer Fashion,' and 'Showbiz' roses in the
east bed and 'Fragrant Cloud' and 'Piccadilly' in the west
bed. At the far west end of the west bed the garden's
collection of old garden roses and English roses includes
the hybrid perpetuals 'Baronne Prevost' and 'Paul

Neyron,' and the English rose 'Wise Portia.' The circular
bed on the west side of the main walk surrounds 'French
Love' standard roses with 'Tropicana' and 'Golden
Slippers;' on the east side, 'Tropicana' standards are
ringed by 'Cherry Vanilla' and 'Jean Boerner.'

Beyond the rose gardens, the formal gardens stretch
south. The climbing rose 'Royal Sunset' at the west end of
the cross-axis starts blooming in April of a good year,
across the walk from a "flowering maple" (actually
Abutilon vitifolium, a Chilean relative of hollyhocks) and
several narcissus. Further south along the west walk are
mature white and pink rhododendrons.

The square beds in the center of the lawns are
frequently full of color: red and yellow Darwin tulips in
the spring, cardinal flower (*Lobelia cardinalis*) and dahlias
in summer. In the beds edging the center walks, 'Hino
Crimson' and 'Koster's Brilliant Red' azaleas provide
sheets of color in spring when the daffodils and grape
hyacinths are ending their show. Their more sedate
companions include Pt. Reyes ceanothus (*Ceanothus
gloriosus*), viburnums, low-growing conifers, and
rhododendrons. The canna 'Wyoming' in a bed along the
west walk is bright orange against bronze. South African
plants include red-hot-poker (*Kniphofia uvaria*),
Agapanthus 'Peter Pan,' montbretia (*Crocosmia* x
crocosmiiflora), and schizanthus.

South of the formal gardens is the Japanese-style
garden. Although it is much more floriferous than a
traditional Japanese garden, it is a lovely small landscape.
In the spring it is particularly colorful along the eastern
edge of the pond, with deep blue mats of *Lithodora diffusa*
hugging the rocks below the large mounds of 'Loder's
White' and 'The Hon. Jean Marie de Montague'
rhododendrons best viewed from the bridge over the
west end. At the north end of the bridge is *Rhododendron*

occidentale, a fragrant native azalea. A gnarled Mt. Fuji cherry (*Prunus serrulata* 'Mt. Fuji') planted by Simpson shades *R. impeditum*. The small dry landscape along the north side of the garden, with a stream of flat stones arranged like fish scales, is a recent addition. A huge European white birch (*Betula pendula*) rises to the east beyond the large rhododendrons.

Head southeast, past a young monkey puzzle tree (*Araucaria araucana*) on your way to the All-America Rose Selections (AARS) display gardens. After the award year, Shore Acres keeps as many of the roses as will fit and grow well in its collections. East of the rose display area, a rhododendron species garden is under development. Along with large-leaved species from the Himalayas are some hybrids including 'Mrs. G. W. Leak,' 'Jingle Bells,' and 'Curlew.'

North of the rhododendron garden is a greenhouse full of tropical plants. Continuing north along the eastern edge of the property is a long, narrow shady garden, divided from the formal garden by a spruce hedge that got out of hand. Below the spruces are hydrangeas; along the east side of the garden are camellias. In the northeast corner of the property, behind the gardener's cottage, are more big hybrid rhododendrons, along with a Mexican orange (*Choisya ternata*), black bamboo (*Phyllostachys nigra*), and hay-scented sweet box (*Sarcococca* sp.).

While you are at Shore Acres, take a few minutes to enjoy Simpson Beach, just down the hill from the garden's southwest corner. It's a classic Oregon coastal inlet with a sandy shore, dramatic rocky headlands, and a freshwater stream.

Central Oregon
and The Dalles

Don't expect gardens the size of those west of the mountains. The gardens here are all quite small because of the challenging climate and soil and the smaller population.

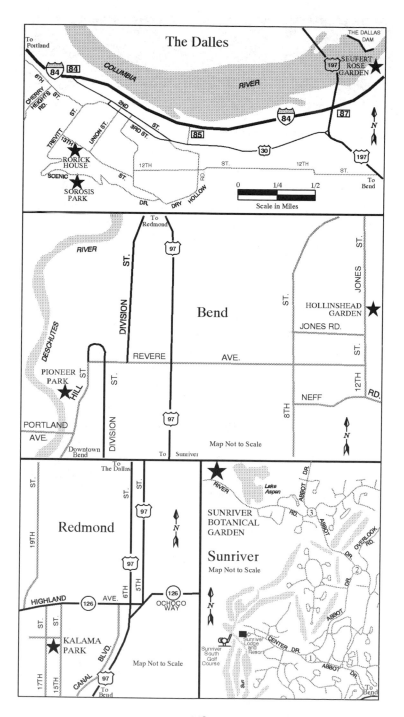

The Dalles

To Portland

COLUMBIA RIVER

THE DALLAS DAM

SEUFERT ROSE GARDEN ★

6TH ST.
CHERRY HEIGHTS RD.
2ND ST.
3RD ST.
TREVITT 13TH ST.
UNION ST.
12TH ST.
12TH ST.
SCENIC DR.
DRY HOLLOW RD.

RORICK HOUSE ★

SOROSIS PARK ★

To Bend

0   1/4   1/2
Scale in Miles

Bend

To Redmond

RIVER

DESCHUTES

DIVISION ST.
HILL ST.
DIVISION ST.

REVERE AVE.

JONES ST.
HOLLINSHEAD GARDEN ★
JONES RD.

ST.
ST.
12TH RD.

NEFF

8TH

PIONEER PARK ★

PORTLAND AVE.

Downtown Bend

To Sunriver

Map Not to Scale

Redmond

To The Dalles

97
97
97

19TH ST.
ST.
6TH ST.
5TH ST.

HIGHLAND 126 AVE.

126 OCHOCO WAY

KALAMA PARK ★

17TH ST.
15TH ST.
CANAL BLVD.

97
To Bend

Map Not to Scale

Sunriver
Map Not to Scale

RIVER ★
Lake Aspen
ABBOT DR.

SUNRIVER BOTANICAL GARDEN

3
OVERLOOK RD.
2
1
ABBOT DR.

Sunriver Lodge and Resort
Sunriver South Golf Course
CENTER DR.

ABBOT DR.
To Bend

Seufert Rose Garden

The Dalles Dam Visitors' Center

Seasons of interest: Summer, early fall

Directions: From Interstate 84, take exit 87 and proceed north (toward the river), following the signs to the Visitors Center. The garden is southeast of the center.

The visitors center and garden are open 9 a.m. to 4 p.m., Wednesday through Sunday, early April until Memorial Day, and after Labor Day through the end of September; and every day from Memorial Day through Labor Day, from 9 a.m. to 5 p.m.

Labels: About half of the roses are labeled.

Background: The Visitors Center, the rose garden, and the grassy area to the north are on land that was part of the Seufert Brothers Cannery (which canned salmon and fruit) from 1886 through 1953, when the land was sold to the federal government for construction of The Dalles Dam. The garden was built some time during the cannery's tenure, probably early in the twentieth century, and the windows of the cannery offices looked out onto it. It was built in a wedge shape because a rail spur ran along the northern edge of the garden from the main rail line to the cannery loading ramp. Remnants of the loading ramp wall can be seen northeast of the garden.

The garden was neglected from 1953 until 1986, when area garden clubs, the Corps of Engineers, and a local boy scout troop restored it. Labels found during restoration indicate that roses were being planted in the garden well into the 1940s, although none survived to the time of restoration. The fence and fence posts are original, as is the brick walk. A flagpole probably stood at the west end of the garden where the urn now sits. The octagonal planter at the east end, now full of miniature roses, was originally a goldfish pond.

What to see: This small, wedge-shaped garden is home to approximately seven dozen roses, including miniatures, modern roses, and old garden roses. The garden does not always get needed care.

Just inside the gate, in an octagonal planter, are miniatures, including 'Bojangles,' 'Funny Girl,' 'Royal Ruby,' and 'Yellow Doll.' The main beds run from the gate along either side of a brick path to an elderly magnolia at the west end. Among older roses are 'Mme. Hardy,' a damask from 1832; 'Mrs. John Laing,' a hybrid perpetual from 1887; and 'Prosperity,' a hybrid musk from 1919. Hybrid teas include 'Dainty Bess,' from 1925, 'McGredy's Sunset' from 1936, and 'Pristine' from 1978.

Rorick House

300 W. 13th
The Dalles
(541) 296-1867

❧

Season of interest: Summer

Directions: From Interstate 84, take the City Center exit (no. 85). In downtown, on 3rd Avenue, turn left on Union (at a traffic light), go up the hill to 13th, and turn right. Proceed two blocks; the house is on the southwest corner of the intersection of 13th and Lincoln streets. The house is open 10 a.m. to 4 p.m. on Friday, Saturday, and Sunday from Memorial Day through Labor Day.

Labels: None

Background: Rorick House, built in approximately 1850, is the oldest house in The Dalles. It was built at Camp Drum by a noncommissioned officer whose name is not known. The military installation became Fort Drum in 1853, and Fort Dalles the following year. The house was used as sergeants' quarters. The federal government sold off Fort Dalles property in 1884. Estell (Eck) and Mae Rorick bought the house from the second set of private owners in 1929 and started a garden. The bricks they used in the garden paths were made locally; originally part of a Catholic school, the bricks were salvaged when the school was torn down in the 1960s. Mrs. Rorick died in 1986, and Mr. Rorick in 1991. He left the property to the Wasco County Historical Society. The property is on state and national historic registers.

The garden is tended by the Mid-Columbia Master Gardeners, who are restoring it in the style of a cottage garden of the 1930s and '40s. Luckily for them, Mrs. Rorick kept detailed garden records.

What to see: This small, old-fashioned garden contains several little gardens. In the front yard, the rockery has been replanted as it was fifty or sixty years ago, with two alyssums, creeping phlox (*Phlox stolonifera*), snow-in-summer (*Cerastium tomentosum*), hollyhocks (*Alcea rosea*), and aubrieta (*Aubretia deltoidea*). Winter jasmine (*Jasminum nudiflorum*) decorates the front fence; roses march along the street side. A trumpet vine (*Campsis radicans*) hugs the front of the shed.

In the back yard, the herb garden perches along the top of the patio wall, as it did in Mrs. Rorick's day. It includes thymes, sages, oreganos, and other herbs. Nearby, along the east fence, are dwarf irises, succulents, and poppies. Along the back fence are daylilies, peonies, scilla, lilacs, hollyhocks, poppies, and roses. In the perennial bed along the west side of the yard are bleeding hearts, daisies, lilies, coral bells, hostas, and lily of the valley.

West of the yard proper are two extra lots. Their stone-edged raised beds are being restored; in the meantime, they are home to roses, lilacs, and iris. In the southwest corner, the fence is interrupted by an Osage orange tree (*Maclura pomifera*).

Sorosis Park

Scenic Drive
The Dalles

❧

Seasons of interest: Summer, early fall

Directions: From W. 3rd Street (eastbound) or W. 2nd Street (westbound) downtown, turn south onto Union, right onto 9th, and left on Trevitt. Proceed to the top of the bluff ; the street will become Scenic Drive. Parking is on the north side of the road, at Kelly Viewpoint. The rose garden is south across the road, at the park's entrance.

Labels: None

Background: Sorosis Park is named for The Dalles Sorosis Club, which successfully led an effort to get this piece of former Fort Dalles property turned into a city park in 1911, and then raised funds to plant the trees and grass. The rose garden was developed in the late 1950s by The Dalles Garden Club with assistance from the city. Roses are planted in memory of deceased members of the club or of the community.

The fountain at the south end of the garden was built with a bequest by Maximilian Vogt, who came to The Dalles in the 1860s and built a fortune of a million dollars by the time of his death in 1911. The fountain, which no longer works, sat at 3rd and Washington downtown until it became a traffic hazard.

The roses are now maintained by The Friends of the Rose Garden, a volunteer group that plans to build a gazebo in the middle of the garden and a rock wall around the edge. The Northern Wasco County Parks Department plans to make curb cuts so that the rose garden is accessible to wheelchairs, and to eventually make the paths wheelchair-compatible.

What to see: The garden's rosebeds, planted with several hundred hybrid teas and floribundas, are in concentric circles along red gravel paths. Each bed is planted either with a single color of rose or with variegated roses. Sorosis Park is a lovely big park with playgrounds and picnic facilities. As long as you've made it to the top of the bluff, enjoy the park and the view.

Kalama Park

17th and Kalama
Redmond
(541) 548-6088 (Oregon State University
Extension Service)

Seasons of interest: summer, early fall

Directions: From Highway 97, turn west onto Highway 126 (Highland Avenue). Turn left on 17th; proceed three blocks; turn left on Kalama.

Labels: The plants are labeled.

Background: The All-America Selections Garden was begun at Hollinshead Garden in 1993, and moved here in 1995.

What to see: The current year's All-America Selection flowers and vegetables are planted in a small plot at the northwest corner of the park.

Pioneer Park

Revere Street at the Deschutes River Bend

Seasons of interest: Late spring, summer

Directions: From Highway 97, turn west on Revere. (The cross streets are named alphabetically from south to north, and Revere is at a traffic light). Just after you cross under the viaduct, turn left on Hill Street. The park is a few hundred feet south on your right. The gardens are north of the lawn and south of the playing fields.

Labels: None

What to see: If you've tired of the yellow-greens and grays of the high desert, Pioneer Park provides bright colors. The gardens start at the north end of the lawn with roses planted in honor of war veterans. In the terraces up the slope to the north, annuals—particularly petunias, pansies, and marigolds—share the space with daisies, hollyhocks, coreopsis, daylilies, pinks, and lupines. In the top terrace are rhododendrons, azaleas, and more roses.

Trees in the garden include western larch (*Larix occidentalis*), ponderosa pine (*Pinus ponderosa*), and wild cherry (*Prunus* sp.).

Hollinshead Garden

Jones Road
Bend
(541) 548-6088 (Oregon State University
Extension Service, Redmond)

Seasons of interest: Summer, early fall

Directions: From Highway 97, turn east on Revere. (The cross streets are named alphabetically from south to north, and Revere is at a traffic light). Turn left on 8th, go one-tenth of a mile and turn right on Jones. Proceed two-tenths of a mile and turn left at the stop sign. After the turn, you will still be on Jones Road. Hollinshead Park is on the right half a block after that turn.

The garden is shown only by appointment through the extension service.

Labels: Many of the plants are labeled.

Background: The garden is on a parcel of farm property left to the city in trust to maintain as a farm. The local master gardeners have planted a demonstration garden here since 1988.

What to see: The primary purpose of the garden is to prove that it is possible to grow flowers and vegetables in central Oregon. The varieties, grown in concentric circles, change yearly. Variety trials are run in the first plot south of the circles, herbs are outside the gate, and perennials run along the outside of the west fence of the garden.

Sunriver Botanical Garden

River Road
(541) 593-4394

❧

Seasons of interest: Spring, summer, fall

Directions: Take Abbot Drive to Circle 3; head west on River Road and, past Lake Aspen, turn right following signs to the Nature Center. The garden is in a fenced area accessible through the Nature Center building.

Open dates are determined by the weather and by Sunriver Nature Center hours, so call ahead. There is an admission fee. Children must be accompanied by an adult.

Labels: Most of the plants are labeled.

Background: The garden was designed by David Danley, a botanist who was the director of the Nature Center when it moved to its current location in the mid 1980s. The garden was built and planted by two volunteers, under the direction of a horticulturist.

What to see: To the outlander, particularly the outlander speeding through on one of the major highways, it may appear that only five kinds of plants grow in central Oregon: pines, sage, juniper, antelope browse, and bunchgrass. This garden demonstrates that other plants are at home here.

Don't expect vast sweeps of color. The garden is small. Many of the plants that can survive the harsh climate are also small, and show their colors in small quantities and for a limited time. Expect to get up close and bend over. The greens tend to be yellowish and grayish. But there is diversity in flower color and leaf shape and texture to enjoy.

Just outside the Nature Center door is a bird-feeding area, with small mountain ashes, a hedge of yellow-

flowered Siberian peashrub (*Caragana arborescens*), and tall Oregon grape (*Mahonia aquifolium*).

The ponderosa pine forest community area is home to squaw carpet (*Ceanothus prostratus*) and several penstemons: the glaucous (*Penstemon euglaucus*), the rock (*P. davidsonii*), and the ash (*P. cinicola*). Out on the open sagebrush steppe area to the north, color is provided by sulfur buckwheat (*Eriogonum umbellatum*), with its small clusters of red to sulfur yellow flowers; blue flax (*Linum perenne*); prairie lupine (*Lupinus lepidus*); mullein (*Verbascum* sp.); and evening primrose (*Oenothera* sp.). A very small desert area has sand lilies (*Leucocrinum montanum*) and two cactuses.

To the east, the riparian region along a little stream includes more lupines, common monkeyflower (*Mimulus guttatus*), mountain juniper (*Juniperus communis*), western blue flag iris (*I. missouriensis*), and shrubby cinquefoil (*Potentilla fruticosa*).

A grove of quaking aspen (*Populus tremuloides* var. *aurea*) along the north wall of the building shelters perennials including western wormwood (*Artemisia ludoviciana*) and *Penstemon rydbergii*. Along the west wall of the Nature Center building are more perennials suitable to the climate: columbines, red and yellow yarrows, beebalm (*Monarda didyma*), chives, and yet another penstemon, the pinleaf (*P. pinifolius*).

✣

Gardens in the Works

As this is written, several gardens are in the planning stages.

Classical Chinese Garden

Block bounded by N.W. 2nd, 3rd, Flanders, and Glisan
Portland
(503) 228-8131

Planned opening: 1999

Directions: From Interstate 405 northbound in Portland, take the Everett Street exit (no. 2B); bear right, and turn right on Everett Street. Turn left on 2nd, and left on Flanders. From Interstate 405 southbound, take the Burnside/Couch exit (no. 2A); turn left on Burnside, left on 2nd, and left on Flanders.

Background: Suzhou, Portland's sister city in China, boasts two of the three most famous Chinese gardens. The City of Portland hired the City of Suzhou's Garden Design Bureau to plan and build this garden. The plan for Portland is not a copy of any single Suzhou garden, but incorporates features from several famous gardens. The development of the garden, with a combination of private and public funds, is in furtherance of Portland's Central City 2000 Plan and development of the River District. The garden will replace a parking lot.

Classical Chinese gardens are walled, urban gardens. Suzhou's design bureau originally planned the garden to be within a wall around the entire square block. At

Portland's request, the wall is in several areas set back to allow plantings between the wall and the sidewalk so that passersby can enjoy a bit of the garden.

All of the buildings will be constructed in Suzhou, dismantled, shipped to Portland, and reconstructed. A team of fifty Chinese craftsmen will come to Portland for six months to put the pieces back together.

What to see: The garden is to be a walled garden around a central lake. Visitors will cross a plaza at the corner of 3rd and Glisan and enter through the main pavilion, crossing an arm of the lake on a covered bridge, and continuing counter-clockwise around the lake on paths and through pavilions. The pavilions range from small covered viewing areas at wide points on bridges to buildings large enough to display artifacts, house a tea shop with food service, and contain meeting rooms.

Although the garden skirts a lake, it will be built on the rocky shoreline and beyond, and not include water plants. The proposed plant list includes many natives of China, including crape myrtle (*Lagerstroemia indica*), windmill palm (*Trachycarpus fortunei*), and Chinese parasol tree (*Firmiana simplex*). Fragrant plants include star jasmine (*Trachelospermum jasminoides*) and lemon daylily (*Hemerocallis lilioasphodelus*). Among fruits to be grown are figs (*Ficus carica*), pomegranate (*Punica granatum*), Japanese banana (*Musa basjoo*), and loquat (*Eriobotrya japonica*).

Sara Hite Memorial Rose Garden

Milwaukie Center
Southeast Kellogg Creek Drive
(503) 653-8100 (Milwaukie Center)

Planned opening: spring, 1998

Seasons of interest: summer, fall

Directions: From McLoughlin Boulevard (Highway 99E), turn east onto Highway 224. Continue to Rusk Road, which is at a traffic light and well marked; turn right.

From Interstate 205 take exit 13 and proceed west on Highway 224. Turn left onto Rusk Road.

Follow signs to Milwaukie Center, North Clackamas Park. The rose garden will be on your left.

Background: The idea for the garden came from Wilma Owings, a Portlander and member of the Friends of Milwaukie Center, who wanted to find a home for her hundreds of roses when she could no longer tend them. She donated a hundred roses, as well as money to purchase more. The garden is named for the late founding director of the center, who encouraged the rose garden project and always had a rose on her desk.

What to see: The garden will have three hundred and fifty roses in twenty-two beds, arranged in a square around a central plaza. Fifty varieties will include hybrid tea, climbing, miniature, and a few old garden roses. A gazebo is planned for the east end of the garden.

The Oregon Garden

Cascade Highway (Highway 213)
Silverton
(503) 653-8875

Planned opening: Some public events may be scheduled starting in 1998. The first phase, of up to 100 acres (of a total of 240), is scheduled to open in 2000.

Directions: From Interstate 5 north of Salem, take the Silverton exit (no. 256). Proceed east on Highway 213. The garden will be on your right as you enter Silverton.

Background: An Oregon Botanic Garden was first proposed in the late 1940s, but did not get past the dreaming stages for almost half a century. The Oregon Association of Nurserymen, mindful of the growing importance of horticulture in the state (which exports more plants than any other), in the early  1990s began planning a major garden that would do more than just showcase ornamental horticulture in formal gardens. The master plan, which includes wetlands as well as more formal gardens, was the result of a five-day collaboration by a group of five landscape architects, three architects, an artist, and a biologist.

What to see: At this writing, the design process is not yet complete.

Jackson & Perkins Garden at Miles Field

South Pacific Highway (Highway 99)
Medford

❦

Planned opening: Spring 1999 (first phase)

Directions: From Interstate 5 southbound, take the Medford-Barnett Road exit (no. 27). At the signal light at the top of the ramp, proceed straight ahead. From Interstate 5 northbound, take the Medford exit (no. 27). At the signal light at the top of the ramp, turn left onto Barnett Road. At the next signal, turn left.

Continue straight through one traffic light; at the next, turn left onto Highway 99. Proceed half a mile and turn left into the Miles Field parking lot.

Background: Miles Field, a stadium owned by Jackson County, has for years been home to baseball; it hosts local high school, American Legion and Babe Ruth, and the Southern Oregon Timberjacks professional teams. The Miles Field Community Renovation Society is currently rebuilding it, and a garden will be planted and maintained by Jackson & Perkins, the Medford rose-growing firm.

What to see: The garden will be along the west edge of the stadium. Among the planned plantings are about twelve hundred roses, as well as several hundred perennials and 250 dahlias.

The garden will be in two parts. Half will be a formal display garden of hybrid tea, floribunda, and miniature roses, including the All-America Rose Selection choices for the current and coming year. In the other half, roses will be planted with lawns, shrubs, and perennials to show how to integrate them into landscapes.

❦

Pioneer Garden

Columbia Gorge Discovery Center
Wasco County Historical Museum and Oregon Trail
Living History Park
The Dalles, Oregon
(541) 296-8600

Planned opening: Possibly spring 1998.

Directions: From Interstate 84 three miles west of The Dalles, take exit 82.

Background: The garden is part of the exhibit on pioneer life. Part will be dedicated to the Walker family, who came to the Oregon Country with the Whitmans, and whose youngest son, Samuel, had a garden that was the envy of other pioneers.

What to see: At this writing, the plans are not yet in final form. They may include, in a 20- x 100-foot bed, a dooryard garden of herbs; early roses the pioneer women would have brought with them; a section of native and naturalized plants, and other flowers the pioneers would have grown; and a section for vegetables and crops.

Japanese Garden

Four Rivers Cultural Center
Ontario
(541) 889-8191

Planned opening: 1999

Directions: From Interstate 84, take the City Center exit (no. 374) and follow signs to the Cultural Center.

Background: The Four Rivers Cultural Center was originally intended to focus on the local Japanese-American population. Its subject has widened to the five local cultures (Basque, European-American, Hispanic, Northern Paiute, and Japanese), but the garden plan has remained Japanese. Designed by Hoichi Kurisu, the garden honors local civic leaders and veterans of World War II.

What to see: Plans call for a one-and-a-third-acre walled strolling garden along the east side of the cultural center. Just outside the entrance, near the center's southeast corner, is a monument stone.

Much of the garden is to be planted along a pond, fed by a stream with three waterfalls. At one corner of the pond will be a zigzag bridge along an iris bed; the path along the pond will also lead to a viewing gazebo. The garden will also have two different stone lanterns, a wisteria arbor, and a thirteen-story pagoda.

The plantings will include, along with the expected pines and magnolias, serviceberries (*Amelanchier* spp.), dwarf Arctic willow (*Salix purpurea* 'Nana'), blueberries (*Vaccinium* spp.) and lingonberries (*V. vitis-idaea*).

General Index

Page numbers for gardens planned but not planted at this writing are listed in parentheses

Albany, 156
Albany College, 71
Albany Olde-Fashioned Garden, 156
All-America Selections (flowers and vegetables), 53, 192, 226
All-American Rose Selections, 84, 86, 170, 177, 215, 217, (235)
Aloha, 74
American Rhododendron Society, 14, 33, 34, 35, 75, 122, 183
American Rose Society, 84, 86
arboretums, 44, 51, 52, 54-55, 61-64, 98-104, 117-18, 119-20, 126-27, 130-32, 143-44, 147-48, 157-58, 163-66, 172-73, 178-82, 186-87, 194-95, 198-200, 204
Ashland, 201-4
Aurora, 115-18
Aurora Colony 115-16
Austin, David, 85
Avery, Joseph C., 169
Avery Park, 169-71

Baker, Patricia, Wildflower Garden, 187
Barker, Burt Brown, 125
Barto, James, 66, 183
Beach, Frank E., 85
Bend, 227-28
Berry, Rae Selling, 65-66, 183
Berry Botanic Garden, 65-69
Bishop's Close, The Garden of the, 61-64
blind, gardens for the, 45, 78, 168
Boehl, Victor, 193
Boehl, Victor, Memorial Rose Garden, 193

botanic gardens, 38-41, 65-69, 136-37, 147-18, 208, 214-17, 229-30, (234)
botanists, 19, 38-39, 134, 208
Brookman, Herman, 70-71
Brown, Alice, 138-139
Brunk House, 145
budget cuts, iv, 108, 162
Bush, Sally, 142
Bush's Pasture Park, 142
Bybee-Howell Territorial Park, 14-16

Camp Arboretum, 157
Capitol, Oregon state, 130-32, 139
Capitol Arboretum, 130-32
Capitol Park, 130, 131
Casey, Marguerite M., Peace Garden, 3, 4
Central Oregon, challenges of gardening in, 218, 229
Central Park (Corvallis), 167-68
Chinese gardens, 54, (231-32)
Chintimini Park, 159
Choshi Garden, 212
City Park (Dallas), 147-49
Clackamas Community College, 51-55
Clark, William, 10, 13
Classical Chinese Garden, (231-32)
coastal climate, 207, 209
colleges, 44, 51-55, 71-72, 126-27, 150-53, 160-66, 178-82
Colonial Dames, 124-25
Columbia County Demonstration Garden, 17-18
Columbus Day Storm, iv, 71, 101, 126, 151, 162, 164, 180
composting exhibits, 43, 53, 73, 110, 141
Condon, Thomas, 178: Condon Oaks, 178, 179
construction, plants and, 71, 91, 163, 180

Coos Bay, 212-17
Coote, George, 160
Corry, Chet, 202
Corvallis, 157-73
cottage gardens, 15, 200, 222-23
Council Crest, 99
Crystal Springs Rhododendron Garden, 33-37
Currey, Jesse A., 84

Dallas, 147-49
Dalles, Fort, 222, 224
Danley, David, 229
Deepwood, 138-41, 142: Deepwood Gardeners, 140
Depression, the (1929-1941), 8, 100, 157, 161-62, 202
Deiss, Ted, 11
Douglas County Demonstration Farm, 192
Duncan, John, 59, 100
Duniway, Abigail Scott, 59
Duniway Park, 58-60

Eastman, Harold, 79
Eastman, Harold, Memorial Garden, 79
Edwards, Rick, 24
Elk Rock, 61-64
Enge, Skip, 15
Environmental Learning Center, 51-54
etiquette of visiting gardens, iv, 106
Eugene, 174-87

Fairhill, Arthur, 126
Fir Acres, 71
Florence, 211
Florence Garden Club Memorial Garden, 211
Fort Vancouver National Historic Site, 23-26
Four Rivers Cultural Center, (237)
Frank, M. Lloyd, 70
friends of gardens organizations, iv, 39, 73, 140, 147, 152, 186, 215, 224

fruit and vegetable
  gardens, 14-15, 17-18,
  23-26, 48-49, 54-55, 73,
  78, 145-146, 192, 200,
  207, 226, 228, (232),
  (236)
Fuller, Germaine, 134
Fuller, Germaine,
  Japanese Garden, 133,
  134, 135
Fulton Display Garden,
  73

Gallagher, A. E. and
  Irene, 211
Gallagher's Park, 211
garden clubs, 15, 45, 59,
  74, 75, 101, 126, 152,
  170, 211, 224
Gardens of Enchantment,
  The, 45
gazebos, 47, 69, 72, 139,
  141, 152, 153, 156, 193,
  (233)
Gentle, Thomas, family,
  151
Gentle House 150-153
geographical specialties:
  Africa, 110, 216; Arctic,
  110, 152-53; Asia, 66,
  109-10; Europe, 102-4;
  Oregon, 38-41, 69, 108,
  110-11, 136, 147-48, 157-
  58, 229-30, (236); Pacific
  Northwest, 157-58;
  South America, 103,
  215, 216; Southeastern
  United States, 40
gifts: of land, 62, 100, 176;
  of money, iv, 91; of
  ornaments, 91, 91-92,
  94, 139; of plants, iv, 59,
  62, 79, 91, 101, 162, 176,
  179, 184
Grants Pass, 193
greenhouses and
  conservatories, 71, 141,
  143, 144
Gresham, 42-44
Gresham Regional
  Library Japanese
  Garden, 42-43
Grotto, The, 3-4
Grove of the States, The,
  119-20
gymnosperms, 99, 101

Halvorson, Tom, 45
Hanke, Winston, 170
Hanley, Claire, 198-99
Hanley, Claire,
  Arboretum, 199-200
Hansen, Connie, 208-9,
  210
Hansen, Connie, Garden
  208-10
Hatfield, Mark O., former
  Senator, 134
Hendricks, Thomas and
  Martha, 183
Hendricks Park, 183-185
herb gardens, 16, 17, 25,
  45, 53, 78, 112, 115-16,
  136, 141, 144, 146, 196,
  200, 223, 228
Heritage Garden, 48-49
hidden gardens, 7-8, 72
Higasha, Art, 147
Hillsboro, 79
historical societies, 14,
  145, 199, 222
Hite, Sara, Memorial
  Rose Garden, (233)
Hollinshead Garden, 228
Holman, Frederick V., 83
Holmes, Edna, Garden,
  70-72
Home Orchard Society,
  14-15, 51, 54
Home Orchard Society
  Arboretum, 51, 54-55
Hoover, Herbert, 124-25
Houser, Wanda, 200
Hoyt Arboretum, 98-104
Hunter, Delbert, 147
Hunter, Delbert,
  Arboretum and Botanic
  Garden, 147

International Rose Test
  Garden, 82-88

Jackson & Perkins
  Garden at Miles Field,
  (235)
Jacksonville, 196-97
Jacksonville Herb
  Garden, 196
James, Del, 184
Japan Society, the, 96-97
Japanese Garden, The
  (Portland), 89-97
Japanese Garden, Four

Rivers Cultural Center
  (Ontario), 237
Japanese gardens, 42-43,
  50, 89-97, 134, 135, 147,
  148, 204, 212, 213, 216-
  17, (237)
Jenkins, Belle and Ralph,
  74-75
Jenkins Estate, The, 74-78
Jensen Arctic Museum,
  150, 152-53

Kalama Park, 226
Kerr, Peter, 61-62
Keyser, C. Paul, 34, 90,
  100
Klager, Hulda, 19-20
Klager, Hulda Lilac
  Garden, 19-20
Knighton, William C., 138

labor, designing to save,
  30, 108, 124, 167
LaCreole Creek, 148
Ladd Circle and Squares,
  29-32, 83
Lane, Harry, Mayor, 83
Leach, John and Lilla, 38-
  39
Leach Botanical Garden
  38-41
Lee, Jason, 134-35
Lewis, Mary, 3
Lewis and Clark, 131
Lewis and Clark College,
  70-72
Lewis and Clark
  Exposition, 61, 83, 139,
  161
Lewis-Brown Farm, 172-
  73
Lincoln City, 208-10
Linfield College, 126-27
Lithia Park, 201-4
Lord, Elizabeth, 124-25,
  139, 142, 143
Lord & Schryver, 124,
  138-39, 140
Lyons, Marshall and
  Ruth, 184

MacNab, James A., 126
Martell, Don, 162
Martin, Jane E., Entrance
  Garden, 35
master gardeners, 18, 22,
  167, 192, 198, 207, 222

Mayer, Father Ambrose, 3
McLaren, John, 202
McLoughlin, John, 25
McMinnville, 127-127
Medford, 198-200, (235)
Metro Washington Park
    Zoo, 105-11
Miles Field, (235)
Milwaukie, (233)
Mingus Park, 212
Minthorn, Henry John
    and Laura, 124
Minthorn House, 124
Mische, Emanuel T., 7-8,
    61-62, 99, 100
Monmouth, 150-53
Moser, Brother
    Ferdinand, 10
Mt. Hood Community
    College, 44
Mt. Pisgah Arboretum,
    186-87

National Sanctuary of
    Our Sorrowful Mother,
    3-4
Newberg, 124-25
North Willamette
    Experiment Station,
    117-18
Northwest Herbal
    Society, 116

Oak Grove, 46-47
old-fashioned gardens,
    19-20, 23-26, 48-49, 124-
    25, 145-46, 151-52, 153,
    156, 222-23, (236)
Old Rose Garden, 197
Olmsted, John, 61, 161
Olmsted Brothers, 7, 59,
    161
OMSI Herb Garden, 112
Ontario, (237)
Oregon Association of
    Nurserymen, 119
Oregon City, 48-55
Oregon City – Tateshima
    Sister City Japanese
    Garden, 50
Oregon Garden, The
    (Portland), 5-6
Oregon Garden, The
    (Silverton), (234)
Oregon Herb Society, 112
Oregon Journal, 33, 99

Oregon State University,
    157, 160-66, 169
Oriental gardens, design
    of, 54, 92-93, 94, 95, 96,
    135, (232)
ornament, garden, 92, 95,
    97, 139, 170, (237)
ornamental horticulture
    trade, Oregon, 117
overgrowth, removing,
    47, 71, 75, 209
Overholser, James L., 171
Owen, George and Enid,
    176
Owen Rose Garden 176-
    77

Palmerton, Orrin, 194
Palmerton Arboretum
    194-95
peace gardens, 3, 4, 13
Peavy, George, 157
Peavy Arboretum, 157-58
Peninsula Park, 7-9, 83
Pioneer Garden (The
    Dalles), (236)
Pioneer Park (Bend), 227
Pittman, Anna Maria, 135
plants: breeding 19, 162;
    transplanting, 91, 163,
    179
Platt, Jane (Kerr), 63
poisonous plants, 21-22
Porter, Lotus Knight, 190
Porter, Lotus Knight
    Garden, 190
Portland: Chamber of
    Commerce, 99; City of,
    29, 58: City of, rose
    awards, 84, 85; gardens
    in, 3-13, 29-42, 58-73,
    80-112, (231); as Rose
    City, 30, 83; Rose
    Festival, 83, 85
prior uses of garden sites,
    5, 52, 58-59, 90-91, 99-
    100, 134

recycling plants and
    garden materials, 52, 91
Redmond, 226
remodeling, garden, 30,
    91
restoration, garden, 8, 75,
    79, 124-25, 140, 209, 214-
    15, 220-21, 222-23 25;

rhododendrons: breeding
    of, 162; gardens, 12, 33-
    37, 67-68, 78, 121-23,
    164-66, 170, 183-85, 186,
    190, 209, 210, 217;
    hybrids, Pacific
    Northwest, 35, 36, 37,
    170-71, 183-85; test
    gardens, 34;
    transplanting of, 34, 91,
    163
Risley Landing Gardens,
    46-47
rock gardens, 36-37, 40,
    41, 63, 68-69, 76, 137,
    141, 207
Rogue River, 194-95
Rorick, Estell and Mae,
    222-23
Rorick House 222-23
Rose Festival, Portland,
    83, 85, 87
rose gardens, 4, 7-9, 29-
    32, 53, 71, 72, 82-88, 135,
    142, 144, 146, 152, 156,
    159, 167-68, 169-70, 176-
    77, 191, 193, 197, 200,
    204, 215-16, 217, 220-21,
    224-25, (233), (235)
rose societies, 79, 84, 85,
    86, 176, 193, 197
Roseburg, 190-92
Roseburg Veterans'
    Administration
    Hospital, 101
roses: as civilizing
    influence, 84; English,
    85; as industry, 94; old
    garden, 88; Portland,
    87; testing, 84, 85, 86
Royal Rosarians, 84, 86

St. Helens, 17
St. Paul, 121-23
Salem, 130-46
Salmon Creek Poison
    Prevention Garden 21-
    22
Sandy, 45
Sauvie Island, 14
Schryver, Edith, 139, 142.
    See also Lord &
    Schryver
Sesquicentennial Rose
    Garden, 133, 134, 135
Seufert Brothers Cannery,
    220

Seufert Rose Garden, 220
Shakespearean gardens, 34, 84, 87
Shore Acres, 214-17
signature plants, 83, 131
Silverton, (234)
Simpson, Louis, 213, 214
Siskiyou Mountains, botanical and geologic interest of, 39
sister cities: Choshi, Japan, 212; Sapporo, Japan, 94; Suzhou, China, 231-32; Tateshima, Japan, 50
site selection, 59, 65, 84, 90, 121
Smith, Cecil, 121-23
Smith, Cecil and Molly, Garden, 121-23
Sorosis Park, 224-25
Southern Oregon Experiment Station, 198-200
Springer, Martha, 134
Springer, Martha, Botanical Area, 133, 134, 136-37
state trees, 119-20
States, Grove of the, 119-20
storms, iv, 163, 180, 203. *See also* Columbus Day Storm; weather
Sunriver, 229-30
Sunriver Botanical Garden, 229-30

Tartar, Mae M., 143
Taylor, A. D., 161-62, 167-68, 169
test gardens: dahlias, 192; fuchsias, 41; rhododendrons, 34; roses, 82, 86
The Dalles, 220-25, (236)
The Dalles Dam, 220
Thornton, Robert Y., 119
Tillamook, 207
Tillamook Master Gardeners' Demonstration Garden, 207
time, effect on gardens, 39, 66, 75, 122
Tono, P.T., Professor, 90, 96

University of Oregon, 131, 178-82, 183
University of Portland, 10-13
urban gardens, 5-6, (231-32)

Vancouver, Washington, 21-26
Vietnam Veterans' Memorial, 101, 104

Wakefield, Emma, 115-16
Wakefield, Emma, Herb Garden, 115-16
walking garden, 145
Washington, gardens in, 19-26
Washington Park (Portland), 80-112
Washington Park Zoo, 105-11
water features 35, 36, 54, 69, 72, 92-93, 110: fountains, 4, 45, 85, 131, 224; pools and ponds, 18, 62, 64, 76, 94, 110, 148, 152, 158, 204, 207, 209, 213, 216, 232*, 237*; streams, 4, 95, 148, 204, 209, 213, 230, (237)
weather: floods, 49, 203; protection from, 11, 209; surviving severe, 84, 101. *See also* Columbus Day Storm; storms
weddings, sites for, 7, 14, 19, 33, 38, 46, 74, 82-83, 98, 138, 142, 150-151, 157, 176, 186, 208, 214
Western Oregon State University, 150-53
wetlands plants, 54, 69, 148, 209, (234)
wildlife habitat, gardens as, 54, 110-11
Willamette University, 133-37
Willamette Valley Herb Society, 115
Willson, H. W., 130
Willson Park, 130-32
Wilsonville, 119-20
Woodland, Washington, 19-20
World War I, 84, 86-87
World War II, 84, 162

zoos, 90-91, 105-11

241

Plant index

* discussed in background section

Page numbers for gardens planned but not planted at this writing are listed in parentheses

abelia, 153: glossy, 54
Abelia x *grandiflora*, 54
Abies: *balsamea*, 54; *balsamea* 'Nana,' 44, 52-53; *concolor* 'Candicans,' 166; *grandis*, 136; *grandis* 'Johnson,' 158; *lasiocarpa*, 40, 100; *nordmanniana*, 166, 182; *pinsapo*, 182; *sachalinensis*, 182
Abutilon vitifolium, 216
Acanthus mollis, 184
Acer: *argutum*, 185; *capillipes*, 13, 204; *carpinifolium*, 104; *circinatum*, 13, 40, 149; *circinatum* 'Little Gem,' 104; *davidii*, 13, 204; *forestii*, 64; *ginnala*, 36, 54; *griseum*, 110, 204; *macrophyllum*, 10*, 35, 182; *negundo* 'Variegatum,' 20; *palmatum*, 4, 50, 64, 72, 75*, 104, 127, 173, 187; *palmatum* f. *dissectum atropurpureum*, 199; *palmatum* 'Sango kaku,' 109; *pensylvanicum*, 204; *platanoides*, 104; *platanoides* 'Globe,' 104; *platanoides* 'Olmsted,' 104; *pseudoplatanus*, 191; *pseudosieboldianum*, 204; *rubrum* 'Autumn Flame,' 118; *rubrum* 'Bowhall,' 118; *rubrum* 'Red Sunset,' 118; *saccharum* 'Newton Sentry,' 64; *sempervirens*, 104; *shirasawanum*, 204; *sieboldianum*, 204
aconite, winter, 76, 103
Actaea rubra, 18
Adiantum pedatum var. *aleuticum*, 62

Aesculus, 120: x *carnea*, 132, 182; x *carnea* 'Briotii,' 22; *octandra*, 180
Agapanthus 'Peter Pan,' 180
Akebia quinata, 210
Albrizia julibrissin, 109, 110, 195
Alcea rosea, 49, 223
Alchemilla mollis, 153
alder: red, 36; red lobe-leaved, 148
alliums, 40
almond, 194
Alnus rubra pinnasecta, 148
Althaea officinalis, 116
alum root, 149
alyssum, 223
amaranth, globe, 146
Amaranthus caudatus, 25
Amelanchier, (237)
andromeda, 76, 79, 92, 118, 135, 152, 184, 204: variegated, 76
anemone, 123
Anemone pulsatilla, 153
angelica, 112, 125
Angelica archangelica, 112, 125
annuals, 6, 13, 45, 78, 87, 144, 152, 156, 215
Antennaria dioica, 137
apples, 14*, 18, 19*, 45, 54, 78, 125: Black Jersey, 15; Cox's Orange, 15; Golden Delicious, 144; Greasy Pippin, 15; Horse, 15; Irish Peach, 15; Mother, 15; Peck's Pleasant, 15; Red Delicious, 144; Sanctuary Delicious, 15; Sops of Wine, 15; Westfield Seek No Further, 15; Winesap, 144; Yellow Transparent, 144
Aquilegia formosa, 153
Araucaria araucana, 20, 103, 217
arborvitae, 132: Rheingold, 137
arbutus, 110
Arbutus menziesii, 103

Arctostaphylos, 40: *canescens*, 136; *uva-ursi*, 152; *viscida*, 158
artemisia, 177
Artemisia: *abrotanum*, 116; *dracunculus*, 116; *lactiflora*, 116; *ludoviciana*, 230
Asarum, 41
Asclepias incarnata, 25
ash, 104: Marshall, 194; mountain, 54, 103, 229; American, 104; European, 103-4, 108; Moravian, 104
Asian pear, 54
aspen, quaking, 230
asters, 20
astilbe, 77, 153, 199, 210
Athyrium: *felix-femina*, 184; *nipponicum* 'Pictum,' 69
aubrieta, 223
Aubretia deltoidea, 223
azalea, 6, 11*, 12, 13, 36, 45, 50, 62, 72, 88, 92, 93, 95, 97, 109, 118, 135, 148, 152, 162*, 163*, 165, 166, 168, 182, 185, 190, 199, 202*, 204, 207, 213, 227: evergreen, 4, 35, 76, 93, 118, 166, 185, 190, 211; Exbury, 210; 'Hino Crimson,' 216; 'Koster's Brilliant Red,' 216; mollis, 36; western, 76
azaleadendron, 171

bamboo, 96, 102, 109, 110, 135, 141, 213: arrow, 18; black, 217; heavenly, 213
banana, 110: Japanese, (232)
baneberry, 18
barberry, 29*, 30, 107*: wintergreen, 54
bay tree, 103, 187
beans, 18, 49, 146: scarlet runner, 25
bear's breech, 184
beautybush, 144, 185
beebalm, 18, 26, 230
beech, 118: copper, 103, 181; European, 103, 144; tricolor, 103; weeping, 103

begonia, 144
Belamcanda chinensis, 53
Bensoniella, 39*
Berberis: darwinii, 53;
  julianae, 54
bergenia, 110, 132
berries, 54, 55, 207, (237)
Betula: albo-sinensis var.
  septentrionalis, 64, 181;
  jaquemontii, 12; pendula,
  43, 103, 217; pendula
  'Dalecarlica,' 168;
  pendula 'Gracilis,' 144;
  pendula 'Trost Dwarf,'
  137
birches, 50, 104, 118, 148,
  165: Chinese paper, 181,
  Chinese red, 64; cutleaf,
  144: weeping, 168;
  European, 43;
  Jacquemont, 12; Trost
  dwarf, 137; white, 103,
  217
bleeding hearts, 4, 63,
  125, 156, 184, 187, 223
bloodroot, 123
Blue Star, 146
blueblossom, 148
bougainvillea, 144
box, 63, 132, 141, 144:
  dwarf, 118, 162*;
  Japanese, 53; sweet, 217
box elder, variegated, 20
Boykinia rotundifolia, 41
Briza media, 53
bromeliads, 110
broom, 200: Spanish, 29*
buckeye, 120: yellow, 180
buckwheat, 24*: desert,
  148; sulfur, 230
Buddleia globosa, 103
bulbs, 4, 44, 64, 79, 87, 88,
  122, 125, 135, 144, 148,
  152, 153, 190, 194, 207,
  209, 215
butterbur, Japanese, 35
butterfly bush, 111, 153,
  168, 195

cactus, 69, 141, 144
calendula, 18, 26, 116, 146
camas, 153
Camassia, 153
camellia, 4, 11*, 12, 13, 32,
  39*, 40, 41, 54, 86*, 88,
  92, 96, 97, 118, 131, 135,
  152, 164, 195, 213, 217

Camellia: japonica, 11, 40;
  sasanqua, 11; sinensis, 11
Campanula carpatica 'Blue
  Chips,' 16
Campsis radicans, 20, 223
candytuft, 200
canna, 132: 'Wyoming,'
  216
Caragana arborescens, 230
cardinal flower, 22, 216
Carpinus betulus, 132:
  'Columnaris,' 12
Carya ovata, 131
cascara, 40
Castanea dentata, 20
catalpa, 9: common, 180
Catalpa bignoniodes, 180
ceanothus, 40: Pt. Reyes,
  216
Ceanothus: gloriosus, 216;
  prostratus, 230;
  thyrsiflorus, 149
cedar, 100*: Alaska
  weeping, 152; Alaska
  yellow, 194; Atlas, 44,
  53, 63, 165, 194; blue
  Atlas, 132, 187, 194;
  deodar, 71*, 77; deodar,
  golden, 194; deodar,
  prostrate, 43; Japanese,
  63; of Lebanon, 127;
  western red, 194
Cedrus: atlantica, 63, 165,
  194; atlantica 'Glauca,'
  132, 187, 194; atlantica
  'Glauca Pendula,' 44;
  atlantica 'Pendula
  Glauca,' 53; deodara, 77;
  deodara 'Aurea,' 194;
  deodara 'Pendula,' 43;
  libani, 127
Celsia reticulata, 148
Centaurea: cyanus, 77;
  moschata, 153
Centranthus ruber, 153
Cerastium tomentosum,
  110, 223
Cercidiphyllum japonicum,
  64, 109, 158, 187:
  'Pendula,' 213; var.
  sinense, 64
Cercis, 195
Chamaecyparis: lawsoniana,
  181; nootkatensis, 194:
  'Pendula', 153; obtusa,
  63, 109, 118, 210: 'Nana

Lutea,' 53; pisifera, 181
Chamaemelum nobile, 146
chamomile, Roman, 146
cherry, 15*, 54: bitter, 158;
  Black Tartarian, 177;
  flowering, 6, 43, 63, 91*,
  92, 93, 103, 113, 132,
  144, 152, 163, 164, 213;
  Kwanzan, 164, 195; Mt.
  Fuji, 217; weeping, 96,
  199; wild, 227
chestnut, true, 20
Chimonanthus praecox, 67
Chinese: fringe tree, 36,
  64; parasol tree, (232);
  scholar tree, 166
Chionanthus retusus, 36, 64
chives, 16, 196, 230
chocolate vine, 210
Choisya ternata, 62, 77, 217
chokecherry: Amur, 103;
  western, 158
chrysanthemum, 210
Chrysanthemum:
  parthenium, 18; x
  superbum, 16
Chrysothamnus nauseosus,
  148
cinquefoil, 111: shrubby,
  230
cistus, 215
Cladastris, 103: lutea, 127,
  166
Claytonia parvifolia var.
  flagellaris, 47
clematis, 140, 146, 153,
  156: prostrate, 69
Clematis montana var.
  rubens, 184
Clerodendrum
  trichotomum, 72, 166
clover, 110: crimson, 24*
colchicum, 77
colewort, 25
columbine, 40, 64, 69, 136,
  140, 146, 153, 177, 184,
  210, 230: McKana
  hybrids, 210; western,
  153
comfrey, 22
coneflowers, purple, 16
conifers, 11*, 12, 44, 54,
  62, 69, 99*, 102, 118, 120,
  127, 136, 137, 179*, 181:
  dwarf 53, 204, 207, 216
Convallaria majalis, 75*,
  153

coral bells, 53, 153, 199, 223
coreopsis, 20, 227
cork tree, Amur, 164
cornflower, 77
Cornus: florida, 54; florida 'Rubra,' 63; kousa, 50, 67, 117, 204; kousa var. chinensis, 102; kousa 'Milky Way,' 35; nuttallii, 54, 103, 149; nuttallii 'Colrigo Giant,' 185; sericea, 103
Cortaderia selloana, 215
Corydalis lutea, 37
Cotinus coggygria, 141, 165
cotoneaster, 109, 111
Cotoneaster lacteus, 168
cover crops, 24*
crabapple: 'Flame,' 125; flowering, 103, 132, 142*, 144, 164, 191; fruiting, 142
crape myrtle, 36, (232)
Crataegus x lavallei, 12
crimson clover, 24*
Crocosmia x crocosmiiflora, 216
crocuses, fall, 153
Crown of Thorns, 144
Cryptomeria japonica, 63, 118
Cunninghamia lanceolata, 12, 163*, 194
Cupressus: arizonica, 181; bakeri, 103, 158; macrocarpa, 158, 215
currants: western, golden, 148; winter, 29*
cyclamen, 67, 68, 123, 199, 208*, 209
Cyclamen: hederifolium 'Album', 123; purpurascens, 123
Cydonia oblonga, 125
Cymbalaria muralis, 63, 184
Cyperus alternifolius, 69
cypress: Baker, 158; Cuyacama, 181; Lawson false, 181; Hinoki, 53, 63, 109, 118, 209; Modoc, 103; Monterey, 158, 215; Sawara false, 181

daffodil, 18, 76, 123, 153, 216: hoop-petticoat, 123
dahlia, 19*, 20, 25, 109, 145*, 146, 192, 215, 216, (235)
daisy, 13, 32, 88, 110, 153, 223, 227: English, 76; Shasta, 16, 25*
daphne, 36, 69, 76: garland, 22; winter, 5, 22, 29*
Daphne: cneorum, 22; genkwa, 185; odora, 5, 22, 29*
darlingtonia, 69
Darlingtonia californica, 69
Darmera peltata, 184
Davidia involucrata, 36, 102, 184
daylily, 32, 77, 88, 156, 190 223, 227: lemon, (232)
dead nettle, 153
delphinium, 71*, 77, 78, 144, 156: wild, 76
dianthus, 45, 71*, 96, 116, 146, 156
Dianthus 'Tiny Rubies,' 96
dicentra, 140
Dicentra spectabilis, 63
Diospyros: kaki, 182; virginiana, 144
Disporum smithii, 68
dodecathon, 76
Dodecathon, 151*
dogwood, 4, 6, 35, 104, 111, 118, 126*, 127, 144, 149, 163, 187, 191, 204, 209: Chinese, 102; eastern, 54; Kousa, 50, 67, 117, 204: 'Milky Way,' 35; Pacific, 54, 103
Doronicum, 77
dove tree, 36, 102, 184
dragonhead, false, 77

Echinacea purpurea, 16
edible flowers, 18, 78
elderberry: red, 69: Pacific Coast, 136; variegated, 168
Eleagnus angustifolia, 110
elecampane, 116
elm, 118, 163*, 164: American, 13, 131, 161*; Camperdown, 13, 43, 131

Emilia javanica, 25
empress tree, 165
Enkianthus, 44: campanulatus, 144
epimedium, 40, 63, 125
Epimedium: x versicolor 'Sulphureum,' 204; x youngicum, 184
Eranthis hyemalis, 76, 103
erigeron, 40
Eriobotrya japonica, (232)
Eriogonum, 148: umbellatum, 230
erythronium, 37, 76
escallonia, 215
Escallonia rubra, 215
eucalyptus, 118
Eucalyptus niphophila, 103, 110
euonymus, 39*, 47: winged, 4
Euonymus alata, 4
Euphorbia: milii, 144; wulfenii, 64
evodia, 118
Exochorda x macrantha 'The Bride,' 77

Fagus sylvatica, 103, 144: 'Atropurpurea,' 103; 'Pendula,' 103; 'Purpurea,' 181; 'Tricolor,' 103
Fatsia japonica, 110
fennel, 112, 196
ferns, 4, 20, 35, 40, 41, 63, 64, 67, 69, 92, 95, 141, 144, 148, 149, 199: Japanese painted, 69; lady, 184; licorice, 41; maidenhair, 62; sword, 41
feverfew, 18
Ficus carica, (232)
fig, 24*, 72, 110, (232)
fir, 67, 100*: alpine, 40, 110; balsam, 44, 54: dwarf, 52; China, 194; Douglas, 10*, 68, 101*, 111, 119, 123, 131, 163*, 164, 180*, 181, 182, 213; Douglas, bigcone, 54; grand, 136; Johnson, 158; Nordmann, 166, 182; red, California, 158; Sakhalin, 182; Spanish, 182; white, 166

244

Firmiana simplex, (232)
flax, 49: blue, 230:
    western, 136, 148; New
    Zealand, 200, 215
Foeniculum vulgare, 112
forget-me-nots, 76, 125,
    146, 153, 209
forsythia, 123, 168
Forsythia viridissima
    'Bronxensis,' 13
four-o'clocks, 25
foxglove, 22, 49, 77
franklinia, 104, 166
Franklinia alatamaha, 166
Fraxinus pennsylvanica
    'Marshall,' 194
fringecup, 35, 136
fuchsia, 41, 132:
    California, 40; hardy,
    18, 19*, 20
Fuchsia magellanica, 18

Galium odoratum, 16, 68
Garrya: elliptica, 136;
    fremontii, 149
gaultheria, 69
Gaultheria shallon, 13
gayfeather, 18
geranium, 140: hardy,
    112, 168; scented, 45, 78
Geranium oregonum, 136
germander, 116
ginger, 41
ginkgo, 22, 110, 131, 182
Ginkgo biloba, 131, 182:
    'Autumn Gold,' 22
gladiolus, 20
Gleditsia, 187: triacanthos,
    103, 110, 195
goldenchain, 191
goldenrod, 136
Gomphrena globosa, 146
grapes, 15*, 18, 54, 55,
    140, 192
grass, 109, 136, 137, 158,
    172*, 200, 204, 207, 213:
    bear 136; blue oat, 18;
    Eulalia, 53; giant silver
    banner, 18; imperial
    bloodgrass, 109;
    ornamental, 12, 13, 16,
    32, 50, 53, 168, 173, 199,
    200; perennial, 18, 109;
    quaking, 53; rye, winter,
    24

groundcovers, 117, 146,
    149, 209*
guava, 54
gunnera, 110, 177

hackberry, 148
Halesia carolina, 68: var.
    monticola, 166
Hamamelis: x intermedia
    'Ruby Glow,' 63; x
    intermedia 'Jelena,' 63;
    mollis, 6, 63, 109
harlequin glorybower, 72,
    166
hawthorn, 29*, 118:
    Carriere, 12
heather, 5, 13, 35, 135,
    187, 208*
Helictotrichon
    sempervirens, 18
hellebore, 103, 123, 208*,
    209
Hemerocallis
    lilioasphodelus, (232)
hemlock, 100*: Canadian,
    181; Canadian dwarf,
    43; mountain, 110;
    weeping, 108*; western,
    181
herbs, 15*, 16, 25, 41, 45,
    78, 115*, 116, 125, 136,
    141, 146, 153, 156, 168,
    196, 200, 223, 228, 236
heuchera, 40
Heuchera, 53, 153:
    micrantha, 149; 'Palace
    Purple,' 16
hibiscus, 118
Hibiscus syriacus, 153
hickory, shagbark, 131
holly, 22, 39*, 40, 45, 104,
    118, 137, 140: hedgehog,
    40; Japanese, 40, 92, 96
hollyhock, 16, 20, 49, 223,
    227: wild, 148
honeysuckle, 20, 72, 111,
    153
hop tree, 103
hops, 25*, 49
hornbeam: European,
    132; European
    columnar, 12
horsechestnut, red, 22,
    132, 182
hosta, 4, 35, 63, 64, 58, 59,
    77, 88, 93, 95, 110, 132,
    140, 177, 199, 223

huckleberry, 40, 108: red,
    69
hyacinth, 153: grape, 76,
    216; wood, 153
hydrangea, 29*, 32, 77, 88,
    125, 209, 210, 217:
    climbing, 72, 76;
    lacecap, 76; oakleaf, 64;
    smooth, 22
Hydrangea: anomala, 72,
    76; arborescens
    'Annabelle,' 22;
    macrophylla, 76;
    macrophylla var.
    normalis, 76; quercifolia,
    64
hypericum, shrub, 209

Ilex: aquifolium 'Ferox,' 40;
    crenata, 40, 53, 96;
    verticillata 'Winter Red,'
    22
impatiens, 20, 88
Imperata cylindrica
    'Rubra,' 109
Inula helenium, 116
iris, 16, 20, 32, 35, 40, 45,
    47, 53, 63, 64, 69, 88, 92,
    135, 137, 140, 146, 153,
    156, 162*, 168, 187, 199,
    213, (237): dwarf, 223;
    Japanese, 210; Pacific
    coast hybrids, 210;
    Siberian, 210
Iris: ensata, 94, 210; x
    germanica 'Florentina,'
    116; innominata, 40, 149;
    sibirica, 210
ivy, 139*, 140: English, 54;
    Kenilworth, 63, 184;
    tree, 45

Japanese spice tree, 103
jasmine: star, (232);
    winter, 6, 223
Jasminum nudiflorum, 6,
    223
Joe Pye weed, 112
Johnny jump-ups, 76
Juglans nigra, 131, 181
juniper: mountain, 230;
    pfitzer, 54
Juniperis: chinensis
    'Pfitzerana,' 54;
    communis, 230
Jupiter's beard, 153

kalmia, 110
Kalmia: *angustifolia*, 40;
  latifolia, 63
Kalmiopsis leachiana, 39*,
  41
Kalopanax, 110
katsura, 64, 109, 153, 158,
  187: Chinese, 64;
  weeping, 213
Kerria japonica, 136, 144,
  153
kinnikinnick, 40, 152
kiwi, 54
kniphofia, 110
Kniphofia uvaria, 216
Kolkwitzia amabilis, 144,
  185

laburnum, 103
lace shrub, 40
lady's mantle, 153
Lagerstroemia indica, 36,
  (232)
lamb's ears, 45
larch, 100*: Chinese, 102;
  European, 44; Polish,
  102; western, 227
Larix: *decidua*, 44, 108;
  decidua var. *polonica*,
  102; *occidentalis*, 127,
  227; *potaninii*, 102
laurel, 125*, 153:
  California, 181;
  mountain, 63, 77; sheep,
  40
Laurentia fluviatilis, 146
Lavandula angustifolia, 116
lavender, 53, 112, 146,
  196: English, 116
leopard's bane, 77
leopard's flower, 53
Leucocrinum montanum,
  230
leucothoe, western, 149
Leucothoe davisiae, 149
lewisia, 37, 40, 47, 69
Lewisia cotyledon, 137
lilac, 19*, 20, 59*, 60, 78,
  125, 140, 145*, 146, 156,
  223: Japanese tree, 60;
  Meyer's, 67; 'My
  Favorite Sensation,' 20;
  Persian, 144
lily, 67, 71*, 108*, 153, 223:
  Asiatic, 77, 199;
  oriental, 177; sand, 230

lily of the valley, 64, 75*,
  153, 223
lime tree, 144
Limnathes douglasii, 184
linden, 182: American, 35,
  131
Lindera obtusiloba, 103
Linum perenne, 49, 230:
  var. *lewisii*, 136, 148
Liriodendron tulipifera, 62,
  120, 131
Lithocarpus densiflorus,
  103
Lithodora diffusa, 216
Lobelia: *cardinalis*, 22, 216;
  siphilitica, 22
locust: black, 194-5;
  honey, 103, 110, 187,
  195; Spanish, 44
loosestrife, gooseneck, 26
loquat, (232)
love-lies-bleeding, 25
lunaria, 35
lupine, 32, 110, 146, 153,
  156, 227: prairie, 230;
  tree, 136
Lupinus, 153: *arboreus*,
  136; *lepidus*, 230
Lychnis coronaria, 153
Lysimachia clethroides, 26

Maackia amurensis, 103
Macleaya cordata, 20
Maclura pomifera, 223
madrone, 103, 202*
magnolia, 62, 77, 103, 118,
  152, 163, 182, 199, 210,
  (237): bigleaf, 109;
  Kobus, 199; saucer, 132,
  195; southern, 131, 132,
  144; star, 195; sweet bay,
  144, 181
Magnolia: *campbellii* var.
  mollicomata, 36; *delavayi*,
  64; *gigantea*, 110;
  grandiflora, 62, 64, 131,
  132, 144; *kobus*, 199;
  liliflora 'Nigra,' 63-64;
  macrophylla, 62, 109, 110;
  sieboldii, 36; x
  soulangiana, 63, 132, 195;
  stellata, 195; *stellata*
  'Jane Platt,' 63; *tripetala*,
  165; *virginiana*, 144, 181
mahogany tree, 110
mahonia, 13, 67, 68, 110

Mahonia: *aquifolium*, 230;
  'Arthur Menzies,' 67,
  213; *nervosa*, 77; *pumila*,
  64
Malus, 132: 'Flame,' 125;
  'Ruby Red,' 164
manzanita: hoary, 136;
  sticky, 158
maple, 13, 93, 95, 96, 104,
  109, 118, 135, 152, 172*,
  185, 191, 204, 213:
  Amur, 36, 54; bigleaf,
  10*, 35, 179*, 182; coral
  bark, 109; Cretan, 104;
  flowering, 216;
  hornbeam, 104;
  Japanese, 4, 50, 72, 76,
  92, 127, 173, 187, 204,
  209; laceleaf, 199;
  Norway, 104; Norway
  'Globe,' 104; Norway
  'Olmsted,' 104;
  paperbark, 110; sugar,
  fastigate, 64; sycamore,
  191; vine, 13, 40, 149
marigold, 20, 227
marshmallow, 116
meadow rue, 40
meadowfoam, 184
*Metasequoia
  glyptostroboides*, 64,
  180*, 182, 187
Mexican orange, 62, 77,
  217
mint, 16, 49, 53, 116, 137,
  146, 196: orange, 116;
  pepper-, 116; spear-,
  116; woolly apple, 116
Mirabilis jalapa, 25
Miscanthus: *sacchariflorus*,
  18; *sinensis*
  'Gracillimus,' 53
mitella, 77
mock orange, 77, 144,
  153, 156
Monarda didyma, 18, 26,
  230
monkey puzzle tree, 20,
  103, 217
montbretia, 216
moss, 91*, 92: Irish, 146;
  Scottish, 146
mugwort, 116
mulberry, 110
mullein, 64, 230: giant, 49
Musa basjoo, (232)

muskmelon 'Nutmeg,' 25
Myrrhis odorata, 116

nandina, purple, 108*
Nandina domestica, 213:
   'Nana,' 108*
narcissus, 71*, 123, 184,
   216
Narcissus bulbocodium, 123
nasturtium, 18
nectarine, 54
Nerium oleander, 21*
New Zealand flax, 200,
   215
nicotiana, 45
Nigella damascena, 49
ninebark, 54
Nyssa sylvatica, 104

oak, 103, 148, 191: bur,
   120; cork, 41; Oregon
   white, 10*, 13, 22, 64,
   126, 143*, 144, 178*, 184,
   187; pin, 165, 181; red,
   108; shingle, 103;
   swamp, 103; tan, 103;
   water, 103; white, 103,
   165; willow, 36, 166
Oemleria cerasiformis, 148
Oenothera, 230
oleander, 21*
olive, Russian, 110
orange, 24*
orange ball tree, 103
orchid, 110
oregano, 223
Oregon grape, 77, 111,
   213, 230
orris root, 116
Osage orange, 223
Osmanthus delavayi, 64
oxalis, 199
Oxydendron arboreum, 185

pagoda tree, Japanese,
   199
palm, 102*, 110, 118:
   windmill, (232)
pampas grass, 215
pansy, 5, 140, 227
Papaver orientale, 153
parrotia, 103
Parrotia persica, 35, 164
pasqueflower, 76, 153
pawpaw, 118
peach, 54

pear, 15*, 45, 54, 78, 124*,
   125: Asian, 54;
   'Bradford,' 104;
   'Chanticleer,' 132;
   'Redspire,' 152
peas, Austrian field, 24*
peashrub, Siberian, 230
pelargonium, 20
penstemon, 40, 41, 69,
   173: ash, 230; glaucous,
   230; pinleaf, 230; rock,
   230; rock 'Diamond
   Lake,' 136
Penstemon: cardwellii, 40,
   136; *cinicola*, 230;
   davidsonii, 230;
   davidsonii 'Diamond
   Lake,' 136; *euglaucus*,
   230; *pinifolius*, 36, 230;
   rydberghii, 230
peony, 44, 53, 62, 63, 64,
   67, 69, 77, 125, 140, 153,
   162*, 168, 200, 223: tree,
   20, 77
periwinkle, dwarf, 75*,
   77, 166
Pernettya mucronata, 54
persimmon, 104, 118:
   American, 144; Kaki,
   182
Petasites japonicus, 35
petunia, 237
Phellodendron amurense,
   164
Philadelphus, 144
phlox, 153: creeping, 223
Phlox stolonifera, 223
Phormium tenax, 200
photinia, 110, 165
Photinia villosa, 164
Phyllostachys nigra, 217
Physocarpus capitatus, 54
Physostegia virginiana, 77
Picea: pungens 'Koster,' 54;
   pungens 'R. H.
   Montgomery,' 137;
   sitchensis, 210
Pieris japonica 'Variegata,'
   76
pineapple, 24*, 54
pine, 12, 13, 50, 77, 93, 97,
   100*, 135, 148, 152, 187,
   (237): Japanese
   umbrella, 123; knob-
   cone, 41; lacebark, 103;
   lodgepole, 158; longleaf

southern, 120;
   maritime, 158; piñon,
   120: singleleaf, 120;
   ponderosa, 227; red,
   120; Scotch, 54, 158;
   umbrella, 20; weeping,
   107*; white, 88; white,
   Himalayan, 109; white,
   western, 158
pink, 110, 227
Pinus: attenuata, 41;
   bungeana, 103; *contorta*
   var. *latifolia*, 158;
   densiflora, 50; *edulis*,
   120; *monophylla*, 120;
   monticola, 158; *palustris*,
   120; *pinaster*, 158;
   ponderosa, 227; *resinosa*,
   120; *strobus* 'Pendula,'
   107*; *sylvestris*, 54, 158;
   wallichiana, 109, 165
Pistacia chinensis, 103
pistachio, Chinese, 103
pitcher plant, 69
plane tree, 202*:
   American, 180; London,
   44, 104, 181, 204;
   oriental, 29*
Platanus, 132: x *acerifolia*,
   44, 104, 181, 204;
   occidentalis, 180;
   orientalis, 29*
plum, 15*, 54: American
   wild, 158; -apricot
   cross, 54; Indian, 148
podocarp, 102*
poison oak, 22*
Polypodium glycyrrhiza, 41
Polystichum muritum, 41
pomegranate, 24, (232)
poor-man's-orchid, 20
poplar, 104: yellow, 120
poppy, 140, 144, 223:
   oriental,153; plume, 20
Populus tremuloides var.
   aurea, 230
potato, 25*, 146
potentilla, 62
Potentilla fruticosa, 230
primrose, 35, 75*, 76, 77,
   123, 184, 209:
   candelabra, 36, 77, 208*,
   210; evening, 230
primula, 67, 68, 69, 184
Primula: alpicola, 68;
   denticulata, 68; *japonica*

Primula (continued) 'Wanda,' 77; sikkimensis, 68; veris x P. 'Sunset Shades,' 185
prune, 15*
Prunus, 148, 158, 199, 227: americana, 158; dulcis, 194; emarginata, 158; serrulata, 97; serrulata 'Kwanzan,' 43, 164, 195; serrulata 'Mt. Fuji,' 217; subhirtella 'Autumnalis,' 97, 103, 132; subhirtella 'Pendula,' 96; virginiana, 158; yedoensis, 132
Pseudosasa japonica, 18
Pseudotsuga: macrocarpa, 54 ; menziesii, 10*, 131, 164, 181, 213
Ptelea trifoliata, 103
Punica granatum, (232)
pussy willow, weeping, 45
pussytoes, 137
Pyrus calleryana: 'Bradford,' 104; 'Chanticleer,' 132; 'Redspire,' 152

Quercus: alba, 103, 165; bicolor, 103; garryana, 10*, 22, 64, 126, 144, 178*, 184, 187; imbricaria, 103; macrocarpa, 120; nigra, 103; palustris, 165, 181; phellos, 36, 166; robur 'Pyramidalis,' 181; rubra, 109; suber, 41
quince, 125, 144, 153

rabbitbrush, gray, 148
red-hot-poker, 216
redbud, 103, 118, 182, 195
redwood: coast, 41, 182; dawn, 64, 165, 180*, 182, 187
Rhamnus purshiana, 40
Rheum x hybridum, 125
rhododendron, 4, 6, 11*, 20, 21*, 29*, 32, 35-37, 40, 45, 47, 50, 54, 62, 63, 66*, 67-68, 69, 72, 76, 78, 86*, 88, 91*, 92, 93, 109, 118, 121*, 122-23, 126*, 127, 131, 135, 148, 152, 162*, 163, 164, 166, 168, 170*, 170, 176, 182, 183-

84, 184-85, 187, 190, 195, 202*, 204, 207, 208*, 209, 210, 211, 213, 216, 227: 'Barto White,' 171; 'Beauty of Littleworth,' 36; 'Blue River,' 35; 'C. B. Van Nes,' 122; 'Cinnamon Bear,' 122; 'Crater Lake,' 35, 184; 'Crystal Springs,' 37; 'Curlew,' 217; 'Cynthia,' 34*, 36; 'Dairy Maid,' 36; 'Double Winner,' 122; 'Elizabeth,' 122; 'Goldfort,' 35; 'Hello Dolly,' 36; 'Jingle Bells,' 217; 'Lem's Cameo,' 36; 'Lem's Walloper,' 36; 'Leo,' 211; 'Little Bert,' 67; Loderi hybrids, 204; 'Loderi King George,' 36, 120, 165; 'Loder's White,' 216; 'Martian King,' 170; 'Matador,' 122; 'Mrs. G. W. Leak,' 217; 'Pawhuska,' 171; 'Pink Pearl,' 77; 'Point Defiance,' 170; 'Queen of Hearts,' 211; 'Ring of Fire,' 171; 'Rosemary Chipp,' 184; 'Sappho,' 165, 170; 'Sir Charles Lemon,' 122; 'Sunspray,' 170; 'Taurus,' 122, 210; 'The Hon. Jean Marie de Montague,' 216; 'Virginia Richards,' 184; 'Yellow Hammer,' 210
Rhododendron, 122: augustinii, 67; augustinii spp. elegans, 12; augustinii 'Tower Coat,' 185; bernicosum, 12; bodinieri, 122; calophytum, 35, 122; davidsonianum, 12, 210; decorum x vernicosum, 68; discolor, 36; emateium, 68; exiumum, 122; fargesii 'Barto Rose,' 184; fastigiatum, 12, 68; flavidum, 12; forrestii var. repens, 122; gymnocarpum, 184; hodgsonii, 68; impeditum,

12, 217; kaempferi, 68; keiskei 'Yaku Fairy,' 122; keleticum, 187; leucaspis, 68; lutescens, 12; macrophyllum, 78; montroseanum, 122; morii, 12; niveum, 185; occidentale, 76, 216-17; orbiculare, 122; ponticum 'Variegatum,' 187; racemosum, 12; racemosum 'Rock Rose,' 184; radicans, 122; ririei, 36; vernicosum, 187; williamsianum, 122; yakushimanum 'Mist Maiden,' 187; yakushimanum x calophytum, 123; yunnanense, 68
rhubarb, 22, 54, 125
Rhus, aromatica, 40
Ribes: aureum, 148; cereum, 148
Robinia: hispida, 44; pseudoacacia, 195
rodgersia, 177
Rosa: x alba, 53; banksiae, 204; banksiae 'Alba,' 177; banksiae 'Lutea,' 177; centifolia, 49; chinensis 'Viridiflora,' 144; damascena 'Ispahan,' 53; damascena 'Semper-florens,' 135*; eglanteria, 49; foetida, 156; gallica, 53; gallica 'Rosa Mundi,' 49; x harisonii, 49; rugosa, 87; wichuraiana 'Albéric Barbier,' 177; wichuraiana hybrids, 7*
rose, 19*, 20, 83-85*, 86-88, 110, 112, 127, 132, 134-135*, 135, 136, 137, 140, 142-43*, 144, 145*, 146, 152, 153, 162-62*, 164, 167*, 168, 169*, 170, 173, 176-77, 182, 190, 191, 193, 195, 197, 200, 202*, 204, 207, 215, 217, 221, 223, 225, 227, (233), (235), (236): 'Agnes,' 197; alba, 88, 177; 'All That Jazz,' 31; arctic, 152; 'Baronne Prevost,' 215; 'Betty Prior,' 12;

'Blaze', 191; 'Bojangles,' 221; Bourbon, 88, 197; 'Cardinal de Richelieu,' 197; 'Carmenetta,' 197; 'Cathedral,' 31; centifolia, 88; 'Charles Lefebvre,' 197; 'Charlotte E. Van Dedem,' 85*; 'Cherry Vanilla,' 216; China, 197; climbing, 4, 53, 78, 79, 86, 135, 153, 159, 170, (233); 'D'Aguesseau,' 88; 'Dainty Bess,' 12, 31-32, 87, 221; Damask, 88, 197, 221; 'Duchess of Portland,' 87; 'Duquesa de Peñaranda,' 31; 'Elizabeth of Glamis,' 31; English, 85*, 88, 132, 135, 170, 177, 215; 'Etoile de Hollande,' 31; 'Fantin Latour,' 88; 'Feu Pernet-Duchet,' 85*; 'Fisherman's Friend,' 88; floribunda, 72, 79, 132, 135, 176, 225, (235); 'Fluffy Ruffles,' 31; 'Fragrant Cloud,' 31, 215; 'Francesca,' 88; 'Frau Karl Druschki,' 7*, 8*, 197; 'French Love,' 216; 'Funny Girl,' 221; Gallica, 78, 88, 197; 'Golden Slippers,' 216; 'Golden State', 85*; 'Graceland,' 31; 'Grand Duchesse Charlotte,' 153; grandiflora, 132, 135, 176; 'Green Ice,' 177; 'Hansa,' 78; 'Harison's Yellow,' 78; 'Heirloom,' 31; 'Henry Hudson,' 184; 'Honorine de Brabant,' 78; hybrid perpetual, 88, 197, 215, 221; hybrid tea, 4, 72, 79, 86, 132, 135, 176, 221, 225, (235); 'Iceberg,' 215; 'Jacques Cartier,' 87; 'Jean Boerner,' 216; 'Juno,' 88; 'Just Joey,' 31; 'La Belle Sultane,' 88; 'La France,' 197; 'Louise

Odier,' 88; 'Mme. Alfred Carriere,' 78; 'Madame Caroline Testout,' 7*, 31, 83*, 87; 'Mme. Ernest Calvat,' 197; 'Madame Hardy,' 221; 'Mme. Isaac Pereire,' 88; 'Maid of Honor,' 31; 'Maman Cochet,' 197; 'Mark Hatfield,' 135; 'Masquerade,' 31; 'McGredy's Sunset,' 221; 'Merci,' 177; miniature ,4, 45, 86, 135, 170, 221, (233), (235); 'Moonlight,' 88; moss, 88, 153; 'Mrs. George C. Thomas,' 85*; 'Mrs. John Laing,' 221; musk, 177; hybrid, 88, 176, 221; 'Narcisse de Salvande,' 197; 'Nestor,' 197; 'Old Blush,' 197; old garden, 78, 88, 135, 156, 215, 221, (233); 'Paul Neyron,' 215-216; 'Piccadilly,' 215; 'Piñata,' 191; 'Pink Favorite,' 31; polyantha, 79, 135; Portland, 87; 'Pristine,' 221; 'Prosperity,' 221; 'Provence,' 135*; 'Quatre Saisons,' 135*; 'Royal Ruby,' 221; 'Royal Sunset,' 31, 88, 216; rugosa, 177, 215: hybrid, 197; 'Showbiz,' 215; shrub, 53, 86, 135, 168, 170; 'Souvenir de Dr. Jarmin,' 88; 'Sparkler,' 31; 'Sterling,' 85*; 'Summer Fashion,' 215; tea, 197; 'The Countryman,' 88; 'The Green Rose,' 144; 'The Portland Rose,' 87, 88; 'Tropicana,' 31, 216; 'Voodoo,' 31; 'Wild Flower,' 88; 'Wise Portia,' 215; 'Yellow Doll,' 221; 'Zepherine Drouhin,' 78
rose campion, 153
rose of Sharon, 153

rosemary, 6, 53, 122
Rubus parviflorus, 69, 110
rudbeckia, 16, 43
rye, winter, 24*

Sabal palmetto, 120
sage, 16, 49, 112, 223
sagebrush, 158
Sagina subulata, 146: 'Aurea,' 146
salal, 13, 67
Salix: commutata, 41; *purpurea*, 109; *purpurea* 'Nana,' (237)
salvia, 173
Salvia verticillata, 184
Sambucus racemosa, 69, 136
Sanguinaria canadensis, 123
sarcococca, 40
Sarcococca, 217
Sarracenia, 69
sassafras, 103
Sassafras albidium, 103
Satureja montana, 116
savory, winter, 116
saxifrage, 69
schizanthus, 216
Sciadopitys verticillata, 20, 123
scilla, 36, 132, 223
sedum, 13, 18, 40
Sedum: 'Autumn Glory,' 184; *oreganum*, 136
sequoia, 100*: giant, 127, 169*, 181; giant weeping, 108
Sequoia sempervirens, 41, 182
Sequoiadendron giganteum, 127, 181: 'Pendulum,' 108
serviceberry, (237)
shooting star, 76, 151*, 187
shortia, 76
silk tree, 109, 110, 195
siktassel: coast, 136; mountain, 149
silverbell, 68: mountain, 166
Sisyrinchium californicum, 47
smoke tree, purple, 141
snapdragon, 156

snow gum, 102-3, 110
snow-in-summer, 110, 223
snowbell: fragrant, 102, 165; Japanese, 12, 36, 181, 209
snowdrop, 123
Solidago canadensis, 136
Sophora japonica, 166, 200
Sorbus: americana, 104; *aucuparia*, 103-4, 108; *aucuparia* 'Edulis,' 104
sour gum, 104
sourwood, 185
southernwood, 116
Spartium junceum, 29*
speedwell, 18
spiderwort, 109
Spiraea prunifolia 'Plena,' 76
spiraea, 104, 153: bridal wreath, 76
spruce, 12, 77, 100: blue, Koster, 54; R. H. Montgomery, 137; Sitka, 210
squashberry, 41
squaw: carpet, 230; currant, 148
Stachys byzantina, 45
starflower, 176
Stephanandra incisa, 29*, 40
stewartia, 39, 182, 184, 210: Japanese, 35, 63, 76, 102
Stewartia: monadelpha, 40; *pseudocamellia*, 35, 63, 76, 102
stock, 45
styrax, 104
Styrax: japonicus, 12, 36, 181; *obassia*, 102, 165
succulents, 223
sumac, fragrant, 40
swallowwort, red, 25
sweet cicely, 116
sweet gum, 63, 156
sweet sultan, 153
sweet woodruff, 16, 68, 110
Swietenia macrophylla, 110
sycamore, 132
Synthyris stellata, 69
Syringa: meyeri, 67; *microphylla* 'Daphne' x

persica, 144; *reticulata*, 60; *vulgaris*, 60

Taiwania cryptomerioides, 63
talinum, 69
tamarack, 127
tamarisk, 194
Tamarix, 194
tarragon, French, 116
tasselflower, 25
Tellima grandiflora, 35, 136
Teucrium, 116
thalictrum, 53
thimbleberry, 69, 110
Thuja: occidentalis, 132; *occidentalis* 'Rheingold,' 137; *plicata*, 194
thyme, 16, 53, 116, 146, 196, 223
Tilia americana, 35, 131
tomato, 49: 'Purple Calabash,' 25; 'White Beauty,' 25; 'Yellow Perfection,' 25
Trachelospermum jasminoides, (232)
Trachycarpus fortunei, (232)
Tradescantia virginiana, 25, 109
Trientalis, 136
trillium, 4, 40, 41, 68, 76, 77, 123, 153, 187
trumpet vine, 20, 223
Tsuga: canadensis, 181; *canadensis* 'Gentsch White,' 43; *heterophylla*, 181; *mertensiana*, 110
tulip, 13, 20, 71*, 76, 153, 216
tulip tree, 62, 120, 131

Ulmus: americana, 13, 131; *glabra* 'Camperdownii,' 13, 43, 131
Umbellularia californica, 103, 181, 187
umbrella tree, 69, 165

Vaccinium, 40, (237): *parvifolium*, 69; *vitis-idaea*, (237)
valerian, common, 166
Valeriana officinalis, 116
Verbascum, 230: *thapsus*, 49

veronica, 173
vetch, 68
viburnum, 13, 29*, 39*, 40, 125, 184, 204, 209, 216: leatherleaf, 153; tea, 97
Viburnum: x *bodnantense*, 13; *edule*, 41; *plicatum tomentosum*, 13, 165; *rhytidophyllum*, 153; *setigerum*, 97; *tinus*, 13
Vinca minor, 75*, 166
viola, 69, 199
Viola glabella, 153
violet, 68, 77, 123, 153: dogtooth, 76; yellow, 76

wallflower, 75*
walnut, black, 104, 131, 181
water lily, 64
watermelon, 25*
weigela, 125, 131, 144, 210: variegated, 76
Weigela florida 'Variegata,' 76
wheat, 25*, 25, 49
widow's-tears, 25
wildflowers, 109, 110, 121*, 148, 153, 158, 187, 200
willow, 109, 111: dwarf Arctic, (237)
winterberry, 22
wintersweet, 67
wisteria, 72, 146
witch hazel ,12, 13, 39*, 40, 53, 62, 63, 103, 104, 209: Chinese, 5-6, 109
wormwood, 196: western, 230

Xerophyllum tenax, 136, 146

yarrow, 18, 43, 88, 146, 195, 230
yellowwood, 103, 127, 166
yew, 63, 139*
yucca, 45, 63, 110

Zauschneria, 40
zelkova, 100, 118, 152, 200
Zelkova serrata, 110, 118, 200
zinnia, 25